BODY INVADERS
Sexuality and the Postmodern Condition

Edited and introduced by
Arthur and Marilouise Kroker

MACMILLAN
EDUCATION

First published 1988

Published by
MACMILLAN EDUCATION LTD
Houndmills, Basingstoke, Hampshire RG21 2XS
and London
Companies and representatives
throughout the world

Printed in Canada

British Library Cataloguing in Publication Data
Body invaders: sexuality and the post
    modern condition. — (Culture Texts).
    I. Body, Human — Social aspects
    I. Kroker, Arthur   II. Kroker, Marilouise
    III. Series
    304 GN298

ISBN 0-333-46840-6
ISBN 0-333-46841-4 Pbk

For Alexis

Art Direction: New John Nissen Mannequins (Brussels).
Photo: Christian d'Hair.

CONTENTS

Panic Bodies

BODY WRITING

BODY INVADERS
Sexuality and the Postmodern Condition

CultureTexts

Arthur and Marilouise Kroker   General Editors

CultureTexts is a series of creative explorations in theory, politics and culture at the *fin-de-millenium*. Thematically focussed around key theoretical debates in the postmodern condition, the *CultureTexts* series challenges received discourses in art, social and political theory, feminism, psychoanalysis, value inquiry, science and technology, the body, and critical aesthetics. Taken individually, contributions to *CultureTexts* represent pioneering theorisations of the postmodern scene. Taken collectively, *CultureTexts* represents the forward, breaking-edge of postmodern theory and practice.

Titles

The Postmodern Scene: Excremental Culture and Hyper-Aesthetics
Arthur Kroker/David Cook

Life After Postmodernism: Essays on Value and Culture
edited and introduced by John Fekete

Body Invaders
edited and introduced by Arthur and Marilouise Kroker

Forthcoming

Panic Science

Forgetting Art

I

BODY INVADERS

1

PANIC SEX IN AMERICA

Arthur and Marilouise Kroker

1. Body McCarthyism

Last winter we received a letter from an American friend who had this to say about the prevailing obsession in the U.S.A. over *clean bodily fluids*:

> Do you remember loyalty oaths? When I was growing up in the U.S. teachers were required to sign them to affirm that they had never been communists. Some, on principle, refused. That, it seemed to me at the time, required courage in the prevailing hysteria over bad attitudes and disloyal ideas. I remembered loyalty oaths last week when I read an article in the *New York Times* about the latest twist in the anti-drug hysteria. Since quite a business has developed in the sale of drug-free urine, now there's talk of compulsory drug testing requiring urination under observation. Well, it seems to me only a matter of time, given the contemporary crisis over clean bodily fluids, until someone will decide teachers have to take urine and blood tests to keep their jobs. Aren't we, after all, the guardians of the good health of the young? But can one, as a matter of principle, refuse to piss in a bottle? It does seem ridiculous. The refusal to sign a loyalty oath was quite dignified; to refuse a common medical procedure would seem silly.[1]

Why the hysteria over clean bodily fluids? Is it a new temperance movement driven by the prevailing climate of reactionary politics which, by targeting the body as a new surveillance zone, legitimizes the widening spread of a panoptic power apparatus and heightens distrust of *our own* circulatory system? Or is it a panic symptom of a more general anxiety about the silent infiltration of viral agents into the circulatory systems of the dead scene of the social: an invasion which succeeds in displacing fear about the threatening external situation into the inner subjective terrain of bodily fluids?

A *urinal politics* would be one that privileges the body anew as the target of the power of the panoptic, sublimates anxieties about the catastrophe without onto the body as text for an immunological discourse, and speaks the discourse of clean bodily fluids with such evangelical zeal because, like the radiating light waves from a long past explosion of a gigantic supernova, it has only now reached the telematic sensors of Planet One. The rhetoric of clean bodily fluids is really about the disappearance of the body into the detritus of *toxic bodies, fractal subjectivity, cultural dyslexia, and the pharmakon* as the terror of the simulacra in the postmodern condition. The intense fascination with sanitizing the bodily fluids, with clean urination for the nation, is also a *trompe-l'oeil* deflecting the gaze from the actual existence of the contaminated body (as the *sine qua non* of the technification of culture and economy in the high-intensity marketsetting) and the obsolescence of bodily fluids as surplus matter in telematic society.

As the insurgent basis of urinal politics in contemporary America, the desperate rhetoric of clean bodily fluids signals the existence of the postmodern body as *missing matter* in the cyberspace of a society dominated by its own violent implosion in loss, cancellation, and parasitism. As the missing matter of the social, the body too is the darkness to infinity whose shadowy presence is recognized both by a Hollywood filmmaker like Stephen Speilberg, who, in his recent acceptance speech at the Oscars, leaned over the podium and effusively thanked "the audience out there in the dark"; and a TV philosopher, Dan Rather, who ends his CBS news broadcasts these days with the little bromide: "Wherever you are, be there" (a direct steal from the movie, *Buckaroo Bonzai's Adventures Across the 8th Dimension*, where Buckaroo cheers up Penny Pretty with the cryptic advice, "Wherever you go, there you are").

The politics of urination under observation are a *recyclage* of the McCarthyism of the 1950s which, this time on the terrain of bodily fluids rather than loyalty oaths, insists on the (unattainable) ideal of absolute purity of the body's circulatory exchanges as the new gold standard of an immunological politics. Less a traditional style of McCarthyism with its refusal of political pluralism and its insistence on *absolute* commitments to America as *the* Holy Community, but a hyper-McCarthyism of the late 1980s with its biological vision of the fundamentalist body: a hyperdeflation of the body to the quality of its internal fluids.

Body McCarthyism would be a biologically-driven politics in which the strategies and powers of society come to be invested on the question of the transmission of bodily fluids and which, if inspired by the deflationary and conservative vision of the fundamentalist body, also feeds parastically on generalized panic fear about the breakdown of the immunological systems of American society. A hygienic politics, therefore, which can be so immediately powerful because it is so deeply mythological, and this because never has power been so deeply subjective and localized as the body is now recycled in the language of medieval mythology. Not sin this time, however, as a sign of the body in ruins, but a whole panic scene of media hystericizations of the secreting, leaking body. The *rubber gloves* the Washington police force insisted on wearing before touching the bodies of gays who were arrested at recent AIDS demonstrations in Lafayette Park across from Reagan's White House; *the sexual secretions* in contemporary American politics where presidential candidates, from Hart to Celeste, are condemned out of hand by a media witchhunt focussing on unauthorized sexual emissions; and *routine testing*, the Reagan Administration's bureaucratic term for the mandatory policing of the bodies of immigrants, prison populations, and members of the armed services who are to be put under (AIDS) surveillance for the slightest signs of the breakdown of their immunological systems.

Ultimately, the politics of Body McCarthyism, which is motivated by panic fear of viral contamination, is steered by a eugenic ideology (William F. Buckley, in an outbreak again of the fascist mind, demands the tattooing of AIDS victims); it responds to a double crisis moment (the *external* crisis as the breakdown of the immunological order in economy (panic money), culture (panic media), and politics (panic Constitution); and the *internal* crisis as the existential breakdown of the American mind into a panic zone when the realization grows that Lacanian *misrecognition* is the basis of the bourgeois ego (the substitution, that is, in the American mind at its mirror stage of an illusory, fictive identity for a principle of concrete unity); it focusses on the illusory search for the perfect immunity system; and it calls up for its solution a whole strategical language of cellular genetics, from AIDS research to Star Wars.

The perfect mirror image of Body McCarthyism is provided, in fact, by the striking relationship between the medical rhetoric surrounding AIDS research and the military rhetoric of Star Wars as parallel, but reverse, signs of fear about the breakdown of the immunological order of American culture. The rhetoric surrounding both AIDS and Star Wars focusses on the total breakdown of immunity systems: AIDS can be perceived in such frightening terms because its appearance indicates the destruction of the internal immunological system of the body (the *crisis within*); while the rhetoric of Star Wars creates, and then responds to, generalized panic fear about the breakdown of the technological immunity systems of society as a whole (the Bomb as the *crisis without*). Both Star Wars and AIDS are theorised in the common research language of cellular genetics, where missiles are viruses and invading antigens body missiles. In both cases, the strategical aim is for the immune systems B-cells (lasers in Star Wars; retroviruses in AIDS research) to surround invading antigens, whether within or without, in preparation for their destruction by cystoxic T-cells or killer cells. Both AIDS research and Star Wars deal with ruined surfaces (the planet and the body), both operate in a common language of exterminism and suppression, and both work to confirm the thesis, first formulated by Michel Foucault in *The History of Sexuality*, that power, today, is principally a product of biological discourse because what is ultimately at stake in power and its applied technologies is the life and death of the species itself.

2. The Pleasure of Catastrophe

We have reached a fateful turning-point in contemporary culture when human sexuality is a killing-zone, when desire is fascinating only as a sign of its own negation, and when the pleasure of catastrophe is what drives ultramodern culture onwards in its free fall through a panic scene of loss, cancellation, and exterminism.

Indeed, there is an eerie resemblance between the *fin-de-millenium* mood of contemporary America and Thucydides' eloquent historical account of the dark psychological outcomes of the plague that devastated Athens in the fifth century B.C. In the curiously detached terms of the classical historian who viewed human affairs through the clinical lens of medicine, thus tracking the unfolding of history as disease, Thucydides noted the upsurge of panic anxiety within the Athenian population as a whole in response to the rapid spread of a seemingly incurable disease, the origins of which were not understood, the epidemiological development of which was baffling to the medical profession of the time, and the protections against which were non-existent. Before the dark menace of the plague (and the rumours that amplified both the numbers and suffering of its victims), there was the immediate and almost complete breakdown of even the most minimal forms of social solidarity. With charity for others guaranteeing only one's own death, friend shunned friend, neighbours acted towards one another on the basis of a ruthless calculus of self-interest, and isolation became the template of the previously democratic public life of Athens as a whole. But even this desperate recourse to radical social isolation was quickly proven futile when it became evident, if only by dint of the corpses in the streets and private dwellings, that if the medical causes of the Athenian plague were as complex as they were unpredictable, then, too, none of the traditional precautions against the spread of this contaminant could provide immunity against the invasion of the body by a disease which was as disfiguring of the surface of the flesh as it was ultimately fatal. In Thucydides' historical account, a panic scene of human psychology at the end of the world emerges: a carnivalesque mood of *bit-*

ter hysteria at already living on borrowed time after the catastrophe, with nothing to lose because one is certain to be cheated of life anyway; and, for those few who unexpectedly recovered from the disease, a curious, if highly unrealistic, feeling of triumph over death itself — a sense of triumph which ultimately, and not uncommonly, found its purchase in the ecstatic belief among the survivors of the disaster that *they would never die of any cause.*

The psychological mood of postmodern America is similar to the Thucydidean account of the dark days of Athens of the fifth century. Here, the invasion of the body by invisible antigens, the origins of which are unknown, the circulation of which is as unpredictable as it is haphazard, and the pathology of which is as disfiguring as it is seemingly fatal, has generated a pervasive mood of living, once again, at the end of the world. Everywhere now the previously suffocated sounds of private anguish become the psychological text of public life: *unhappy consciousness* at being trapped in bodies which are pleasure palaces first, and torture chambers later; a triumphant, if unrealistic, sense of *disbelief* among those portions of the American population previously unaffected (heterosexuals) that the fate of the gay community is less a moral judgement on sexual preference than an ominous early warning system of the relentless, and inevitable, spread of viral infections by the medium of bodily fluids; depression to the point of *cluster suicides* among the young at the mythological significance of invading retroviruses in breaking down the body's immunity system; an *absence of charity*, to the point of viciousness for fun, in seeking to isolate oneself from viral contaminants; and a *will to hyper-materialism*, to judge by the inflation of commodity values from the stock exchange to the art market, as an excessive sign (that in the age of panic money when exchange value turns into *implosion* value) that everything has lost its real value.

Between a melancholy sense of fatalism and a triumphant, but unrealistic, sense of immunity from viral contamination, these are the psychological poles of panic sex at the *fin-de-millenium*. The tragic sense of human sexuality today is that it is the scene of a violent and frenzied implosion, where sexual activity is coded by the logic of exterminism, where consciousness is marked by an intense fear of ruined surfaces, where the body is invested (as a passive host) by a whole contagion of invading parasites, where even history is recycled as *the* reality-principle as everyone is compelled to live in fear of their own sexual biographies, where the disappearance of reciprocity and love as the basis of human sex is driven onwards by a media-induced state of panic anxiety about the transmission of bodily fluids, where if advertisers are to be believed, it is just the hint of catastrophe which makes sex bearable in the age of the death of seduction, and where, anyway, natural sex has suffered a triple alienation. First, there was the disappearance of organic sex into discursive sexuality (when, as Michel Foucault said in *The History of Sexuality*, we must pass through what is said about sex, the discourse of sexuality, in order to know our own sex in the modern episteme). Then, the disappearance of biological motherhood with the alienation of the womb (under the double pressure of the technification of reproduction and the subordination of the ovaries to the sovereignty of private property contract as in the Baby M case). And finally, the vanishing of seduction itself into a whole ideological scene of the body redoubled in an endless labyrinth of media images.

It is not just the phallocratic signifier of semen either which is the hint of potential catastrophe in sex today. If the British Government is accurate in its recent billboard campaign against AIDS which dot the English countryside ("Don't Die Out of Ignorance") it is *all* the bodily fluids — blood, saliva, any puncturing of the surface of the skin — with even razors and pierced ears as no-go zones.

Panic sex in America is the body in the postmodern condition as a filter for all the viral agents in the aleatory apparatus of the dead scene of the social, and where, if the body is marked, most of all, by the breakdown of the immunological order, this also indicates, however, that there is a desperate search underway for technologies for the body immune: from *panic fashion* (the "New Look" in the Paris fashion scene); and *panic science* (the deep relationship between AIDS and Star Wars research) to *panic policy* (the urinal politics of contemporary America) and *panic eating* (the double occurence in America today of a schizoid regime of dietary practices: the explosion of eating disorders, from bulimia to anorexia, on the one hand; and, on the other, an intense fascination with the recuperation of the healthy mouth, culminating with the recent High Fashion edict that the slightly robust woman's body is back as a counter-aesthetic in the age of AIDS and disappearing bodies.

First, then, the end of telic history (with the serialty of the Bomb), followed by the implosion of the social into a panic site (with the triumph of signifying culture in the era of promotional culture), and now there is the implosion of human sex itself into a catastrophe scene. The result is the production of a *cynical sex*, of sex itself as an ideological site of disaccumulation, loss, and sacrifice as the perfect sign of a nihilistic culture where the body promises only its own negation; where the previously reflexive connection between sexuality and desire is blasted away by the seductive vision of *sex without organs* — a hyperreal, surrogate, and telematic sex like that promised by the computerized, phone sex of the Minitel system in France — as the ultimate out-of-body experience for the end of the world; and where the terror of the ruined surfaces of the body translates immediately into its opposite: *the ecstacy of catastrophe and the welcoming of a sex without secretions as an ironic sign of our liberation.*

So that is what we get when sexuality is negation and when, under the pressure of the logic of exterminism, pleasure is coded by the seductive vision of the hyperreal: *sex without secretions.* Accordingly, the generation of bodies fit for the waiting time of post-catastrophe: parasited from within by retroviruses that circulate in the bodily fluids; and tattooed from without by the panic signs of the high-intensity market-setting — the body infolded in time, like a *world strip* from particle physics across which run indifferent rivulets of experience. With the body coded by the bleak (but fascinating, because reversible) exchange-process of host and parasite, post-modern consciousness, like a pulsar, also alternates between repulsion and seduction over the fate of the body as (both) a terroristic sign and a pleasurable scene of its own exterminism. At the *fin-de-millenium*, sex — like power, history, money, and the unconscious before it — is always triumphally suicidal as the sign of its darkest seduction.

At least, this is what the fashion scene hints at as the basis of the deep relationship, today, between sexuality and the pleasure of catastrophe. Recently, there was an interesting article in the British edition of the fashion magazine, *Elle*, that focussed on Dior's newest collection as a way of analysing, more generally, fashion as an early warning system of major cultural transformations. Modelled on Dior's first post-World War II fashion line which, dedicated to his mother, used previously rationed material to excess as a way of privileging the consumer body to excess so necessary for the expansionary political economy of the 1950s, the *New Look* of the 1980s uses material to excess again, but this time to highlight (and parody) the flouncey, all virginal, little-girl look so privileged now in a fashion scene which circulates in the shadow of AIDS and where what counts is "innocence not experience." The *New Look* is a perfect adaptive response to the parasited body in the postmodern condition. It is coquettish, little-girl innocence for a generation of women who have everything to fear from the transmission of bodily fluids, and who can simultaneously resist and artistically parody the parasited body with all the excessive, fashion signs of virginal sexuality. Like the return of *crinoline*, which is really a fun costume for the big party at the fin-de-millenium, the New Look, which is everywhere in Paris haute couture, is both an early warning system signalling a major shift in consumer subjectivity away from the serial sex of the late twentieth-century, and a master parody on the impossibility of the body immune in the age of lost innocence. Dior's *New Look* is a cynical sign-play on our knowledge that we are trapped in bodies which are contamination chambers for all the invading antigens of hypermodern culture — a whistling through the graveyard parody on an end-of-the-world culture which is marked by the negation of sex into a killing zone: a zone of ruined surfaces, weakened solidarity, and a prevalent mood of viciousness for fun as the bitter, passive nihilists (the growing majority among the middle classes of North America) take revenge on the weak — the poor, the unborn, the young, the old, the sick, those in prisons and in mental asylums — for their own despair over their botched and bungled instincts.

3. Panic Scenes

And so, postmodern culture in America is what is playing at your local theatre, TV set, office tower, or sex outlet. Not the beginning of anything new or the end of anything old, but the catastrophic, because fun, implosion of America into a whole series of panic scenes at the *fin-de-millenium*.

Panic God: This is Jimmy Bakker and what the press love to describe as the "heavily mascaraed Tammy Faye". Not just TV evangelicals brought to ground by a double complicity — Jerry Falwell's will to money and Jimmy Schwaggart's will to power — but Jimmy and Tammy as the first, and perhaps the best, practioners of the New American religious creed of *post-Godism*. TV evangelicism, then, is all about the creation of a postmodern God: not religion under the sign of panoptic power, but the hyper-God of all the TV evangelicals as so fascinating and so fungible, because this is where God has disappeared as a grand referent, and reappeared as an empty sign-system, waiting to be filled, indeed *demanding* to be filled, if contributions to the TV evangelicals are any measure, by all the waste, excess and sacrificial burnout of Heritage Park, U.S.A. An excremental God, therefore, for an American conservative culture disappearing into its own burnout, detritus, and decomposition. For Jimmy and Tammy's disgrace is just a momentary *mise-en-scene* as the soap opera of a panic god reverses field on itself, and everyone waits for what is next in the salvation myth, American-style: Jimmy and Tammy in their struggle through a period of dark tribulations and hard trials on their way to asking forgiveness (on Ted Koppel's *Nightline* show on ABC). As Jimmy Bakker once said: "In America, you have to be excessive to be successful." Or, as Tammy likes to sign out all her TV shows: "Just remember. Jesus loves you. He *really, really* does."

Panic Politics: If Gary Hart could implode so quickly, actually be *lasered* by the media and disappear as a political candidate in 72 hours, that is because Hart was first the beneficiary, and then the victim, of the postmodern politics of the simulacrum.

In the American politics of 1984, the inflation of Hart's sign-value was predictable. Not because of his neo-liberalism and not because of his *real* political constituency (he had none), but because a TV-subordinated politics required that Mondale — a real modernist *recit* — have a believable opponent in the primary game. And so, Hart, who in 1984 could understand media politics with such precision that he actually pioneered a new style of TV barnstorming just perfect for a postmodern politics when, in the absence of money for ads and time for organization, he flew from airport to airport through the South and West, stopping only for instant TV interviews and then immediately flying on to the next airport, this postmodern Hart — a serial candidate in a sidereal and topological politics — could be inflated instantly by the media under the empty sign of "new ideas".

But the media always incites flagging interest in its images by reversing field on itself. Here, transgression is the law in an estheticized reality. And so, Hart was *field-reversed*: first, his name; then, his age; later, his military record; and, finally, the sign-value of Hart was imploded by bringing it to ground by means of a curiously nostalgic surveillance of that old modernist signifier: his nightly sexual habits. In the end, Hart turned out to be a modern kind of guy who did not understand at all the secret of cynical power in the age of panic politics, and who had not meditated on Baudrillard's fatal insight that the secret of the great priests, politicians, and master strategists was always to understand that power was dead, that power in the postmodern condition has only the cynical existence of a perspectival simulacra. And they were killed, like Hart, when they forgot that secret, that in the age of dead power, power is interesting only on its dark side of disaccumulation, excess, and waste.

In his last press conference, Hart insisted that the private be held separate from the public and that Americans — to parody Sargent Friday in *Dragnet* — are interested in the issues, just the issues. *This is perfectly mistaken.* In panic politics of the postmodern kind, where power is always cynical and purely symbolic, and where the media is parasitical of *all* living sources of energy, it is *only* the private lives of candidates that are interesting, and that is because issues in the simulacrum are increasingly projections of the President's central nervous system onto the text of the body politic. Anyway, when American culture is increasingly experienced as a fuzzy set — where individual particles have no meaning apart from their patterning within larger and more abstract statistical totalities — then temporary political coherency for an imploding America can only be provided by *technological holograms*: like Reagan's presidential "State of the Union" addresses in the United States, or Thatcher's televised kitchen homilies about Britain as a family grocery store. In any case, in his now infamous interview in the *New York Times*' Sunday magazine, it was obvious that Hart was doomed when he said that Kierkegaard was his favorite philosopher. A presidential candidate of the cynical, neo-liberal kind should have been reading Derrida, Bataille, Baudrillard, and Nietzsche as keys to understanding the postmodern politics of the USA today, that is, the poststructuralist politics of *all text, no sex.*

Panic TV: This is Max Headroom as a harbinger of the post-bourgeois individual of estheticized liberalism who actually vanishes into the simulacra of the information system, whose face can be digitalized and fractalized by computer imaging because Max is living out a panic conspiracy in TV as the real world, and whose moods are perfectly postmodern because they alternate between kitsch and dread, between the ecstasy of catastrophe and the terror of the simulacra. Max Headroom, then, is the first citizen of the end of the world.

The

Body

Doubled

New John Nissen Mannequins (Brussels).
Photo: Christian d'Hair.

La Specola museum, Florence
Photo: Liberto Perugi

2

THESES ON THE DISAPPEARING BODY IN THE HYPER-MODERN CONDITION

Arthur and Marilouise Kroker

Thesis 1. Body Aesthetics for the End of the World

If, today, there can be such an intense fascination with the fate of the body, might this not be because the body no longer exists? For we live under the dark sign of Foucault's prophecy that the bourgeois body is a descent into the empty site of a dissociated ego, a "volume in disintegration", traced by language, lacerated by ideology, and invaded by the relational circuitry of the field of postmodern power. And if there is now an insistent demand for the recovery of "subjectivity", this would indicate that hyper-subjectivity has because *the* condition of possibility for the operation

No. 42 Study for *Temple Project*, 1980, New York, Francesca Woodman

of power at the fin-de-millenium. An ultra subjectivity for an entire society in ruins living on the excess energies of (its own) "borrowed power", becomes interesting only because it is so deeply parasitical of a culture, whose key technological feature is, as Michael Weinstein claims, that *the mind is on its way to being exteriorized again*. The struggle for the happy return of subjectivity would then be complicit with the deepest grammar of power in the postmodern condition, and, for a culture living under the sign of Bataille's general economy of excess, the body to excess would be its perfect analogue.

Everywhere today the aestheticization of the body and its dissolution into a semiurgy of floating body parts reveals that *we* are being processed through a media scene consisting of our own (exteriorized) body organs in the form of second-order simulacra. And subordinations of the body to the apparatus of (dead) power are multiple. *Ideologically*, the body is inscribed by the mutating signs of the fashion industry as skin itself is transformed into a screen-effect for a last, decadent and desperate, search for desire after desire. *Epistemologically*, the body is at the center of a grisly and false sense of subjectivity, as knowledge of the body (what Californians like to call "heightened body consciousness") is made a basic condition of possibility for the operation of postmodern power: the "cynical body" for a culture of cynical power. *Semiotically*, the body is tattooed, a floating sign, processed through the double imperatives of the cultural politics of advanced capitalism: the *exteriorization* of all the body organs as the key telemetry of a system that depends on the *outering* of the body functions (computers as the externalization of memory; *in vitro* fertilization as the alienation of the womb; Sony Walkmans as ablated ears; computer generated imagery as *virtual perspective* of the hyper-modern kind; body scanners as the intensive care unit of the exteriorization of the central nervous system); and the *interiorization* of ersatz subjectivity as a prepackaged ideological receptor for the pulsations of the desiring-machine of the fashion scene. *Technologically*, the body is subordinated to the twofold hypothesis of hyper-functionality and ultra refuse: never has the body (as a floating sign-system at the intersection of the conflation of power and life) been so necessary for the teleonomic functioning of the system; and yet never has the body (as a prime failure from the perspective of a technological society that has solved the problem of mortality in the form of technique as species-being) been so superfluous to the operation of advanced capitalist culture. In technological society, the body has achieved a purely *rhetorical* existence: its reality is that of refuse expelled as surplus-matter no longer necessary for the autonomous functioning of the technoscape. Ironically, though, just when the body has been transformed in practice into the missing matter of technological society, it is finally free to be emancipated as the rhetorical centre of the lost subject of desire after desire: the *body as metaphor* for a culture where power itself is always only fictional.

Indeed, why the concern over the body today if not to emphasize the fact that the (natural) body in the postmodern condition has *already* disappeared, and what we experience as the body is only a fantastic simulacra of body rhetorics? An *economic* rhetoric that would target the body as a privileged site for the acquisition of private property, and invests the consuming body with ideologies of desire (the "possessive individual"), a politico-juridical theory of rights (contractual liberalism), and even a media world (the abstract electrobody of the advertising scene). A *political* rhetoric that would constitute anew the public body in the form of "public opinion" as an elite substitution for the missing matter of the social, and massages, manipulates, and mediates public opinion at will, feeding it back to the political body in a dadaesque stream of message-response discharges. A *psychoanalytical* rhetoric that would desperately require the recovery of the subject as the site of the big reality-sign of the "unconscious", and recuperates the language of sexual desire and transgression as a way of marking the body with a whole language of sublimation, projection, and censorship, even tracing divisions between the body of prehistory (the *somatic* experience of the pre-oedipalized phase of childhood experience) and the body of post-history (the symbolically saturated world of *thetic* experience). A *scientific* rhetoric that would speak now of the existence of the teleonomic body at the intersection of genetic biology, structural linguistics, and cybernetics. And even a *sports* rhetoric that would celebrate the commodification to excess in publicity culture of particular body parts: 'arms' (baseball); 'feet' (soccer); 'shots' (hockey); and 'jumps' (basketball).

But if there is such a proliferation of body rhetorics, might not this, too, mean that, like sex before it, the body has now undergone a twofold death: the death of the *natural* body (with the birth of the languages of the social and, before them, the Foucauldian verdict of the "soul as the prison of the body"); and the death of the *discursive* body (with the disappearance of the body into Bataille's general economy of excess)? This would mean that we have entered the scene of panic bodies for the fin-de-millenium. Panic bodies living on (their own) borrowed power; violent, and alternating, scenes of surplus energy and perfect inertness; existing psychologically on the edge of fantasy and psychosis; floating sign-systems of the body reexperienced in the form of its own second-order simulacra; a combinatorial of *hyper-exteriorization* (of body organs) and *hyper-interiorization* (of designer subjectivities); and incited less by the languages of accumulation than fascinating, because catastrophic, signs of self-exterminism, self-liquidation, and self-cancellation. Panic bodies: an inscribed surface onto which are projected all the grisly symptoms of culture burnout as the high five-sign of the late 1980s. This is why, perhaps, the perfume industry (those advance outriders of hyper-modern theory) are manufacturing a new scent — *POISON* — for the olfactory pleasures of panic bodies; and why, if there can be now such widespread concern about viruses, this is symptomatic of a broader public panic about dead power as a body invader — the projection of evil within in the form of viruses as postmodern plagues.

Thesis 2. Blurred Images of Panic Bodies Moving to Escape Velocity at Warp Speeds

Smudged Images

Francesca Woodman's *Space* sequence is an exact photographic description of the exteriorization of the body in the hyper-modern condition. In the same way that the Irish painter Francis Bacon said that it is only by "smudging the image" that we can begin to capture the (disappearing) essence of the real today, Woodman's *Space* photography is a perfect dialetic of the blurred image. The image of the woman inside the case whirls in a dancer's pose as if to reflect that it is her imprisonment in this zone of surveillance (the

From *Space²*, *Providence, 1975-1976,* *Francesca Woodman*

glass case is the *reverse image* of Foucault's panoptic gaze) that gives her a certain magnetic, almost celestial, presence. But then perhaps we are all prisoners now of a panoptic power in negative image, and the blurring of the image of the dancing figure indicates exactly that limit placed on our freedom where the aestheticization of the body begins. Unless it is the opposite? Not the limit as the division *en abyme* between surveillance and emancipation but, as Foucault hinted in "A Preface to Transgression", the limit experience which only works to confirm the impossibility of transgression?

And so the woman framing the case is a *trompe-l'oeil*, distracting our gaze from the absence in the *Space* sequence of any border between inside and outside, between the limit and transgression. What we have in *Space* is not, as Rosalind Krauss has claimed in her interpretation of this work, an illustration of the "edge" in architectural practice, but the reverse. *Space* is the site of an endless body slide: an indeterminate optical refraction between the image of the reclining woman and that of the dancing woman, between the aesthetics of the "inert" and energy to excess, between the limit and transgression. What is this then, if not another meditation on immobility and frenzy as the key aesthetic moments of the hyper-modern condition: a violent and hallucinogenic scene of the un-bound sign of the aesthetic operator flashing across the simulacrum like the trace of the "virtual particle" before it? Woodman's *Space* sequence is a photographic practice *in situ* of the body living between fantasy and psychosis, and of the disappearance of the border in the visual architec-ture of today's (mediated) bodily practices.

It is the very same with Woodman's study for *Temple Project* which is an evocative lament for the body as a metaphor for the ruins within and without. Here, the body undergoes instant metamorphosis into the ruined columns of classical antiquity — the body actually becomes the site of classical ruins — because, in western culture, it never existed anyway. It was always the empty scene for the play of aestheticized power: some-times a "perspectival appearance" (Nietzsche); sometimes a "language trace" (Derrida); sometimes a disappearing sign of the "hyperreal" (Eco); some-times an optical "after-image" (Levin); and sometimes only a "solar anus" (Bataille). *Temple Project* is so wonderfully parodic of the modernist representation of power because it is about panic bodies that are always aestheticized when most abstract, and exhibit all the pathological symptoms of a culture to excess when they are inscribed within their own (image) simulacra.

And, of course, *Temple Project*, like the *Space* sequence before it, is gender specific. It is about women's bodies as the negative image of the ruins within the postmodern scene. Because now as ever, the play of power within and against the text of women's bodies is an early warning sign of a grisly power field that speaks the language of body invaders. As privileged objects of a domination that takes as its focus the inscription of the text of the body, women have always known the meaning of a relational pow-er that works in the language of body invaders. This is not, though, the wager of an old patriarchal power that announces itself in the transcen-dent and externalized language of hierarchy, univocity, and logocentricity, but a power field that can be multiple, pleasurable, and, indeed, fully em-bodied. Woodman's photographs are a scream that begins with the terri-ble knowledge women's bodies have always been postmodern because they have always been targets of a power which, inscribing the text of the flesh, seeks to make of feminine identity something interpellated by ideology, constituted by language, and the site of a "dissociated ego". Thus, if Wood-man's photographic practice is prophetic of the fact that, when power speaks in the language of a body invader, then the ruins within are also made complicit with the end of the emancipatory project, this may issue from her insight that women's bodies have always been forced to dwell in the dark infinity of the limit and transgression as serial signs: exchange-able and reversible poles in a power field that can be hyper-subjective be-cause it is also hyper-simulational. Women's bodies are an inscribed text, this time in skin, not philosophy, a preface to (the impossibility of) trans-gression.

Once the human body leaves this planet...

So what is it to be then? Carol Wainio's brilliant artistic vision of the simulational body of the late twentieth-century (*Untitled/Sound*) where the body actually disintegrates as it moves at warp speeds across the mediascape, and sound too (most of all?) is experienced as a relational power-field? Or not the body as an aesthetic operator traversed by the sound waves and frenetic imaging-systems of the mediascape (where the body is still contained by technology), but the body as its own simulacrum?

Untitled (Sound) 1986 Carol Wainio.
Photo: R. Max Tremblay, S.L. Simpson Gallery

Recently *High Performance*, a Los Angeles art magazine, published an important interview with Stelarc — a body artist from Australia and latterly Japan — who evidently follows Nietzsche in thinking of the body as a "dancing star".[1] Moving one step ahead of medical technology in using medical instruments to film the insides of his own body, Stelarc observed that in amplifying the sounds of his body — blood flows, muscles, heartbeats — he made of his own interiority an "acoustical landscape". Stelarc actually makes his body its own simulacrum: an acoustical scene; a "musical situation" (*Deca-Dance: Event for Three Hands*); a "primal image of floating in 0-G" (*Sitting/Swaying: Event for Rock Suspension*); and evolutionary detritus (*The Body Obsolete*). For Stelarc, like Nietzsche before him, the body may be a bridge over the abyss, but where Nietzsche, the last and best of all the modernists, turned back to a tragic meditation on the death of God, Stelarc makes of his own body its own horizon of sometimes repulsive, sometimes fascinating, possibilities. He actually makes of his body an experiment in thinking through the endless sign-slide between torture/pleasure (*Event for Obsolete Body*), sensuality/exterminism ("What people saw was the internal structure of my body on a video screen as well as the sealed external body"); and skin/deskinning technologies ("new bodies" for people who manage to escape the 1-G gravitational field of planet One.)

STELARC'S THE BODY OBSOLETE*

The imagery of the suspended body is really a beautiful image of the Obsolete body. The body is plugged into a gravitational field, suspended yet not escaped from it.

My body was suspended by hooks with ropes from an 18-foot diamond inflated balloon. My body sounds were transmitted to the ground and amplified by speakers. I got sick — turned purple — the body sounds changed dramatically.

Sitting/Swaying — Event for Rock Suspension, Photo by Kenji Nozawa, Tamara Gallery, Tokyo.

THE BODY AS SIMULACRUM

In our past evolution, the body has been molded in a 1-G gravitational field. The notion of designing the body for new environments fascinates me. Is it possible to create a thing to transcend the environment? Unplugging the body from this planet... Over four-million years, the body developed a response against viruses, foreign bodies, etc. But technology is just a couple of hundred years old. The first phase of technology contained the body

Handswriting, Stelarc, Maxi Gallery, Tokyo. Photo by Akihiro Okada, *High Performance*, Issue 24/1983.

whereas now miniaturized tech can be implanted into the body. If the tech is small the body acts as if it were not there. It becomes a component. Once the human body leaves this planet we have an excuse to invent a new body — more expanded and variable.

---

* All quotations are taken from *High Performance*, "The Body Obsolete", with Paul McCarthy interviewing Stelarc, Volume 6, Number 4, 1983, pp. 14-19.

Thesis 3. *Ultra Oedipus:* The Psychoanalytics of the Popular Viruses of (our) Bourgeoisie

In the late 1980s, we are beyond Deleuze and Guattari's theses in *Anti-Oedipus: Capitalism and Schizophrenia* that power in the postmodern condition (the "body without organs") operates by transforming the body into a screen for all the pulsating signs of the fashion scene, by conflating power and seduction, and by dehistoricizing and delocalizing the body until it merges with all the relays and networks of the desiring machine of the *socius.*

Today it's this and more. Never has power been so deeply subjective and localized as the body is now recycled in the language of medieval mythology. In medieval times, extreme anxiety about the public situation was typically projected in the sign-language of sin onto the body as the enemy within. Indeed, as Umberto Eco hints in *Travels in Hyperreality,* the medieval scene was marked by a whole litany of cardinal sins for an apocalyptic age in which the body was made the truth-sayer of the ruins without. Now, as late twentieth-century experience comes under the big sign of the medievalization of politics, we witness an almost daily series of media hystericisations of the body:[2] Coke (the seeming addiction of the whole middle class in a media-defined drug frenzy); AIDS (panic fear about sexually transmitted diseases); a nation of "drunk drivers"; and even "missing kids" (who make even milk cartons a metaphor for a spreading panic fear about the "missing family" of traditional American mythology).

In a key political essay, "Anxiety and Utopia"[3], Franz Neumann argued that neo-fascism American-style would be marked by a twofold psychological movement: the *externalization* of private stress in the form of the projection of residual anxieties about the missing ego of the bourgeois self onto the "enemy without" (scapegoating of the weak by the politically powerful is the keynote of the contemporary politics of ressentiment); and the desperate search for *authoritarian political leadership* which would offer (at least) the media illusion of a coherent political community.

No longer under the sign of the political economy of accumulation but in the Bataillean scene of the general economy of excess, the psychological dissolution of the bourgeois ego follows exactly the *reverse* course to that theorised by Neumann: no longer the projection of the existential crisis (the missing matter of the old bourgeois ego) onto the enemy without, but the *introjection* of the public crisis (the death of the social and the self-liquidating tendencies of the economy of excess) onto the "enemy within." A whole contagion of panic mythologies (AIDS, anorexia, bulimia, herpes) about disease, panic viruses, and panic addictions (from drugs to alcohol) for a declining culture where the body is revived, and given one last burst of hyper-subjectivity, as the inscribed text for all the stress and crisis-symptoms of the death of the social.

Everyone benefits from this resurrection of the "medieval body" positioned as a passive screen for all the hystericizations and panic mythologies of the (disappearing) public realm. When the scene of general cultural collapse is shifted onto the terrain of subjectivity, the political results are predictable. The return of an authoritarian regime in labour relations and the disciplinary state are legitimated anew as political elites (responding to programmed public moods in the form of opinion polls) and economic elites (the valorized leaders of late modernity) shift the crisis without onto the previously private terrain of the body. Images of the sinful body, then, for a political scene where the elites get exactly what they want: the media monopolize the rhetoric for the just-nominated addiction of the week; political elites inscribe the body with the disciplinary agenda of the conservative mood (mandatory drug-testing as a privileged site for focussing on the "enemy within"); economic elites recycle the labouring body of primitive capitalism; and reactionary moral elites (from family therapists to the new fundamentalist outriders of sexual repression) transform fear and anxiety about panic addictions and panic viruses into repressive political retrenchments: against feminism, against gays and lesbians, and against the young. In the politics of decayed vitality for the twilight time of the twentieth-century, even the missing bodies of (our) Yuppies — the ascendant class-fragment of late capitalism — are happy: the nomination of the body as a crisis-centre fit for the immediate entry of the therapeutic agencies of the state and vulnerable to a moral wash of guilt and repentance is the *trompe-l'oeil* necessary to disguise, and repress, the fact of the "disappearing body" as the fate of late modernity. And the return of hyper-subjectivity is only a certain indication of the presence now of body invaders — from the fashion scene and panic viruses to the proliferating signs of consumer culture — as the language of postmodern power.

Thesis 4. Structural Bodies

> With the end of the *bound* sign, the reign of the emancipated sign begins, in which all classes acquire the power to participate... With the transition of the sign-values of prestige from one class to another, we enter the world of the counterfeit in a stroke, passing from a limited order of signs, where taboos inhibit "free" production, to a proliferation of signs according to demand.
>
> J. Baudrillard,
> "The Structural Law of Value and the Order of Simulacra"

Good Health without a Body

> Health might be treated as a symbolic circulating medi-
> um regulating human action and other life processes... We
> treat the health complex as strategic in a society with an
> activistic orientation.

T. Parsons, "Health and Disease"

Talcott Parsons, the bourgeois social theorist, provided a privileged understanding of the hyper-modern body when, at the end of his life, he
developed a series of key theorisations about the creation of the "structural" body as the way in which we now reexperience our organs in the
form of their second-order simulacra. For Parsons, late modernity is marked
by the organization of social experience within the symbolic (genetic) apparatus of the "structural paradigm": Baudrillard's world of the unbound
sign. Typified by "instrumental activism" as its central moral code, by "institutionalized individualism" as its theory of (bourgeois) emancipation,
and by the *"vis mediatrix"* as its cultural ideal, the structural paradigm
is driven onwards by the liquidation of the social, and the exterminism
of the "bound sign" in the cultural excess of a system that has the proliferation of "circulating media of exchange" as its basic cultural apparatus and
the language of "nomic necessity" as its grammar of power.

In instrumentalist language that was a perfect mirror-image of the culture of technicisme he sought to describe (and celebrate), Parsons insisted
that health no longer has a *natural* existence, but only functions in the
purely simulated form of a generalized, symbolic, and circulating medium
of exchange. Health is outside the body, reconstituting it as a relational
field of power (the "health complex") which the body is compelled to
traverse. Stripped of health as a natural referent, the hyper-modern body
is regulated by a health complex that imposes a specific *normative* definition of health ("the teleonomic capacity of an individual living system to
maintain a favourable, regulated state that is the prerequisite of the effective performance... of functions"); legitimates an ominous politics of illness as "societal disturbance"; embodies a fully *technicist* ideology (the
professionalization of medical practice); privileges health as a strategic and
materially inscribed method of social control; is invested with a specific
"will to truth" (bio-technology as emblematic of Foucault's "power and
death over life"); and, finally, subordinates the body to a threefold axis of
power: a market-steered pharmaceutics of the body; a culturally inscribed
definition of public (and private) health norms; and a politics of health
as cultural telemetry.

Parson's world, which is, after all, only the most recent, and eloquent,
expression of the advanced liberal theory of the body, is that of *"cynical
health"* for a cybernetic culture where the body, disappearing in the in-

terstices of the structural paradigm, reappears in the form of an after-image of the health complex. Like Baudrillard's emancipated sign before it, health has lost its representational capacity. Health in the hyper-modern condition is a complex and proliferating sign-system invested by the language of bio-technology, horizoned by the species-dream of genetic biology, steered by the relentless imperatives of market-accumulation, and coded by a relational power field that speaks only the language of the *teleonomic capacities* of the structural paradigm. The health of the "structural body" does not exist except as a purely relational and symbolic term: the processed world of the health complex (health without bodies) in which we come to know the truth about our (disappearing) bodies. Here, Stelarc's fascinating, yet chilling, vision of the new body which leaves this planet is revealed to be not an instance of futurism, but of history. The scanned body of medical telemetry is both the condition of possibility for and justification of the rhetoric of (teleonomic) life in late modernity.

Intelligence without Minds

> As a generalized symbolic medium of interchange, we conceive intelligence as circulating. It can be acquired by individuals — for example, through learning, and it is spent as a resource which facilitates the solution of cognitively significant problems. It should, however, be clearly distinguished from knowledge. Just as money should be distinguished from concrete commodities.
>
> T. Parsons, *Action Theory and the Human Condition*

It is the very same with intelligence which, in the late twentieth-century, floats free of its organic basis in the mind (which was always a purely discursive concept anyway) and is on its way to being exteriorized. Here, Parsons refuses the humanist vision of the thinking subject (as, perhaps, the ideological fiction of classical liberalism), and speaks instead of the relational, disembodied, and purely cybernetic world of intelligence (the ideological fiction of the MIND in the last days of liberalism). Intelligence is the emancipated sign of knowledge in the hyper-modern condition. Like money before it (the perspectival fiction at the end of the *natural* order of the commodity economy), intelligence can be "contentless" because it is a relational process owned by no one, but that takes possession of the mind-functions of teleonomic society.

Existing at the edge of the death of knowledge and the triumph of the negative image of dataism, intelligence refers to the exteriorization of consciousness in late modernity. Possessing only a purely symbolic value (*prestige*); convertible into the exchange-value of *influence*; emblematic of the victory of *science as the language of power*; and controlled by the leading elites of *technocracy*, the valorization of intelligence is a certain indication that we are living the great paradigm shift prefigured by the exteriorization of mind as the dynamic momentum of technological society.

The exteriorized mind of technocracy is endlessly circulating (the radical semiurgy of data in information society function by tattooing the body). This is the world of panic science where consciousness is metaphorical (intelligence has no value in use, but only value in exchange); where information is regulatory of energy in a new cybernetic order of politics; and where EXTERIORIZED MIND is, itself, only a medium across which the shuttling of techno-bodies in search of a brain function takes place. A world of computer enhanced individualism; or as Parsons would boast in a language which is all the more chilling because so hyper-pragmatic:

> Intelligence is not knowledge but the capacity to mobilize what it takes to produce or command knowledge.[4]

An already elegant tombstone, then, for *our* imprisonment in the new world of panic science.

Thesis 5. What About Me? The Body Exteriorized

Why then be sad as the body is unplugged from the planet? What is this if not the more ancient philosophical movement of immanence to transcendence as the body is on its way to being exteriorized again? Behind the popping outwards of the organs lies a power field which is only the darker dream of a bad infinity. With the threnody of screams, there are also sighs of pleasure, as the body is reborn in its technified forms:

Alienated Wombs: the ideological constitution of birth which is marked by the medicalization of the woman's body and the breaking into the body of a whole technological and juridico-discursive apparatus typified by the exteriorization of reproduction in the form of *in vitro* fertilization and technologies of genetic reproduction. In bio-technology at the *fin-de-millenium*, the womb has gone public, alienated from nature, inscribed by eugenics, bonded to public law, and made fully accessible to the exchange-principle. Or, as Mair Verthuy has said about feminism and bio-technology:

> ... We have become a bio-society without even noticing it. Genetic manipulation is a daily event in our universities, in industrial laboratories, military installations. Reproductive technologies are listed on the stock market... Already female foetuses are aborted in greater number than male; femicide is a fact of life in China; work is being carried out to predetermine the sex of the foetus; lactation can be developed in males; artificial placenta exist; it will soon be possible to implant an embryo in any abdomen: male, female; animal, human... Now men can procreate.[5]

Virtual Heads: A story in the *New York Times* illustrates perfectly the obsolescence of the body in the new universe of virtual technology. The United States Air Force had uncovered a critical flaw — the inadequacies of the body reflexes of pilots — in the creation of ultra-sonic jet fighters. According to the aircraft designers, the human body is no longer capable of absorbing, yet alone responding, to the "information environment" of jet fighters moving at hyper-speeds. From the perspective of aerial technology, the human body *is* obsolete and, as Stelarc predicted, what is desperately required is a new body fit for the age of ultra-technologies. In fact, this is just what the designers have created, at least beginning with the *heads* of fighter-pilots. To compensate for the inability of human vision to match the speed and intensity of the information environment of jet-fighters, designers are planning to equip pilots with virtual heads: special helmets which block out normal ocular vision and, by means of a video screen projected on the inside of the mask, feed the pilot at a slowed-down and selective pace specific, strategic information about his aerial environment: altitude, presence of other aircraft, speed, target range. A system of perspective vision, therefore, for the advanced outriders of teleonomic society.

Computer Enhanced Individualism: "Escada was the first to bring computers into the design room. Why? To respond to the rise of individualism in today's world. The incredible union of electronics and artistic talent makes possible the creation of more colours than any human eye has ever seen. Moreover, this technology makes the matching of colours — even on differing fabrics, patterns or designs — exact."

Escada Ad., *Vogue*, 1986

"It was as if fashion dreams were bubbling out of the underground..."

Vogue, October 1986

Man Ray Fashion Photograph, 1938. ©Vis-Art 1987.

The Capezio Woman[6]

The Capezio ad is also about the body debased, humiliated, and inscribed to excess by all the signs of consumer culture. The woman is prostrate and silent as if to emphasize the reduction of her body to a shoe tree. And, like a manic fantasy which follows from knowing ourselves only through a psychotic simulacra of bodily images (the advertising machine), the woman's body, from her facial expression ("devilishly") to the positioning of her limbs, intimates that subjectivity itself is now colonized. And why the shoes to excess? A twofold hypothesis: the advertisement is hyper-functional from the viewpoint of primitive accumulation (more product per image); and the prostrate body is all that is left after being inscribed as a background text for shoes: an object of parody, a site of impoverishment, a social remainder. Just because it runs to excess and, indeed, states openly about the humiliation of the body what other ads only suggest, the Capezio woman is a perfect sign of the "structural body" of the 1980s. The Capezio woman is, in fact, the advertising equivalent on the dark side of Francesca Woodman's *Space* sequence.

All the while, though, there is that sigh of lament from the hidden recesses of subjectivity, another (bodily) image of women waiting to be born once again in remembrance of love lost and recovered, another *no* in the "war of the images" against the structural body.

Notes

1. "The Body Obsolete", an interview with Stelarc by Paul McCarthy, *High Performance*, Volume 6, No. 4, 1983, pp. 14-19.

2. We are grateful to Kim Sawchuk, Julia Emberley, and Peter Kulchyski for their helpful comments on the body mythologized. The thesis on *Ultra Oedipus* is an elaboration of the discussion of panic sex and body invaders in *The Postmodern Scene: Excremental Culture and Hyper-Aesthetics*, (New York: St. Martin's Press, 1986); and (Montréal: New World Perspectives, 1986).

3. Franz Neumann, *The Democratic and Authoritarian State: Essays in Political and Legal Theory*", (Glencoe: Free Press, 1957), pp. 270-300.

4. Talcott Parsons, *Action Theory and the Human Condition*, (New York: The Free Press, 1978), pp. 137-138.

5. Mair Verthuy, "Is There Life After Specificity?" *Canadian Journal of Political and Social Theory*, Vol. 10, No. 3, 1986, pp.189-191.

6. The *Capezio* ad was produced by Ross and Harasym, photo by Shun Sasbuchio.

3

THE YEAR 2000 HAS ALREADY HAPPENED

Jean Baudrillard

I

I once again take up Canetti's proposition: "A painful idea: that beyond a certain precise point in time, history was no longer real. Without being aware of it, the totality of human race would have suddenly quit reality. All that would have happened since then would not have been at all real, but we would not be able to know it. Our task and our duty would now be to discover this point and, to the extent that we shall not stop there, we must persevere in the actual destruction." (*The Human Province*)

There are different plausible hypotheses as to this disappearance of history. Canetti's expression, "...the totality of the human race would have suddenly quit reality," irresistibly evokes, for our contemporary imaginary, astrophysics, the "speed of liberation" (velocity) necessary for a body to escape the gravitational force of a star or a planet. According to this image, we may suppose that the acceleration of modernity, technical, factual, mediatory, the acceleration of all economic, political and sexual exchanges — all that we denote fundamentally under the term "liberation" — has carried us at a speed of liberation, such that we have one day (and in this case, we can, as Canetti does, speak of a "precise" moment: as in physics, the point of "liberation" is exactly calculable) escaped from the referential sphere of the real and of history. We are truly "liberated," in all senses of the word, liberated to such an extent that we have left, through speed (the accelerated metabolization of our societies), a certain space/time, a certain horizon where the real is possible, where the event is possible, because gravitation is still strong enough so that things can think themselves, return to themselves, and thus have some duration and some consequence.

A certain slowness (that is to say, a certain speed, but not too much), a certain distance, but not too much, a certain "liberation" (energy of rupture and change), but not too much, are necessary to produce that sort of condensation, of significant crystallization of events that we call history, that sort of coherent deployment of causes and effects that we call the real.

Beyond this gravitational effect which maintains bodies in an orbit of signification, once "liberated" by sufficient speed, all the signifying atoms lose themselves in space. Each atom goes in its own direction towards infinity, and loses itself in space. That is precisely what we are living in our actual societies, which endeavour to accelerate all bodies, all messages, all processes in all senses, and which in particular have created, with the modern media, for each event, each narrative, each image, a space of the simulation of trajectories to the infinite. Each fact, each trait, political, historical, or cultural is endowed, through its power of mediatory diffusion, with a kinetic energy which breaks itself from its own space, for always, and propels it into a hyperspace where it loses all meaning, since it will never return. It is thus not necessary to write science-fiction: we have as of now, here and now, in our societies, with the media, the computers, the circuits, the networks, the acceleration of particles which has definitively broken the referential orbit of things.

As for history, one must look at its consequences. The "narrative" has become impossible, since it is by definition (re-citatum) the possible recurrence of a sequence of sense. Today each fact, each event, through the impulse to diffusion, through the injunction to circulation, to total communication, is liberated solely for itself — each fact becomes atomic, nuclear, and pursues its own trajectory in the void. To be diffused to infinity, it must be fragmented like a particle. Only thus can it attain a velocity of non-return, which will distance it definitively from history. Each event becomes inconsequential, because it goes too fast — it is too quickly diffused, too far, it is seized by the circuits — it will never return to testify to itself, nor to its meaning (sense is always a testimony). Moreover, each cultural and factual set must be fragmented, disarticulated, in order to enter the circuits, each language must be resolved into 0/1, into binary terms, in order to circulate no longer in our memory, but in the memories, electronic and luminous, of computers. No human language can resist the speed of light. No historical event can resist its planetary diffusion. No meaning can resist its acceleration. No history can resist the centrifugation of facts by themselves, the delimitation of space-time (I would even say: no sexuality can resist its liberation, no culture can resist its promotion, no truth can resist its verification, etc.).

This is what I call simulation. But I must specify that simulation is double-edged, and that what I advance here is none other than an exercise in simulation. I am no longer in a state to "reflect" on something, I can only push hypotheses to their limits, snatch them from their critical zones of reference, take them beyond a point of no-return. I also take theory into the hyper-space of simulation — in which it loses all objective validity, but perhaps it gains in coherence, that is, in a real affinity with the system which surrounds us.

II

The second hypothesis concerning the disappearance of history is in some sense the inverse of the first — it will no longer have to do with acceleration, but rather with the slowing-down of processes. It comes once again from physics.

Matter retards the passage of time. More precisely, slows it down. This phenomenon increases as the density increases. The effect of this slackening would be to extend the length of the wave of light emitted by this body to the extent that it will be received by the external observer. Past a certain limit, time is stopped, the length of the wave becomes infinite. The wave no longer exists. The light goes off.

Here also the analogical transfer is not difficult. You have only to think "masses" instead of "matter," and history instead of "time." You would then know that there would simply be a slowing down of history when it touches the astral body of "the silent majority." Our societies are dominated by this process of the masses, not so much in the demographic or sociological sense of this term, (as in the sense of reaching a critical point, a point of no-return), no longer in acceleration (first hypothesis), but in inertia. Here then is the most important event of our modern societies, the most subtle and most profound trick of their history: the advent, in the very course of their socialization, of their mobilization, of their productive and revolutionary intensification (these societies are all revolutionary in terms of past centuries), the advent of a force of inertia, of an immense indifference, and of the silent power of indifference. What we call the masses. This mass, this inert material of the social, does not arise from a lack of exchange, information, and communication, but on the contrary from the multiplication and saturation of exchange, information, etc. It is born of the hyper-density of the city, of merchandise, of messages, of circuits. It is the cold star of the social and, surrounding this mass, history chills, slows down, events succeed one another and are annihilated in indifference. Neutralized, immunized by information, the masses in turn neutralize history and play (act) as a screen of absorption. They themselves have no history, no sense, no conscience, no desire. They are the potential residue of all history, of all meaning, of all conscience, of all desire. All these good things, as they spread in our modernity, have fomented a mysterious counterpart of which the misunderstanding (the misunderstanding of this inertial force, of this power of inertia, of this inverse energy) today details all political, social, and historical strategies.

This time, it is the contrary: progress, history, reason, desire can no longer find their "speed of liberation." These can no longer snatch themselves from a body too dense, that irresistibly slows their trajectories, that slows time to the point that, as of now, the perception, the imagination of the future escapes us. All social, historical, temporal transcendence is absorbed by this mass in its silent immanence. We are already at the point where political and social events do not have sufficient autonomous energy to move us, and thus they unfold as in a silent film for which we are, not individually, but collectively, irresponsible. History ends there, and you may see how: not because of lack of character, nor of violence (there will always be more violence, but we must not confound violence and history), nor of events (there will always be more events, thanks to the media and information!), but of a slowing down, indifference, and stupefaction. History can no longer surpass itself, it can no longer envisage its own finality, dream its own end; it wraps itself in its own immediate effect, it exhausts itself in its own special effects, it falls back on itself, it implodes in actuality. Finally, we cannot even speak of the end of history, for it will not have time to rejoin its own end. Its effects accelerate, but its sense slackens, ineluctably. It will end by stopping and by extinguishing itself, like light and time at the outskirts of a mass infinitely dense.

Whether the universe is in indefinite or retractile expansion towards an infinitely dense and infinitely small original nucleus, depends on its critical mass (on which speculation itself is infinite, as the "invention" of new particles). Analogously, whether our human history be evolutionary or involutionary depends perhaps on the critical mass of humanity. Has History, the destiny of the species, attained the speed of liberation necessary to triumph over the inertia of the mass? Are we, like the galaxies, caught in a definitive movement that distances us one from another at a prodigious speed, or is this dispersion to infinity destined to end, and the human molecules to approach one another according to an inverse movement of gravitation? Can the human mass, which increases everyday, control a pulsation of this kind?

Humanity too has had its big bang: a certain critical density, a certain critical concentration of humans and of exchanges controls this explosion that we call history — dispersion across space-time of nuclei once dense, hieratic and almost intemporal. Today, we have to deal with the inverse effect: the surpassing of the threshold of the critical mass (population, events, information) controls the inverse process of the inertia of history and politics.

In the cosmic order, we do not know if we have attained a speed of liberation such that we would be in a definitive expansion (this will no doubt remain eternally uncertain). In the human order, of which the perspectives are more limited, it could be that the very energy of the liberation of the species (the demographic, technological acceleration, the acceleration of exchanges in the course of centuries) creates an excess of mass and of resistance which goes faster than the initial energy, and which would thus drag us in an unrelenting movement of contraction and inertia.

(I have forgotten to mention that the mass-effect also depends on simulation. The masses are today our model of social simulation, where the social realizes itself beyond all hopes, but also where it exasperates itself and annihilates itself in its own magnifying mirror. The masses are the purest product of the social, and its most perverse effect.)

III

Third hypothesis, third analogy. This time I will no longer take my examples from physics, but from music; what interests me is still the "vanishing point," the point of disappearance, of evanescence of something — that point of which Canetti speaks, beyond which all has ceased to be real...

Where does the point of a useless sophistication of the social begin? Where does the point of such a realisation of the social, which is also that of its collapse, begin?

It is exactly as with stereophonic effects. We are all obsessed (and not only in music) with high fidelity, obsessed by the quality of the musical "rendering." On the console of our systems, armed with our tuners, our amplifiers and our speakers, we regulate the bass and the treble, we mix, we combine, we multiply the tracks, in search of an impeccable technique, an infallible music. I still remember a control room in a recording studio where the music, diffused on four tracks, came at once in four dimensions, and of a sudden seemed viscerally secreted in the interior, with a surreal relief... It was no longer music. Where is the degree of technological sophistication, where the threshold of "high fidelity" beyond which music as it were disappears? For the problem of the disappearance of music is the same as that of history: it will not disappear *for want of music*, it will disappear in the perfection of its materiality, in its very own special effect. There is no longer judgment, nor aesthetic pleasure, it is the ecstasy of musicality.

It is also thus with history, there too we have gone beyond that limit where, as a result of informational sophistication, history as such has ceased to exist. Immediate diffusion at high rates, proliferation of special effects, and of secondary effects, fading... and this famous Larsen (feedback) effect, produced in acoustics by the too great proximity of a source and a receptor: you find it again in history in the form of a too great proximity and thus of a disastrous interference of an event and its media-diffusion: whence a sort of short-circuit between cause and effect, or between object and experimental subject in the micro-physical experience (and in the human sciences!), all things which entail a principle of radical uncertainty about the truth, about the very reality of the event. Like the too-high fidelity, technological perfection entails a principle of radical uncertainty about the reality of the music. Canetti says it well; beyond that nothing is real (any longer). It is this which today causes the "little music" of history also to escape us, it disappears into the excess of its own referent (which plays like "deterrence," like dissuasion), it vanishes into the microscopic, into the instantaneity of information; it, too, is seized by the principle of uncertainty.

At the very heart of information is the event, the history of which is haunted by its (own) disappearance. At the heart of hi-fi is music, haunted by its disappearance. At the heart of the most sophisticated experimentation is science haunted by the disappearance of its object. At the heart of pornography is sexuality haunted by its own disappearance. Everywhere, the same effect of the "rendering," of the absolute proximity of the real: the same effect of simulation.

By definition, this "vanishing point," the point on this side of which *there was* history, *there was* music, *there was* a meaning to the event, to the social, to sexuality (and even to psycho-analysis — but even this last has also long ago so passed beyond this point of exasperation, of perfectionist affectation in the theory of the unconscious that the concept has vanished therefrom), this point is irrecuperable. Where must we stop the stereo perfection? The limits are constantly extended, since they are those of technical obsession. Where must we stop information? To the collective fascination, we can only oppose a moral objection, which does not make much sense either.

This point that we cannot locate, the passing beyond of it is thus irreversible (contrary to what Canetti implicitly hopes). The situation immediately becomes an original one. We will no longer find music prior to the stereo (unless by an effect of supplementary simulation), we will no longer find history prior to information and the media. The original essence (of music, of the social...), the original concept (of the unconscious, of history...) has disappeared because we will never be able to detach these from their model of perfection, which is at the same time their model of simulation, of their forced assumption in a transgressed truth, which is also their point of inertia and their point of no-return. We will never know what the social or music were, before becoming exasperated in their useless perfection today. We will never know what history was before becoming exasperated in the technical perfection of information, or before vanishing in the multiplicity of codes — we will never know what all things were before vanishing in the realization of their model...

IV

That we leave history in order to enter into simulation (but we enter it, in my opinion, as much through the biological concept of the genetic code as by the media, as much through exploration, which for us acts as a space of simulation, as by the concept of the computer as a cerebral equivalent, as cerebral *model*, etc.) is not at all a despairing hypothesis, unless one speaks of simulation as a higher form of alienation. Which I will certainly not do. History is precisely the place of alienation, and if we leave history, we also leave alienation (not without nostalgia, one must say, for that good old dramaturgy of subject and object).

But we can as well offer the hypothesis that history itself is or was only an immense model of simulation. Not in the sense of all this having been only wind, or that events would always only have the meaning that we give them (which could be true, but of no direct interest here). No, I speak rather of the time in which it unfolds, of this linear time where events supposedly succeed one another from cause to effect, even if the complexity is great. This time is, at the same time, that of the end (of an eschatological process in whatever form: Last Judgment or revolution, salvation or catastrophe) and of an unlimited suspension of the end. This time, where only a history can take place — that is a succession of not insane facts, but all in disequilibrium towards the future — is not that of ceremonial societies, where all things are accomplished at the origin and where ceremony retraces the perfection of this original event, perfect in the sense of all being fulfilled. In opposition to this order where time is completed [*accompli*], that is, simply not existing in the sense in which we understand it, the liberation of the real time of history (for it is a "liberation," a deliverance from the ritual universe wherefrom the linearity of time and death gradually arises) can appear as a purely artificial process. What is this difference (*aufschiebung*), what is this suspense, why does what must be fulfilled do so at the end of time, at the end of history? There is here a projection of a model of reality that must have seemed perfectly invented, perfectly fictitious, perfectly absurd and immaterial for cultures which had no sense whatsoever of a differentiated "expiration," of a waiting, of a gradual sequence, of a finality... A scenario which will in fact have quite a bit of difficulty imposing itself, being so little evident, and in such contradiction to all fundamental exigency. The first epoch of Christianity would have been marked by vehement resistance, even on the part of the believers, to see the coming of the kingdom of God carried forward into an indefinite future. The acceptance of this "historical" perspective of salvation, that is of its unfulfillment in the present, does not go without violence, and all the following heresies would agree on this leitmotif: the immediate demand of the Kingdom of God, the immediate fulfillment of the promise. Something like a defiance of time. We know that entire collectivities have gone so far as to die so as to hasten the advent of the Kingdom. Since this last was promised them at the end of time, it was only a matter of ending time immediately.

All history has been accompanied by a millennial defiance of the temporality of history. The will to see things accomplished immediately, and not in terms of a long detour, is not at all a regressive phantasm of childhood. It is a defiance of time which is born with time itself. With linear time, that is, simply with the birth of time, two contradictory forms are born: the one which consists of following the meanderings of time and of constructing a history, the other which consists of accelerating the course of time, or of brutally condensing it so as to arrive at its end. To the historical perspective, which continually displaces its stakes onto a hypothetical end, has always been opposed a fatal exigency, a fatal strategy of time which wants to continue non-stop to annihilate time and short-circuit the Last Judgment. We cannot say that one of these two powers has actually prevailed over the other, and in the very course of history the question has remained a burning one: ought we or ought we not to wait? Since the messianic convulsion of the first Christians who, weary of waiting for the promised kingdom of Heaven, wished to hasten the advent (the millennium) by their own death; beyond the heresies and revolts, there had always been the desire of the anticipation of the end — eventually by death, by a kind of seductive suicide which aims at diverting God from history. It is the same fatal strategy as that of the ascetic: to entrap God by death, or by realized perfection (the Carthares as well), and thus place Him before his responsibilities, those of beyond the end, those of fulfillment.

If we think about it, terrorism does nothing else. It attempts to (en) trap power by an immediate and total act, without waiting for the end of history. It puts itself in the ecstatic position of the end, and thus hopes to introduce the conditions of the Last Judgement. It is nothing of the sort, of course, but this defiance of history has a long history, and it always fascinates, for, profoundly, time and history have never been accepted. Even if they are not disposed to set up a fatal strategy of this kind, people remain profoundly conscious of the arbitrary, the artificial character, indeed of the fundamental hypocrisy, of time and of history. They are never duped by those who ask them to hope.

Even outside of terrorism, is there not a glimmer of that violent adventist [*parousique*] exigency in the global phantasm of catastrophe which hovers over the contemporary world? Demand for a violent resolution of reality, precisely when this last escapes into hyperreality? Which hyperreality puts an end to the very hope of a Last Judgment (or of revolution). If the ends glimpsed escape us, if even history has no chance whatsoever of realizing them since they would have ended in the meantime (it is always the story of Kafka's Messiah: he arrives too late, one day too late; this slippage is unbearable), then so much for playing the precession of the end, so much for short-circuiting the advent of the Messiah. It has always been the demonical temptation: to falsify the ends and the calculation of the ends, to falsify time and the occurrence of things, to hasten the end — in the impatience of accomplishment, or by the secret intuition that the promise of accomplishment is, anyway, also false and diabolic.

V

The denial of history would thus be that of a fastidious and artificial duration — all *Aufhebung* is experienced [*ressentie*] as *Aufshiebung* — a denial of time as artifact. A denial which one can easily locate in its religious and militarist forms, in its individual and terroristic forms, but which is also perceptible in massive comportments of retreat, of the suspension of the historic will, including the apparent inverse obsession of historicising everything, of achieving everything, of memorizing everything of our past and of that of other cultures. Isn't there here a symptom of a collective prescience of the end of the event and of the living time of history, so that one must arm oneself (as it were) with all of artificial memory, all the signs of the past in order to confront the absence of the future and of the glacial time which awaits us? Have we not the impression that mental and intellectual structures are being buried, enshrouded in memories, in archives, far from the sun, in quest of a silent efficiency or an improbable resurrection? All thoughts are entombed with the prudence of the year 2000. They can already smell the terror of the year 2000. Our societies instinctively adopt the solution of those cryogenics that preserve things in liquid nitrogen while waiting for the discovery of a mode of survival. They are like that luxurious and funereal merchandise that we enclose in the subterranean sarcophagus at the "Forum des Halles" as the museum of our culture, for the future generations after the catastrophe. These societies which expect nothing more of a future advent, and which place less and less confidence in history, these societies which entomb themselves behind their prospective technologies, their stocks of information and in the immense alveolate networks of communication where *time is finally annihilated by pure circulation* — these generations wil never perhaps awake, but they don't know it. The year 2000 will perhaps not take place, but they know nothing of it.

VI

What is lost for us in its actual form is what we used to call the work of the negative. In "change" (social, economic, informational) based, at bottom, on the model of biogenetic innovation; that is to say, on a redistribution of molecular schemas, there is no longer, as in history, the work of the negative (it is the same for the image: there is no longer a negative, this time in the photographic sense, in the digital and numerical image). But what has been lost well before this, as Benjamin would say, is the aura, the glory of the event. For centuries, history saw itself under the sign of glory and of the search for glory, therefore under the sign of a very strong illusion, of a sumptuous capital which circulates through the generations, and to which man voluntarily sacrifices himself. This virtue seems today derisory, and its pursuit no longer signifies. We no longer pursue glory, but identity; not the exaltation of play, but the verification of existence. Events no longer serve as anything but proofs, history has little by little collapsed into the field of its causes and its effects, and events have fallen under the blow of one reason, one structure, one causality, one finality. Whereas the task had been once to lose oneself in a prodigious dimension, the task today is, on the contrary, to give proof of our existence (or of the justice of a cause, etc...). The prodigious event, the one which does not measure itself in terms of its causes, which creates its own scene, its own dramaturgy, no longer exists. The only existing events are those which have a meaning that goes further than their meaning, which are to some extent produced only to verify a law, a correspondence of forces, a structure of a model. It is doubtless there, in this analytic unfolding, in this loss of glory, of the power of illusion, in this loss, for men and for events, of their immortality, it is there that modern history is born, but there also is the germ of its disappearance.

It is possible that not only has history disappeared (that is to say that there is no longer a work of the negative, nor quite a historic reason — not even a prestige of the event, nor thus a historic aura) but that *we must further feed* [*alimenter*] *the disappearance of history.* That is, everything happens as if we were continuing to fabricate history, when we are only, in accumulating the signs of the social, the signs of the political, the signs of progress and of change, *feeding the end of history.*

Socialism (our French socialism) is the best example of this managing of the end of history. It is also the first victim in this derisory simulation. In certain societies, custom demanded that the condemned be hanged on a dead tree — through symbolic necessity: this dead tree was to some extent vital; and one had to nourish the dead with death. History is like this tree. Defunct, it reclaims its victims to nourish its own disappearance. From the heroic and dramatic, it has become sarcophagus and necrophilic. And socialism is this strange victim, this "strange fruit" balancing itself on the dead tree of history. Otherwise innocent of all specific crimes, it would still have fallen to socialism, by the very bankruptcy of historic reason, to administer as it were the end of history. Which is why it is so rich in signs of the past and signs of change, and so poor in events. For socialism (it has this in common with communist regimes, where history has definitively stopped), the final event (revolution) has swung from the future (the revolutionary indeed) to the past. It has taken place. It will therefore never again take place. It remains for us to accommodate ourselves to the time left to us, which is seemingly emptied of sense by this reversal. The end of this century is before us like an empty beach.

Translated by Nai-fei Ding and Kuan-Hsing Chen.
Original text from Jean Baudrillard, "L'an 2000 ne passera pas," *Traverses*, 33/34, 1985, pp. 8-16. We thank Jean Baudrillard for reading the text and Larry Grossberg for his help with this translation.

II

BODY MAPS

Fashion Holograms

In a postmodern culture typified by the disappearance of the Real and by the suffocation of natural contexts, fashion provides *aesthetic holograms* as moveable texts for the general economy of excess. Indeed, if fashion cycles now appear to oscillate with greater and greater speed, frenzy and intensity of circulation of all the signs, that is because fashion, in an era when the body is the inscribed surface of events, is like brownian motion in physics: the greater the velocity and circulation of its surface features, the greater the internal movement towards stasis, immobility, and inertia. An entire postmodern scene, therefore, brought under the double sign of culture where, as Baudrillard has hinted, the secret of fashion is to introduce the *appearance* of radical novelty, while maintaining the *reality* of no substantial change. Or is it the opposite? Not fashion as a referent of the third (simulational) order of the real, but as itself the spectacular sign of a parasitical culture which, always anyway excessive, disaccumulative, and sacrificial, is drawn inexorably towards the ecstasy of catastrophe.

Consequently, the fashion scene, and the tattooed body with it, as a Bataillean piling up of the "groundless refuse of activity". When the sign of the Real has vanished into its (own) appearance, then the order of fashion, like pornography before it, must also give the appearance of no substantive change, while camouflaging the *reality* of radical novelty in a surface aesthetics of deep sign-continuity. Fashion, therefore, is a conservative agent complicit in deflecting the eye from fractal subjectivity, cultural dyslexia, toxic bodies, and parallel processing as the social physics of late twentieth-century experience. Ultimately, the appearance of the tattooed body is a last seductive, ventilated remainder in the reality of the implosion of culture and society into what quantum physicists like to call the "world strip", across which run indifferent rivulets of experience.

patchworks

fragments on fashion
threads of thought
discursive lines

product   text
process   texture
affect   textuality

when i/je think of fashion. i/je think of it as the interface between being and not-being: as a face that has two surfaces: the one posed of flesh and bone – real, substantial, firm and solid: but this other, the production of an imaginary face or mask, rather, it is an extens does not attempt to hide a true face, rather. it is a utopian gesture. or f my body, a vision of possibilities. a utopian aesthetic makin y the basis of a practical and personal aesthetic something fluid and unmaking my identity. there is being and not-being. neither one the go between of being and not-being, neither than the other: m s more absolute or definitive than the other: m sense of self has been reduced to a molecula configuration of interchangeable parts that a re highly energized, highly mobile, and h ighly unstable – ready to re-arrange th emselves as quickly as the urban pa ce and fastly closing space of con sumer imag-escapism demands it. i/je am aware to some extent th at there is little existential space enough for critical distance: the post-modern syndrome operatin g and working on the basis o f a spatial disorientation th at affects both the practice of criticism, as much as the c ritical faculties of practice in the case of fashion, this is the production of an æs thetic practice – style in a p ure sense – at the same time i t is the production of an æs thetic for practical consump tion. the body as text exerci ses the production of knowled ge through the æsthetic pract ice of fancy dress during wh ich the body dresses up in t he possibility of being someo ne: the then knowledge of that someone in turn produces the b eing that desires to be dressed up or down. this is an indeter minable process that loses the point of origin from which it b egan until the self no longer exists but only substitutes and metaphors of being – •i/je am like…•– a romantic conception of the self radically al tered into a post-mod ern production of the not-self: •i/je am not this but that….•i/ je am like somethi ngelse….•i/je ne ver simply am anymore tha n i/je was t o begin with

4

THE FASHION APPARATUS
AND THE DECONSTRUCTION
OF POSTMODERN SUBJECTIVITY

Julia Emberley

The production of a not-self we could call a *displaced sense of originality*. In an effort to retrieve a sense of an original self, the urban consumer creates the self-image of a personal aesthetic, or a style that signals originality, so as to distinguish itself from the uniform conformity deployed by the fashion apparatus that threatens and succeeds in denying self-knowledge and self-expression. Fashion — the production of seasonal products for mass consumption — is bracketed by style-consumers as mundane, ordinary and devoid of a creative drive desperately needed by the individual-subject searching for personal style. The fashion apparatus and its strategies for producing consumption depend on this "negative" reaction to the products it makes available; the fashion apparatus operates on the basis of its own denial, producing its own lack so as to (re)produce desire(s) for the image(s) that will fill the w/hole of the self and its experience of being. Fashion produces the not-being or the anti-fashion subject.

A British fashion magazine describes the anti-fashion tendency inherent in the fashion conscious subject as follows:

> To be fashion conscious or 'fashionable' is still deemed
> to make you 'fickle', 'shallow', 'dumb', 'ephemeral', 'fascist',
> 'fashist' (and some people do aspire to this!!!) — But in
> the real inner reaches of your outer limits... anything is
> possible — even liking clothes...[1]

Fashion has a bad reputation and the consumer implicitly or explicitly knows that there exists a fashion that could be characterized as *homogenous* — clothing rack after clothing rack of the same article of clothing with marginal variations in cut, colour and shape — and *expressionless*, precisely because of the repetition that neutralizes the effect of being unique or individual; and finally, *totalizing*, in that the fashion display insists on a coherent coordination of the parts, whether they be colour-coordinated or shape-coordinated along similar or dissimilar lines, into a whole that gives rise to the "total look".

What fashion offers in order to escape the regime of fashion is diversity, and the freedom of choice to create an individually unique style that is specially marked with personal and artistic idiosyncracies.

Inscribed in the fashion ethic is the insistence that fashion does not want to restrict individual imagination or imperialize the body for its own interest. What the fashion apparatus offers, then, is not fashion, per se, but the opportunity for the individual to create a fashion, to liberate oneself from the fetters of a mundane daily existence that denies pleasure, joy, a sense of self and an experience of being. And yet, in order to produce the space of desire for that "liberation" the fashion apparatus must ensure that sufficient alienation, self-loathing, boredom and sterility exist. In the necessary production of its own contradictions, the fashion apparatus holds the subject within a spectrum of choices which close at the extreme ends of total freedom on the one hand, and absolute control on the other.

The Body as Text and the Texture of the Body

In a passage from William Faulkner's novel *As I Lay Dying*, Addie, the character whose bodily-consciousness is the "I" of the text, describes the process of sexual and spiritual celebration and alienation that occurs between herself and her lover, a local preacher, and between herself and her husband, Anse. In the following excerpt, clothing becomes the dominant metaphor for shaping the experience of Addie's body to various forms of her sexual being in the religion of her world, her family and her self:

> ...I would think of sin as I would think of the clothes we both wore in the world's face, of the circumspection necessary because he was he and I was I; the sin the more utter and terrible since he was the instrument ordained by God who created the sin, to sanctify that sin He had created. While I waited for him in the woods, waiting for him before he saw me, I would think of him as dressed in sin. I would think of him as thinking of me as dressed also in sin, he the more beautiful since the garment which he had exchanged for sin was sanctified. I would think of the sin as garments which we would remove in order to shape

and coerce the terrible blood to the forlorn echo of the
dead word high in the air...
Then it was over... I would never again see him coming
swift and secret to me in the woods dressed in sin like a
gallant garment already blowing aside with the speed of
his secret coming.
But for me it was not over, I mean, over in the sense of
beginning and ending, because to me there was no beginning nor ending to anything then.[2]

Modernist obsessions with the internal and intensive experience of disintegration surface in this passage as a description of the disintegration of
Addie's subjectivity. The interface between her "self" and "the world's face"
is the surface of her body — its flesh — a common boundary between
two spaces of opposing identities that cause her body to implode and dis-
integrate under the pressure of their irreconcilability. This passage also has
the appearance of being characteristically post-modern, in that the body
has been turned inside out and exploded out to the surface where experience has become an outer garment, an extension that inscribes the
body with meaning(s). Here, the body is an open space, an open text, with
"no beginning nor ending"; a body inscribed by the vestimentary symbols of a dead and meaningless corpus of religious doctrine: dressed in
sin, stripped of her soul, Addie is re-dressed with guilt, shame and sin.
The texture of Addie's body has been re-contextualized as a religious text.
Stripped naked and re-clothed, the heurmeneutic body uncovers its in-
timacy, secrecy and hidden meaning, in the same way the preacher dis-
closes and interprets the original scripture in order to recreate, or rather
reproduce, or better still refashion wo/man in the image of the model woman: the unidentified god, the god with no body, the nobody.

Addie's experience of sexual and spiritual alienation described and inscribed through the metaphorical agency of clothing, translates in the
present world economy of fashion as fashion's complicity in the concrete
manufacture of alienation. The fashion apparatus operates on the basis of
a primary contradiction: it claims to fabricate within you your being, your
individual sense of expression, while at the same time forcing you, through
its freedom of choices, to conform to the market uniformity of seasonal
products; what is produced here is alienation, alienation from self and one
another because of the way fashion negates life, by becoming the dominant
repository of what it means to live and to have a "life-style".

Being fashionable inverts life into the concrete manufacture of alienation *from* life, thereby inducing a process of mechanical reproduction.
There is no umblical cord here to be severed but rather an electrical plug
to be plugged into the wall to turn on the blow dryer, the iron, the wash-
ing machine, the electric toothbrush and other therapeutic commodities
that will make you feel better about yourself and loved as only your benevo-

lent mother could love you: the guise of the benevolent state that perpetually keeps you at a conveniently arrested stage of irresponsibility and juvenility, so as to answer your every need and in so doing produce a reality of the real through the image: to produce the real image.

* * *

> The spectacle is the moment when the commodity has attained the *total occupation* of social life. Not only is the relation to the commodity visible but it is all one sees: the world one sees is its world. Modern economic production extends its dictatorship extensively and intensively. In the least industrialized places, its reign is already attested by a few star commodities and by the imperialist domination imposed by regions which are ahead in the development of productivity. In the advanced regions, social space is invaded by a continuous superimposition of geological layers of commodities. At this point in the 'second industrial revolution', alienated consumption becomes for the masses a duty supplementary to alienated production. It is *all the sold labor* of a society which globally becomes the *total commodity* for which the cycle must be continued. For this to done, the total commodity has to return as a fragment to the fragmented individual, absolutely separated from the productive forces operating as a whole.[3]

The globalizing tendency of fashion to dominate a world perspective moves both intensively and extensively — moving inward into "the real inner reaches" (the immediate, daily and local experience of the supermarket check-out counter or bank lineup that mitigate against an "ideal" existence) and moving outward into "the outer limits": space, the East, the exotic, and the Third World. Within a global framework the fashion apparatus circulates and recirculates the language of representation of the Other both on the level of the person and body (anonymously) and on the level of the nation, but with de-politicized neutrality or impersonality. The imaginary vehicles of a "first world" fashion apparatus can be seen to impersonate a Third World "reality". This process personifies the living experience of the Third World in the one-dimensional persona of the paper real-image.

Economic exploitation of the Third World in the fashion industry is well known at the level of clothing production where cheap labour and the comparatively low cost of raw materials, natural fibres and fabrics have been and continue to be easily appropriable commodities for purposes of augmenting the scale of western capital and profits. That these forms of economic exploitation have recently reterritorialized into the sphere of cultural imperialism, signifies an important and complex moment in the socio-economic relations of the West and the Third World. Consider briefly Christian Dior's latest make-up line, entitled *Les Coloniales*. The advertisement contains the framed face of a woman that has been un-naturally whited except for the exotic colours encircling the eyes like the plumage on a wild parrot. It is also interesting to note the use of *anthuriums* with their drooping phalluses that surround her face. The image signifies a colonial elite or the imperialist class of phallocracy. While the geographical space represented is that of the Third World, the indigenous inhabitants have been displaced. This displacement follows from an initial displacement previously used by the fashion apparatus where the native black woman, for example, is eroticized on the basis of her exotic-otherness and exploited for her representational value as such. Having burned out the commercial value of this image, the fashion apparatus has returned to the western image-scape and a hyper-subjected representation of the western white-faced woman. The western woman, whose already white face has been layered with an artificial white mask, has been re-eroticized in this advertisement as an exotic-other, western-subject. The result of this otherization of the western subject is the double displacement of the black Third World subject. And also, a reconfiguration of the Other has taken place where the Other becomes for the western subject an interior danger projected out to the surface, in this case in the form of a white mask, in order to exorcise the fear of difference and alienation by covering over its real presence, both to itself and within the Third World.

There are two co-extensive strategies of power at work in the fashion apparatus I would like to draw attention to: first, the continuing cultural imperialism of the Third World by the western fashion apparatus that transgresses national, political and social boundaries in order to discover new material for its creative exploits and in so doing produces an image — an aesthetics of poverty — of the Third World for first world audiences, consumers and producers that displaces other discursive and visual realities of the Third World (thereby masking the relations of exploitation, oppression and imperialism that exist on socio-economic and political levels between these two worlds); and secondly, to bring home the immediate concerns of the local urban space where a kind of aesthetic "gentrification" is taking place and pushing the ghetto, the site of a violent creative energy, (punk, for example) further and further to the margins of the urban-scape, to the point on the horizon where the landmass disappears from view. Relations of exploitation and oppression are masked and made invisible by an aesthetics of poverty, sterility, waste and death produced by the fashion apparatus. These two strategies, the one reaching out globally, extensively and the other turning inward, intensively, form a complicit w/hole where the fashion apparatus fragments the identity of the consumer-subject along divided lines and boundaries of an (inter-)national and local being.

A Fashion Text: John Galliano's "Visions of Afghanistan: Layers of Suiting, Shirting and Dried-Blood Tones"

For purposes of theorizing the productive and non-productive effects of the fashion apparatus, I have chosen a fashion text from the popular British fashion magazine, *Harper's and Queen*. The March 1985 publication of *Harper's and Queen* presents a spring collection, entitled "SPRING-LOOSE", with an opening portrait that exemplifies, both in its discursive and visual text, the strategies and techniques involved in producing an aesthetics of poverty, waste and death that displace the internal and external problems of exploitation, imperialism and alienation manufactured by the demands of western late capitalism.

The discursive text:

Foucault's distinction between the utopia and the heterotopia, quoted in the following passage, provides a useful model for discussing the discursive effects of Galliano's fashion text:

> *Utopias* afford consolation: although they have no real locality there is nevertheless a fantastic, untroubled region in which they are able to unfold: they open up cities with vast avenues, superbly planted gardens, countries where life is easy, even though the road to them is chimerical. *Heterotopias* are disturbing, probably because they secretly undermine language, because they make it impossible to name this *and* that, because they shatter or tangle common names, because they destroy 'syntax' in advance, and not only the syntax with which we construct sentences but also that less apparent syntax which causes words and things (next to and also opposite one another) to 'hold together'. This is why utopias permit fables and discourse: they run with the very grain of language and are part of the fundamental dimension of the *fabula*; heterotopias desiccate speech, stop words in their tracks, contest the very possibility of grammar at its source; they dissolve our myths and sterilize the lyricism of our sentences.[4]

Fashion promises the utopic experience, an untroubled region designated the "free-world" where the individual liberates her self from the burden of a regulated and mundane existence and transforms daily life into an ideal of endless and fantastic possibilities of being in the world. And yet, its strategy for producing the desire(s) for this utopic experience can only be described, I think, as heterotopic: a multiple and diverse field of discontinuous and incongruous spectacles lacking in syntactical continuity. In the specific case of *Harper's and Queen*, we have John Galliano's "Visions of Afghanistan: Layers of Suiting, Shirting and Dried-Blood Tones", a title and image that is both thematically and syntactically heterotopic; in the incongruous catalogue of words 'suiting, shirting and dried-blood tones', "and" signifies the production of a coherent list of three related elements that is not born out by this particular chain of signifiers; words differ from themselves — the unconventional conversion of articles of clothing, suits and shirts, into activities of ways of dressing and the peculiar mixture of the concrete dried-blood as a modifier for the impressionistic 'tones' — and words differ from one another — though the sequence begins with an alliterative homology between 'suiting' and 'shirting' the sequence is disrupted and stops dead in its tracks by the modifier 'dried-blood' used to designate the dominant colour motif. An unusual choice for a colour preference because of its disturbingly human, or rather, inhuman referent: the reification of the body as commodity where blood, in this case, is valued for its colour potential in the circuit of exchange between production and consumption and, in the process, loses its connection to human life and the living body — a deadly transformation of the real into the imaginary.

In the syntax of Galliano's title we find the heterotopia, a heterogeneous splitting and fracturing which is translated in the "world of fashion" as a multiple and spectacular field of types and tropes that circulate on the surface of visual and textual representations. The fashion-effect of his title dismantles narrative continuity of presentation because syntax is broken, dismembered, shattered and replaced by a "layered effect" — horizontal syntax, discontinuous and fragmented, gives way to a vertical effect of imaginary and semantic layers. In fashion, images cut across traditional barriers of limits of representation and efface, along the way, differences and historical specificities, thus producing, instead, a unitary effect of congenial pluralities that apparently 'hold-together' without contradictions.

What is also interesting in the title of Galliano's text is the site of Afghanistan as the mythical image-scape from which he draws creative insight. But this mythical landscape is not properly a site of utopian possibilities and the dream world of a benevolent otherworldliness; more accurately, it is a distopic vision which embodies a spatial and mythical coherence that is characteristically nightmarish — the nightmare of Third World poverty with its threat of extinction because of famine, disease and war that make it difficult and even impossible to stabilize minimal living conditions for the large groups of indigenous people.

Galliano's incongruous visionary criteria demonstrates more than a heterotopic shattering of a relationship between life and language. Afghanistan,

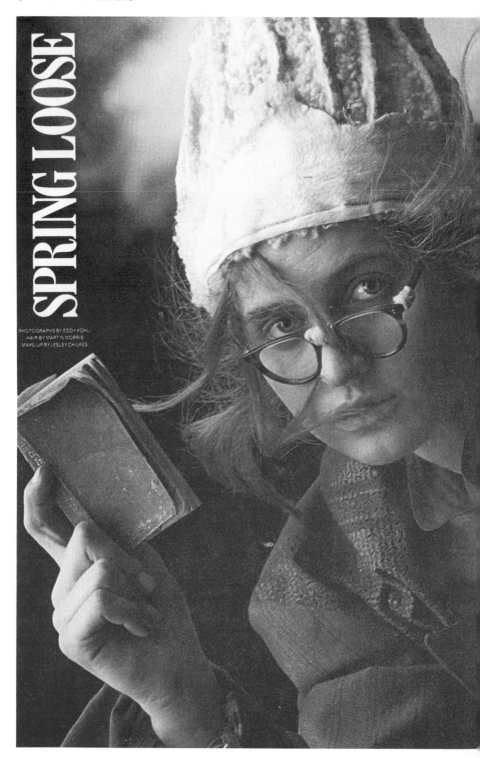

SPRING LOOSE

PHOTOGRAPHS BY EDDY KOHLI
HAIR BY MARTIN MORRIS
MAKE-UP BY LESLEY CHILKES

BRAVE NEW LONDON MAKES THE BIGGEST VIBES IN '85. MODERN PSYCHADELIA MOVES IN WITH A REVIVAL
OF OP-ART PRINTS AND SKINNY RIBS. BRANDISH A BARE MIDRIFF WITH CATSUIT LEGGINGS
AS A SECOND SKIN. COLOURS RUN RIOT THROUGH BLUE, AQUAMARINE AND LIME TO PINK, ORANGE AND
BURGUNDY. TAKE A HINT FROM THE HIPPY TRAIL AND ADD IT TO THE TECHNOLOGICAL EIGHTIES

PRINTED COTTON AND SUITING THREE-QUARTER LENGTH COAT, £450; striped waistcoat, £170; deep burgundy
tton voile overshirt, £122; sheepskin hat, £50; broken glasses, £5, all by John Galliano, from Browns, 23 South Molton Street, Wi

IN GALLIANO'S VISIONS OF AFGHANISTAN: LAYERS OF SUITING, SHIRTING AND DRIED-BLOOD TONE

the site of creative exploitation, represents a distopic heterotopia: a *dis-heterotopia* where the borders of obliteration, evaporation and extinction converge in the single image of dried-blood. In a similar way the first world experiences the possibility of its own evaporation and extinction through the threat of nuclear war: to bring home the distopia to the mythical homeland of the West. If this image-scape has any spatial roots in the imaginary, it is in the mythological dream-scape of the nightmare where the fear of dying, resonances of death, and dried-blood tones predominate.

The visual text:

When looking at the picture of the woman in the introductory fashion portrait I am struck by the unconventionality of the fashion model, model woman; s/he is not beautiful, perfect, smoothed and glossed over in ways that conventionally exemplify the fashion magazine object(ive). S/he has the face of one sandworn, rough, lined and marked by imperfections — the impression contrived is one of being make-up-less, though the effect of no make-up is one that has clearly been produced theatrically. Her hair shoots out in all directions, scattered, unruly, Medusa-like — the appearance of one who cares little for appearance; but again it is a calculated disarray. Her spectacles sit precariously on her face, dislodged from direct contact with her eyes, they appear broken and worn, a prop for the histrionics of an "adventure narrative". In the list of clothes and prices provided by the fashion magazine in the upper right hand corner, I am surprised to find a reference to the glasses; the description reads "broken glasses £". A joke? The fashion consumer can pay for the appearance of a broken commodity, a brand new pair of glasses dressed up with medical tape applied in band-aid fashion to the bridge and the arm joint: the production of a purchasable broken commodity and one that "works" in that it produces the desirable fiction-effect.

The multiple points of view on fashion — aesthetic, socio-economic, political — converge and separate, bind together and blur apart; vision extends outside the immediate photographic spectacle and returns to the spectacle at hand: broken spectacles, broken vision, short-sighted or far-sighted, the wide gaze and the limited point of view. Galliano's "visions" of Afghanistan telescope that vast geographical and cultural spatial distance between the West and the Third World, hold the bridge between these worlds together with little more than a band-aid, in order, perhaps, to keep the (in)stability of those "visions" both imaginary and intact. But his visions explore and exploit, occluding utopian hallucinations or dreams with a distopic series of representations, like the old text she protects under her arm, bound together by a pretty ribbon, so as to keep it from falling apart, intact but inaccessible. And what does the very old and worn text contain? Traditional knowledge, historical understanding? A different currency in the exchange of "seeing" where to "see" is to know, to acquire knowledge. In her other hand she holds open another worn text but the invasion of the western gaze disrupts her activity. She has the look of one caught in the act, guilty, paranoid and party to clandestine activity.

If I were to put a narrative to this visual text, it would be in the genre of the adventure story, a story of intrigue and danger, the crossing of unwelcome and hostile boundaries, the near possibility of being caught, trapped in an underworld of surreptitious cultural exchange where her flight dramatizes the bringing of knowledge to the Third World or an illicit activity, such as reading texts that are traditionally restricted to "men's eyes only" — a James Bond scenario, except that the central character is a woman, and one whose aesthetic practice loosens the bonds of a conventional feminine identity. Her role mimics that of the male hero, but her heroism is one that appears to take larger risks. The unwelcome and hostile boundaries that s/he must cross-over are ideological, sexual, psychological and social as well as spatial and temporal. Her symbolic existence plays out a dangerous and terrifying composition. To read this scene allegorically would be to see the risk wo/men take in moving out of conventional identity-burdened spaces into new and exciting spaces that are liberating but at the same time frightening; once the mask has been chosen s/he must wear it in perpetuity lest the cover becomes discovered and rendered unconvincing and improbable. Her constant mobility, paramount to the illusion of her "self", threatens to become undone by the close of the camera shutter that catches the image, fixing her irrevocably.

The nihilistic experience of post-modernism we could attribute to its erasure of history, to the destruction of the cycle of life and death by levelling experience onto a continuous plane of "change", that is constituted by the eternal reproduction of the "same", albeit, in an apparently new set of clothes; the cycle is no longer a cycle but an unbroken chain of death and mechanical reproduction, a "vacunt" (Sex Pistols) reproduction of the image that glosses over and smooths out the sur-face of the w/hole body effacing under the conditions of its transformations into the idealism of "being", imperfections, anomalies, differences, mortalities even, all of which have been pushed under, buried under the weight of a systematic and mechanical "womb-to-tomb" post-modern life-style — the parody of which is to be found in the death-like appearance of punks whose ghastly shades of white and black and skeleton disfigurations of the body remind us of another meaning embedded in the phrase "late capitalism".

The relationship between Fashion and Death is an old one. In Giacomo Leopardi's "The Dialogue of Fashion and Death" (1824), Fashion persuades her sister Death that she is a worthy and important accomplice to Death's desires and aims and, significantly, that her success depends on the desire for immortality (where immortality is the refusal and denial of death's finality and inevitability). In the first passage quoted, Fashion makes clear her capacity and talent for bringing the body closer to its destruction. In the second passage, Fashion explains her distinctive relationship to the desire for immortality on the part of her subjects, that eventually becomes their demise. In dialogue with Death, Fashion explains:

> ...you from the very start went for people and blood, while I content myself for the most part with beards, hairstyles, clothes, furniture, fine houses and the like. But in fact I have not failed... to play a few tricks that could compared with yours, as for instance to pierce ears, lips and noses, and to rip them with the knicknacks I hang in the holes; to scorch the flesh of men with the red-hot irons I make them brand themselves with for beauty's sake; to deform the heads of infants with bandages and other contraptions, making it a rule that everyone in a certain country has to have the same shape of head... to cripple people with narrow boots; to choke their breath and make their eyeballs pop with the use of tight corsets... I persuade and force all civilized people to put up every day with a thousand difficulties and a thousand discomforts, and often with pain and agony, and some even to die gloriously, for the love they bear me.[5]
>
> Little by little, but mostly in recent times, I have assisted you by consigning to disuse and oblivion those labours and exercises that do good to the body, and have introduced or brought into esteem innumerable others that damage the body in a thousand ways, and shorten life. Apart from this I have put into the world such regulations and customs that life itself, as regards both the body and the soul, is more dead than alive... And whereas in ancient times you had no other farmlands but graves and caverns, where in the darkness you sowed bones and dust, seeds that bear no fruit; now you have estates in the sunlight; and people who move and go about on their own feet are, so to speak, your property and at your disposal from the moment they are born, although you have not yet harvested them... Finally, as I saw that many people had preened themselves with the wish to be immortal, that is, not to die completely, since a fair part of themselves would not fall into your hands, however much I know that this was nonsense, and that when they or others lived in the memories of men, they lived, so to speak, a mockery, and enjoyed their fame no more than they suffered from the dampness of their graves... The result is that nowadays, if anyone dies, you may be sure that there is not a crumb of him that isn't dead...[6]

The fashion apparatus presents the style of immortality, a brand new life-style where nothing decays or gets old, masking death, waste, poverty and absence. Punk, on the other hand, localizes the style war on the urban-scape, producing an anti-aesthetic style that engages the violence, waste and poverty of the urban-other. The cynicism of punk effectively amplifies the "hate-system", reinscribing violence onto the body in an exaggerated fashion by piercing the flesh with safety-pins and perpetrating violence in the "punk-boot" that kicks back the waste of the bourgeoisie picked out of their garbage cans and retrieved from foot to hand to foot again in a violent gesture designed to scare the shit out of "them".

The final cooptation and colonization of punk-style by the fashion apparatus as a style that has come to signify a subversive and sub-cultural way of life on the urban front, and the definition of its cultural parameters produced by this process of signification, raises questions as to whether it is possible to ad-dress fashion as a potentially subversive activity. While anti-fashion may have sporadic and intermittent success at exposing the dominant and repressive fashion discourse or "life-style", the reproductive tendencies of post-modern late capitalism effectively neutralize and dissolve its potential through an inevitable re-creation of its process. The fashionability of "style-wars", characteristic of the emergence of other transgressive urban forms such as grafitti and break-dancing during the late 70s, as well as punk, has become the dominant critical mode of the post-modernist trend.

What is generally understood as a clash of identifiable styles can also be read as a style war against the very notion of identity and the final closures that are placed on the urban subject. In an effort to break away from the ultimate closures that are placed on bodily-consciousness by the fashion apparatus, a certain stylistic madness is emerging where all possible and imaginable styles converge on the fashion subject; covered in layers of historical differences, the subject bears the weight of a heterogeneous and multiple explosion of styles. The result, one could imagine, would be the final collapse and implosion of the body, burnt-out from the pressures of the post-modern pace.

The desire for closure emerges as a desire for death where death, itself, embodied in the confrontation of punk, on the one hand, and in the aesthetics of poverty produced by the dominant style apparatus on the other, has come to be our *life-style*. To be fixed within the confines of one, single identity, and to desire immortality through the perpetuation of an image, is, in the final instance, to be condemned to a living death. In the words of Buffo the clown, from Angela Carter's *Nights at the Circus*:

> It is given to few to shape themselves, as I have done, as
> we have, as you have done, young man, and, in that mo-
> ment of choice — lingering deliciously among the crayons;
> what eyes shall I have, what mouth... exists a perfect free-

dom. But, once the choice is made, I am condemned, therefore, to be "Buffo" in perpetuity. Buffo for ever; long live Buffo the Great! Who will live on as long as some child somewhere remembers him as a wonder, a marvel, a monster, a thing that, had he not been invented, should have been, to teach little children that *truth* about the filthy ways of the filthy world.[5]

Notes

1. From *i-D* magazine, No. 32, December/January, 1985-6.

2. William Faulkner, *As I Lay Dying* (New York: Vintage Books, 1930, 1957), pp. 166-7.

3. Guy Debord, *Society of the Spectacle* (Detroit: Black and Red, 1983), #42.

4. Michel Foucault, *The Order of Things: An Archeaology of the Human Sciences* (New York: Vintage Books, 1970), p. xxiii.

5. Giacomo Leopardi, *The Moral Essays, Operette Morali* (New York: Columbia University Press, 1983), p. 51.

6. Giacomo Leopardi, *The Moral Essays*, p. 53.

7. Angela Carter, *Nights at the Circus* (London: Picador, 1984), p. 122.

Acknowledgements

I would like to thank *Harper's and Queen* magazine for allowing me to reproduce work from their March, 1985 issue. (Fashion photograph by Eddy Kohli).

5

A TALE OF INSCRIPTION/FASHION STATEMENTS

Kim Sawchuk

"... so many political institutions of cryptography."

Jacques Derrida
Scribble (writing-power)

Still Life

Let me begin with two allegories, two dreams, for it is precisely the question of allegory and representation in relationship to the social sciences, particularly cultural studies and feminism, which is at issue in this paper. The first is taken from literature, the second from experience.

In Franz Kafka's short story, "In the Penal Colony", an explorer is invited to the colony to observe and report on its system and method of punishment. At the colony, the explorer is introduced to a machine, a fantastic machine upon which the condemned are placed and their punishment meted. However, prior to their placement on this machine the condemned have been told neither their sentence nor their punishment; knowledge of their transgression and the lesson they are to learn from it will be inscribed on their bodies by vibrating needles as the inviolable dictums of the community such as "Honour thy Superiors" or "Be just" are written into their flesh in a beautiful and decorative script.[1]

Meanwhile, it is November in Toronto, and my mother visits me. We travel to Harbourfront which is packed with holiday shoppers. The crowds circulate throughout the complex amongst the glittering gold and silver decorations in a frenzy of buying and selling. Mannequins have been strategically placed throughout the mall to draw attention to and create desire for the fashions that are for sale.

As we approach these dolls our sensibilities are startled. What we have taken to be plastic models are, in fact, flesh and blood women imitating replicas of real women; representations of representations, women who cannot move, cannot respond to the excited gestures of this mob of consumers. Having exchanged their mobility for a wage, they are compelled to stand in awkward poses for extremely long durations of time while curiosity seekers gaze at them, poke fingers in their direction to force a smile, a movement, and photograph this spectacle of female beauty.

The Object of Fashion

Fashion: what, or whom, are the objects of its discourse? It is a subject without the institutional support or legitimacy granted to other academic subjects, save a few obscure accounts of changes in dress and costume, fleeting references to fashion in the history of European commerce and trade, and the occasional semiotic analysis.[2] What is most conspicuous is the lack of material on the subject, a subject which raises both metaphysical and political questions.

Perhaps this is because, as a topic, we do not know how to frame it, how to address the questions it asks of us. Films, books, photographs, paintings, are all bound by a border that renders them analysable. However, the question of what constitutes the field of fashion is far more ambiguous. As I will argue, it is a phenomenon which threatens the very stability of segregated zones: man/woman, subject/object, the personal/ political, reality/illusion. The body, lying in both the realm of the public and private, is a metaphor for the essential instability of objects in their relationship to each other. Like a fence, or the bar between signified and signifier, it is bound to both, but the property of neither.

As Kafka's allegory reminds us, when we are interested in fashion, we are concerned with relations of power and their articulation at the level of the body, a body intimately connected to society, but which is neither prior to it, nor totally determined by it. For example, in the 1950's Frantz Fanon commented on the French colonial government's attempt to destroy Algerian society by outlawing the veil under the guise of liberating Algerian women.

> The way people clothe themselves, together with the traditions of dress and finery the custom implies, constitutes the most distinctive form of a society's uniqueness, that is to say, the one that is most immediately perceptible.[3]

Whether naked or clothed, the body bears the scatalogical marks, the historical scars of power. Fashionable behaviour is never simply a question of

creativity or self-expression; it is also a mark of colonization, the "anchoring" of our bodies, particularly the bodies of women, into specific positions, and parts of the body in the line of the gaze.

In this respect, it is ironic that the French Fashion conglomerate Christian Dior's summer make-up line was titled "Les Coloniales". "Les Coloniales" with an 'e' on the end to signify woman as the colonized subject at the same time as she is elevated to the level of the exotic. European woman, whose unveiled white skin, blue eyes exuding "the coolness of water and shade", peers from behind a cluster of bright red flowers. From a distance, these flowers seem to be a traditional headscarf. On closer inspection it is clear that they are anthuriums, whose phallic resemblance cannot be coincidental. The bloody history of French colonialism and the Algerian war is magically transformed, re-written with the stroke of eyebrow pencils and lipgloss. The white light of the camera attempts to erase the lines and creases of this history which might be sedimented on the face of this woman; "White mythology," a cool and distant look has displaced the face of the desert. "Les Coloniales" is an appropriate third metaphor in our triumverate of allegories.

Theoretically, it is tempting to interpret Kafka's allegory, Harbourfront, and "Les Coloniales", as relatively clear examples of how ideology functions; patriarchal ideology to repress women, white mythology to distort the reality of colonialism. However, these images are more paradoxical than is obvious at first sight. "Fashion", like "woman" is not an undifferentiated object in-it-self which suddenly appears on the stage of history; nor should it be easily reduced to a mere reflection of social and economic developments, to what Freud called a "master key" which seems to account for the manifestation of the object. Within both Marxism and feminism there is the tendency to treat the object as simply a reflection of social movements, or as an index of the horrific effects of capitalism. It is this analysis which currently dominates the feminist and Marxist interpretation of fashion and popular culture.

For example, Anne Oakley, in her section on fashion and cosmetics in *Subject Women*, says that certain styles of dress reflect specific ideologies. In periods of feminist rebellion, women have called for changes in dress towards "a plainer, more masculine style of dress."[4] In the modern era, types of dress, such as work boots or spike heels indicate either the radical or conservative nature of female subjects in a relatively transparant manner.

Furthermore, women's relationship to fashion and the fashion industry is said to reflect the positioning of women within patriarchal capitalism. Women in European cultures have been socialised to be passive objects: they "appear," while men "act." Many feminists draw upon John Berger's *Ways of Seeing*,[5] in which he argues that the history of European painting shows that the looks of women are merely displays for men to watch, while women watch themselves being looked at. This determines relationships between men and women, women's relationship to other women, and women's relationship to themselves.[6] Whenever women look at themselves, they are acting like men. Laura Mulvey's seminal article "Visual Pleasure and Narrative Cinema", develops this concept of the gaze in its three manifestations, objectification, narcissism, and fetishism, as predominantly gender-determined and male, in relationship to film.[7] Like the women at Harbourfront, whether through economic necessity or their internalization of patriarchal values, they turn themselves into objects for this gaze and further reinforce this phallic economy of desire.

Women's love of clothes, cosmetics, jewellery, their obsession with style and fashion, reinforces the myth that we are narcissitic and materialistic. In turn this reinforces capitalism, which depends upon this obsession with our bodies for the marketing of new products. Griselda Pollack's work expands on this thesis by showing how the solidification of the identity between a woman's body and the notion "for sale" is an extension of the tradition of European high art within popular culture.[8]

There is an element of truth to these arguments, given the historical development of the advertising and clothing industry. But they tend to fall within the trap of decoding all social relations within patriarchy and capitalism as essentially repressive and homogeneous in its effects. As Teresa de Lauretis explains, the visual world is treated as a series of static representations. It is assumed that images are literally absorbed by the viewer, that each image is immediately readable and meaningful in and of itself, regardless of the context, the circumstances of its production, circulation and reception. The viewer, except of course for the educated critic who has learned to see beyond this level of deception, is assumed to be immediately susceptible to these images.[9]

However, fashion, like social being, is constituted through the effects of language, through the circulation and vagaries of discourses which affect the very nature of its images and its objects. Derrida writes:

> Whether in the order of spoken or written discourse, no element can function as a sign without referring to another element which itself is not simply present. This interweaving results in each "element" — phoneme or grapheme — being constituted on the basis of the trace within it of the other elements of the chain or system. This interweaving, this textile, is the *text* produced only in the transformation of another text. Nothing, neither among the elements nor within the system, is anywhere ever simply present or absent. There are only, everywhere, differences and traces of traces.[10]

It for this reason that I emphasize that these inscriptions of the social take place *at* the level of the body, not *upon* it. We must take care in our own theoretical discourse not to position the body or the social in a relationship of radical alterity to one another. Neither fashion nor woman can be seen as objects determined simply by two variables, such as sex and class, for they are constructed in this fabric of intertextual relations. At any specific historical juncture, fashion is located in a discourse on health (corsets, suntanning, fitness), beauty (ideal shapes of breasts, buttocks or lips), morality and sexuality (dress as sign of one's moral fibre), the nation and the economy (the question of the veil in Algeria), and location (climate, geography, seasonal variations), to name only a few possibilities. These discourses involve the body, produce the body as a textured object with multidimensional layers, touched by the rich weave of history and culture.

The intertextual constitution of subjectivity and objects has repercussions for what has been the standard Marxist and feminist interpretation of fashion; fashion as a reflection of the social onto the body, fashion as the repression of the natural body; fashion simply as a commodity to be resisted; fashion as substitute for the missing phallus. Derrida's description of intertextuality is, I believe, theoretically related to the concept of allegory developed by Walter Benjamin, and to Freud's critique of previous methods of dream analysis. Both writers challenge the relative transparency of the object as simple sign, symbol or icon.[11]

In *The Interpretation of Dreams*, Freud noted that the difference between his theory and past methods of dream analysis was that for him, "...memory is not present at once, but several times over, that is, laid down (*neiderlegt*) in various species of indications [*Zeichen*, lit. signs]..."[12] He emphasized that dream interpretation must begin its analysis "en detail," not "en masse," as dreams are of a composite character, and as such, are often confusing.[13] He suggested that there were three understandings of this relationship, and three techniques of dream analysis: the symbolic, which "seems to be a relic and a mark of a former identity;"[14] decoding, which "treats events as a kind of cryptography in which each sign can be translated into another sign having a known meaning in accordance with a fixed key"[15] and a third method which is one of interpretation, of deciphering.

> My procedure is not so convenient as the popular decoding method which translates any given piece of a dream's content by a fixed key. I on the contrary am prepared to find that the piece of content may conceal a different meaning when it occurs in different people or in various contexts.[16]

The memory of events, and of history, is never completely transparent; it is constantly rewritten or overdetermined by present cultural practices. For this reason, language and culture should not be understood as symbolic, for this implies that they are fixed within the chain of signification or in relationship to the "signified." It is this critique of culture as symbolic (i.e., expressive) that is at play in Benjamin's cultural analysis.

Benjamin's study of baroque drama and its allegorical nature critiques the concept of the symbol from the perspective of its ahistoricity. "The measure of time for the experience of the symbol is the mystical instant in which the symbol assumes the meaning in its hidden, and if one might say so, wooded interior."[17] Instead, allegory treats each object as a cultural ruin in which the temporality of all life is encapsulated. Quoting Dante, Benjamin noted that the basic characteristic of allegory is its absolute fluidity, where "any person, any object, any relationship can mean absolutely anything else".[18]

> The basic characteristic of allegory, however, is ambiguity, multiplicity of meaning; allegory and the baroque, glory in richness and meaning. But the richness of this ambiguity is the richness of extravagance; nature, however, according to the old rule of metaphysics, and indeed, also of mechanics, is bound by the law of economy. Ambiguity is therefore always the opposite of clarity and unity of meaning.[19]

A shop window, a photograph, or the line of a song, these fragments or ruins are the most significant aspect of any dream or culture. It is this potential richness of objects, their infinite number of associations, and their possible reconstellation in another field which makes dream analysis, and all interpretation, tentative rather than subject to rational decoding.

The "meaning" of cultural phenomena is neither expressive of one or two primary social relations, nor is it "symbolic". One cannot assume that a crucifix worn by Madonna is an expression of her essentially Christian nature, or that the wearing of high heels reflects a woman's identification with a patriarchal sexual economy.[20] Part of the challenge of alternative fashion adherents has been to dislodge and re-appropriate the traditional significance of fetishised objects. Spike heels, fishnet stockings and crucifixes juxtaposed with black leathers and exaggeratedly teased hairdos were all adopted as costumes by punk women. Not only did this condense different and often disparate styles, but it pushed the most common indices of femininity to their extreme limits, in order to draw attention to its artificiality and construction. Of course, as in the case of Madonna, these trends were re-appropriated by capitalism and the fashion industry as quickly as they appeared, necessitating yet another transformation in style for those interested in establishing an alternative to the industry.

Feminist criticism must regard events, objects, images, as cultural signs or allegories which do not have one fixed or stable meaning, but which derive their significance both from their place in a chain of signifiers, a chain which is itself unstable because of the constant intervention of historical change. Allegories are like the fragments of a dream in which remembrances of the past leave their historical traces, at the same time overdetermining future interpretations of events by an individual subject.

This makes the question of political or aesthetic judgment more complex than the discourses of Marxism and feminism which have only allowed the dichtomization of the world into polarities; man/woman, capital/labour, bourgeiosie/proletariat. Judgments have to be made within the context of discursive situations making a fixed position on any one issue problematic. For example, as Fanon notes in the case of Algeria, the veil was assigned a significance by the colonist that it had not had. "To the colonist offense against the veil, the colonised opposes the cult of the veil."[21] In other words, it was the highly charged atmosphere of the national liberation struggle, as well as the attempt by the French to "Westernise" Algerian women which lead to the polarization of positions.

Likewise, within the history of the dress reform movement, judgments about 'fashion' itself must be understood in the context of our predominantly Christian heritage. Contrary to the assumption of Anne Oakley, an anti-fashion discourse cannot be assumed to be inherently feminist, for it has often been tied to a discourse which is intent on repressing women's potentially subversive sexuality and returning them to the proper sphere of the home. In many writings from the late 19th and 20th centuries, fashion was anthropomorphized into a tyrant, who was said to deprive all, and women in particular, of their freedom and money, block them from more fulfilling pursuits, jeopardize their health, and drop them into the stagnant waters of immorality. As Pope Pius said in 1940, women who were bowing to the tyranny of fashion were "like insane persons who unwittingly threw themselves into fires and rivers."[22] In fact the dress reform movements of the early 20th century were often less concerned with making women more comfortable than with returning them to the proper sphere of the home; they were part of the movement for social purity. Just as improper dress indicated a woman's lack of reason and her immorality, a proper form of dress was said to enhance her "natural" beauty, emphasizing her health and freshness, and promising her fecundity.[23]

A woman's concern for the aestheticization of her body was seen as a sign of her unreasonableness, her potential weakness in contrast to the rationality of men. The argument for austerity in dress and the return to more neutral forms not only valorizes what is seen as characteristic of men (their rationality), but there is the possibility that an anti-fashion sentiment feeds into an already existing discourse of woman's superficiality, duplicity, and the threat that her sexuality poses to men.

Not only does this discourse falsely believe that there is a natural beauty, a core of being beyond socialization, but this position can be accused of a typically 'masculinist' belief that one can be transcendent to one's body; to one's culture, and immune to the seductions of the material world. Although one should not invest one's identity in crass consumer behaviour, it is nevertheless true that you are what you eat, wear, and consume; as Spinoza said, there is no separation between the formation of mind and its ability to recollect, to remember, and the impingement of the senses onto our subjectivities. To believe otherwise is to engage in a Cartesian opposition between the 'in-itself' and the 'for-itself'.

The problem in all of these cases is not that we respond in a sensual manner to the world, but the fixing or territorialization of desire into a restricted economy: the closure on erotic pleasure that the culture industry can create by reinforcing and fixing very specific notions of what is desirable in women, in men, in sexuality, in clothing, and its hegemonic control over the "imaginary" through its domination of cultural mediums. While promising Nirvana to all, the restricted economy limits the flow of goods and services to those with access to capital thus reproducing the forms of class domination; it creates desires while denying them and making them dependent on the flow of capital. In phrasing the necessary critique of capitalism, one must be careful not to lapse into a discourse of economy and restraint, which opposes the ethics of thrift, hard work, and self-discipline to the 'immorality' and 'decadence' of capitalism. As Nietzsche says in *The Will to Power*, "residues of Christian value judgments are found everywhere in socialistic and positivistic systems. A critique of Christian morality is still lacking."[24] Perhaps capitalism's only saving grace is the decadence that it produces, its excesses and surpluses, that allow the person who delights in its cast-offs to live a parasitical existence on its margins.

To assume that all clothing is reducible to the fashion industry in this restrictive sense, and that all looking, and aestheticization of the body is an objectifying form of commodification is simplistic. As Marx himself noted, objectification is part of the process that allows human beings to create themselves, their social relations, and their history.[25]

As Laura Mulvey has argued the film industry has capitalised on scopophilic pleasure. However, one must be careful in transferring paradigms from film theory, which tends to concentrate solely on the notion of the look, and on the eye as the primary organ of experience. Clothing, the act of wearing fabric, is intimately linked to the skin, and the body, to our tactile senses. As author Jean Rhys reflects, women have been sensitized to the relationship between their personal and cultural history as it is inscribed in their clothing. "It is as though we could measure the degree of happiness of particular events in her life through the clothing she was wearing and the rooms she inhabited."[26] Fashion and clothing — being stylish — can also be a poetic experience, intimately connected to the history and remembrance of the lived body. Again it was Freud who suggested the importance of material objects, of memories of clothing, jewellery, in triggering memory and overdetermining thought and action in both the waking and dream states. Because the fashion industry is constantly resurrecting histories and cultures, placing us all in a perpetual schizophrenic present, the experience of fashion and clothing is contradictory for women. It is, perhaps, this longing for a world of fantasy, this desire for the return, and the smell and touch of the body which the fashion industry (in fact all of our sentimental culture) capitalizes on. The acts of shopping, of wearing an article of clothing, of receiving clothing as a gift, can be expressions of recognition and love between women, or between women and men, which should not be ignored, though they may fail to transcend the dominant phallic economy of desire.

Simulation and Representation: The Object in Postmodern Culture

The foregoing analysis is not intended to suggest that we totally reject a Marxist analysis of the commodity or the feminist analysis of patriarchy; but the metaphysical assumptions in place within these discourses must be rethought, rearticulated, reinscribed, for they have produced a history of theoretical closure regarding fashion.

The latter, I believe, has come about for two reasons. First, it seems as if the idea of fashion has been articulated so closely with women, the body and the personal, and therefore with doxa, unreason, and the inessential, that it has been ignored by academic institutions dominated by a sort of antiseptic Platonism. Secondly, and concomitantly, the study of fashion has required a methodological shift in the social sciences: not just a shift from the idea of cultural phenomenon as symbolic or expressive of some fundamental social relation, but away from a metaphysics of presence which favours denotation over connotation, as in semiotics, and use-value over exchange value, as in Marxism. This critique of the metaphysics of presence links the work of Benjamin and Derrida to that of Baudrillard. Some aspects of feminist thought, which criticize fashion on the basis of its 'misrepresentation' of women, and advocate a return to the 'natural' body, and 'natural' beauty have also had to be abandoned. Moving beyond these polarizations makes possible a more in-depth reading and understanding of fashion.

A discourse of representation, which is connected to the concept of the symbol, is inappropriate for an analysis of fashion; yet as we have seen, this is the basis of the majority of writings on fashion. What the phenomenon of women imitating models brings into play is the question of the real, of the referent, as in any sense originary in (post-) modern culture. The live mannequins mentioned in my second allegory do not startle us simply because these women have been reified into a stationary position; they shock us precisely because we are living in an age which anticipates an image. The present era, the age of the postmodern, marks a collapsing of the space of these borders. Reality, the referent, is called into question at that juncture where artificial signs are intertextually mixed with 'real elements.'

In this sense, Kafka's allegory, "In the Penal Colony," does not signify a modern form of repressive, administrative power; what it seems to signal is the end of a mapping of a predetermined code of the social onto the body. The latter was a judicial form of power based on the notion of the pre-existing authority of the norm, or the rules of a cohesive community over the individual body. It is the system of justice and control of the explorer, rather than the keeper of the machine, who will triumph in the postmodern era, the age of late capitalism. Gone is the archaic writing machine which treats the body as a *tabula rasa* upon which a predetermined message is scrawled. In the present age, forms of self-discipline anticipate the self-colonization of the body and its enslavement in an intertextual web.

Baudrillard's writings explore the demise of any transcendental posture that one may be tempted to adopt in cultural critique. He states:

> The first implies a theology of truth and secrecy (to which the notion of ideology still belongs), the second inaugurates an age of simulacra... in which there is no longer any God to recognize His own, nor any judgement to separate the true from the false, the Real from Artificial resurrection, since everything is already dead and risen in advance.[27]

The power of late capitalism is in the imaginary, where subjects are maintained in a circuit of desire and anxiety. Baudrillard's work echoes Kafka's sentiments, and is seminal for further discussions of the implications of the fashion industry within the present economy. "Abstraction today is no longer that of the map, the double, the mirror, or the concept. Simulation is no longer that of a territory, a referential being or sub-stance. It is the generation by models of a real without origin or reality; hyper-reality."[28]

Fashion, with its lack of commitment to this world, with its attempt to create clothes, figures, looks that are irreverent, towards any form of natural beauty, is emblematic of this "precession of simulacra", and the dis-simulation of the logic of the symbol and representation. Baudrillard terms this collapse and instability of border an implosion — "an absorption of the radiating model of causality, of the differential mode of determination with its positive and negative electricity — an implosion of meaning. This is where simulation begins."[29]. Where simulation begins, the notion of representation ends. The failure of the distinction between poles marks the age of the politics of simulation, embodying both the potentially liberating collapse of old borders, while at the same time making possible hegemonic manipulation through control of capital flow and the production of new technologies.

However, the history of this implosion, this circuitry, is not simply a modern phenomenon. Baudrillard's radical deconstruction of these poles is both epistemological and historical. In fact, the archeology of this tendency for the implosion of the space between the imaginary and the real can be seen in the relationship between the naked body and the development of clothing styles. As Anne Hollander shows in her book, *Seeing Through Clothes*, styles of the female body have changed; indeed, the figures admired and hence idealized within the tradition of nude art are themselves shaped by current clothing styles. For example, in Europe, the upper body, i.e. the breasts, was strictly corsetted to emphasize the sweeping outward curve of the belly. Nude paintings which were thought to reflect the natural shape of the body, in fact retain the shape of these clothes; what is depicted by the artist as a "natural body", a representation of a woman's figure, is itself overdetermined by these fashions.[30] Thus, a neat causal relationship between an object and its transcription in some form of "writing" is problematic. It implies that there is an objective reality outside of the critic or artist — a natural body as the originary site — depicted or distorted by mass culture; but images are not mimetic of a natural world prior to representation. As Barthes says, "your body, the thing that seems the most real to you is doubtless the most phantasmic."[31] Not only does a feminist politics based on a notion of representation, on a return to the natural body, or neutral forms of dress, ignore the pleasures involved in the possession of an article of clothing, but the impossibility of this return to the represented.

This process is exacerbated in the era of postmodernism, where technologies make possible the doubling of life, giving a new force to the powers of the imaginary and the memory trace to dominate and completely substitute the real. Baudrillard's social theory, like Derrida's philosophy and Freud's psychoanalysis, signals the continual collapsing of the scene and "the mirror," the prerequisite for any notion of representation as reflection or imitation:

> ... instead there is the scene and the network. In place of
> the reflexive transcendence of mirror and scene, there is
> a smooth, non-reflecting surface, an immanent surface
> where operations unfold — the smooth operational sur-
> face of communication.[32]

This smooth operational surface which ruptures the depth model implicit in classical Marxist humanism inaugurates a different notion of causality: neither 'expressive,' nor simple structural, it questions the possibility of isolating all determinations of a given phenomenon, object, or event.

All of the social sciences have been predicated on a notion of system, either as a relatively stable set of signifiers, as in semiotics, or upon the isolation of a community, as in Marxism, in which human activity is localizable in space and time, generalizable because common meanings are shared amongst its members. Baudrillard's analysis of postmodernity, or late capitalism, throws these assumptions into question. As Philip Hayward notes in "Implosive Critiques," Baudrillard problematizes the notion of a cohesive social upon which the disciplines are based.[33] In a world of fluidity and fragmentation in which the stable boundaries of traditional communities such as the family, the church and the nation are in constant disruption, relocation, and solidification into exaggerated forms, we need a new methodology to complement these transformations.

One way to approach the fragmentation of the social is to study cultural signs as allegorical objects which have a multiplicity of possible meanings rather than any one fixed interpretation. This is not simply an idle, idealistic or nihilistic pursuit. As Elizabeth Cowie explains, meaning is never absolutely arbitrary in any text.

> Rather, the endless possible signification of the image is
> always, and only a theoretical possibility. In practice, the
> image is always held, constrained in its production of
> meaning or else becomes meaningless, unreadable. At this
> point the concept of anchorage is important; there are de-
> veloped in every society decisive technologies intended
> to fix the floating chains of signifieds so as to control the
> terror of uncertain signs.[34]

The contradiction within any analysis is that in order to communicate, one is faced with having to "modify" a text; that is, to classify and identify the regime of codes which govern its production, while being vigilant to their inevitable mutation. Benjamin's concept of allegory, like Derrida's notion of intertextuality, is a strategy of reading which opens up the possibility of deciphering, rather than decoding, the fashion object and other cultural texts. Decoding, as Freud explicated, implies that there is a master system to which all signs can be returned; deciphering, on the other hand, implies that we are cognizant of the instability of all meaning.

This method, or anti-method — *allegoresis* — takes cultural sign objects as emblematic. As Benjamin said "Allegories are, in the realm of thoughts, what ruins are in the realm of things."[35] Like all forms of cultural production, fashion cannot be considered a mere expression of the current *Zeitgeist*, for it is a constituent relational element in the fabric of the social.

Conclusion

Capitalism and the Colonization of the Imaginary

I began this excursion into a discussion of fashion with two dreams, supplemented by a third; a dream of inscription of the social, the mapping of a typically modern form of power onto the body, and its eclipse in the era of postmodernism with its dependence on an abstract disembodied form of self-discipline; secondly a dream of a woman caught, trapped, embedded within a circuitry of power, of competing discourses which not only position her, affect her, but name her "Woman" as distinct in nature and temperament from "Man", thus naming her as both subject and object; thirdly, a dream of a resurrected past, capitalism's cannibalization of the other, its treatment of them as already dead museum pieces, and its resurrection of them as fashion — the colonialism of advanced capitalism powered by the energy of seduction and desires.

The use of allegory in relationship to fashion and postmodernism is appropriate, given postmodernism's use of allegory as a form of artistic practice and criticism, and given the breakdown of stable communities upon which the social sciences base their use of representation as a concept for giving meaning to behaviours. In the place of 'real communities' and the 'social', a simulated community is born; tribes of consumers who buy Tide, T.V. families on shows such as Family Feud, the world in Harmony as in the Coke commercials, a world that we may not feel compelled to conform to but which offers itself to us as a type of hyper-reality. Capitalism operates in full knowledge of the power of the imaginary, of our desire to join into these masquerades, and re-creates the social as a series of dreamworks, much like the landscapes analysed by Freud in *The Interpretation of Dreams*.

The imaginary, as Freud, Lacan, and Althusser knew, must be taken seriously because it has very real effects; any rigid separation between the two realms is impossible. In fact, both zones, if indeed there are only two, are always overdetermining, collapsing in on each other. It is the imaginary which informs what is to be our experience of both past and future. Hence, the colonization that capitalism achieves is also an imperialism of the imagination — not just domination over such physical spaces as the third world.

Indeed, as postmodernist forms of architecture such as the Eaton's Centre in Toronto, the new Air Canada Building in Winnipeg, and the West Edmonton Mall indicate, this resurrection of defunct fictions can either be a pleasurable fantasy or a nightmare. In these architectural dreamscapes one can experience life in a Paris café, on a beach in Miami or in a submarine, without ever having to leave one's province or suburb. On the other hand, many other pieces of postmodern architecture are a direct reaction to the monumentalism of modernist style, which reduced every city to the megalopolis, and flattened every indigenous horizon to "the Same".

Postmodernism fluctuates between the poles of kitsch and a return to the local. It is both a form of populism, and a totally artificial rendering of history and space. Pee Wee Herman's America is the best example of this hyper-reality: it results in more livable spaces at the same time that it degenerates into a celebration of consumer culture.

Likewise, postmodern thought does not merely extoll naively what Frederic Jameson describes as the superficial and artificial surface. It is pragmatic in its realization that the modernist valorization of the real and of authenticity was insensitive to the superficial. Modernism tended to be a romantic discourse, it longed for a return to some prehistoric origin, and positioned itself, as educated critic outside and above the culture it criticised — in the place of God. While modernism valued what it took to be the essential, the real, the substantial over the ephemeral, the imaginary, the formal, postmodernism has been engaged in questioning these divisions, and this transcendental position. As I have argued, this was a most dangerous abdication of power. Postmodern thought realises the full ability of capital to capitalize on every alternative discourse, every act of charity, every emotion and sentiment. Therefore it forces one to adopt the strategy of guerilla warfare, of insurgency, interference and destabilization, rather than the archaic model of revolution that is a part of the language of classical Marxism.

Most importantly, postmodernism enjoins us in the necessity for engaging in a cultural politics, politics that exploits the media, that is based on a language of celebration and ecstasy, as in the most recent efforts of the Toronto Arts Community in bringing attention to the need for sanctions against South Africa. It is not surprising that the most interesting theoretical works and reflections on the state of contemporary culture and politics have come out of art and literary magazines such as *ZG, October,*

Impulse, Borderlines, and the French "fashion magazine" *Pole Position*; and that significant interventions in photography and art have come from women such as Mary Kelly, Cindy Sherman, Martha Rosler, Lynne Fernie, and Christine Davis, who have attempted to grapple with these issues, particularly the issue of the representation of women. They do not necessarily offer positive images of women, but they do question the notion of "Woman" as a natural construct. They do not offer solutions, but instead force the readers of their works to develop skills in interpreting and reading. It is important to transmit skills that will allow consumers of capitalism to understand the power of images in general and to question the notion of the immutability of that which we take to be real. It is at this juncture that aesthetic judgment and politics meet.

Notes

1. Franz Kafka, "In The Penal Colony", *The Penal Colony: Stories and Short Pieces*, trans. Willa and Edwin Muir (New York: Schoken Books, 1961), pp. 191-230.

2. The most interesting recent work on fashion is by Valerie Steele, *Fashion and Eroticism* (New York: Oxford University Press, 1985). Roland Barthes, *The Fashion System* (New York: Hill and Wang, 1983), is another seminal piece, although it is rife with difficulties for the reader because of its extremely technical semiotic approach to the topic. Barthes' own critique of this work can be found in *The Grain of the Voice: Interviews 1962-1980*, trans. Linda Coverdale (New York: Hillard and Wang, 1985). As well, I recommend Kathy Meyers, "Fashion N' Passion", *Screen*, vol. 23 # 3 (October, 1983), pp. 89-97., and Rosetta Brooks, "Fashion: Double Page Spread," *Cameraworks*, #17 (Jan./Feb., 1980), pp. 1-20.

3. Frantz Fanon, "Algeria Unveiled", *A Dying Colonialism*, trans. Haaken Chevalier (New York: Grove Press, 1965), p. 35. Read Fanon's piece in conjunction with the essay by Jacques Derrida, "White Mythologies", *Margins of Philosophy*, trans. Alan Bass (Chicago: University of Chicago Press, 1982). This "white mythology" contained in the most trivial of objects, the fashion photo for a cosmetic company, is integrally connected to another "white mythology", the history of metaphysics. It is the metaphysical position which privileges the notion of Reason over the emotional and the sensual which I will argue has relegated the topic of fashion to the inessential. Derrida, p. 213.

4. Anne Oakley, *Subject Women* (New York: Pantheon Books, 1981), p. 82.

5. John Berger, *Ways of Seeing* (Harmondsworth: Pelican, 1972).

6. Oakley, pp. 45-47. See also, E. Ann Kaplan, *Women and Film: Both Sides of the Camera* (New York: Methuen, 1983). She says: "The construction of woman as spectacle, internalized, leads women to offer their bodies in professions like modelling and advertising, and film acting, and to be generally susceptible to demands to be made a spectacle." (p. 73).

7.   Laura Mulvey, "Visual Pleasure and Narrative Cinema," *Women and the Cinema: A Critical Anthology*, eds. Karyn Kay and Gerald Pearcy (New York: E.P. Dutton, 1977), p.p. 412-428.

8.   Griselda Pollack, "What's Wrong With Images of Women?" *Screen Education*, 3 24 (Autumn, 1977).

9.   Teresa de Lauretis, *Alice Doesn't: Feminism, Semiotics, Cinema* (Bloomington: Indiana University Press, 1984), p. 38. De Lauretis' work provides a clear and cogent summary of many of the theoretical debates within both Marxist-feminist and semiotic analysis as they pertain to the question of the representation of women in film images.

10.   Jacques Derrida, *Positions*, trans. Alan Bass (Chicago: University of Chicago Press, 1981), p. 26.

11.   Walter Benjamin, *The Origins of German Tragic Drama*, trans. John Osborne (London: New Left Books, 1977). Given Benjamin's very clear sympathy with the concept of allegory over and against the classical notion of the symbol, it is unfathomable how Lukacs could so misread Benjamin's work. Lukacs, pp. 40-44. Paul de Man's work on allegory and symbol should be read in conjunction with Benjamin. As de Man notes in relation to European literature "... in the latter half of the eighteenth century... the word symbol tends to supplant other denominations for figural language including that of allegory." Paul de Man, "The Rhetoric of Temporality", *op. cit.*, p. 188. For examples of how deeply the concept of the symbol permeates Marxism's understanding of culture as symbolic, see William Leiss, Stephen Kline and Sut Jhally's excellent study, *Social Communication in Advertising: Persons, Products and Well-Being* (Toronto: Methuen, 1986), pp. 55, 66.

12.   As quoted in Jacques Derrida, "Freud and the Scene of Writing", *Writing and Difference*, trans. Alan Bass (Chicago: University of Chicago Press, 1978), p. 206.

13.   Sigmund Freud, *The Interpretation of Dreams*, trans. James Strachey (Harmondsworth: Pelican, 1976), p. 178.

14.   *Ibid*, p. 468.

15.   *Ibid*, p. 171.

16.   *Ibid*, p. 179. This distinction originally was brought to my attention in a footnote in a friend's Masters Thesis. Forest Barnett Pyle, "Walter Benjamin: The Constellation of a Cultural Criticism", University of Texas at Austin 1983, p. 51. Pyle attributes this distinction to Gayatri Spivak, but does not reference a source. I have traced the distinction to Freud.

17.   Benjamin, p. 165.

18.   *Ibid*, p. 175.

19.   *Ibid*, p. 177.

20.   The work of Louis Althusser still provides the most important critique of this notion of causality, relating it to the philosophical legacy of Hegel within Marxism. Louis Althusser, *Reading Capital*, trans. Ben Brewster (London: New Left Books, 1970).

21. Fanon, pp. 47-48.

22. Jeanette C. Lauer and Robert Lauer, *Fashion Power: The Meaning of Fashion in American Society* (New Jersey: Prentice-Hall Inc., 1981), pp. 73-101.

23. *Ibid*, p. 80.

24. Friedrich Nietzsche, *The Will to Power*, trans. Walter Kaufmann and R.J. Hollingdale (New York: Random House, 1968), p. 17.

25. I owe this reading of Marx to another friend, Lori Turner. Lori Turner, "Marx and Nature," unpublished manuscript, York University, 1986, p. 8.

26. Jean Rhys, *Good Morning Midnight* (New York: Harper and Row, 1930), p. 113. See the anthology, *The Female Body in Western Culture: Contemporary Perspectives*, Susan Rubin Suleiman, ed. (Cambridge: Harvard University Press, 1983).

27. Jean Baudrillard, *Simulations*, trans. Paul Foss, Paul Patton and Philip Beitchman (New York: Semiotext(e), 1983), pp. 12-13.

28. *Ibid*; p. 2.

29. *Ibid*; p. 57.

30. Anne Hollander, *Seeing Through Clothes* (New York: The Viking press, 1978), pp. 97-104.

31. Barthes, *Grain of the Voice*, p. 365.

32. Jean Baudrillard, "The Ecstacy of Communication", *The Anti-Aesthetic: Essays on Postmodern Culture*, Hal Foster, ed. (Washington: Bay Press, 1983), p. 127.

33. Philip Hayward, "Implosive Critiques", *Screen*, vol. 28, 3-4-5- (July-Oct., 1984), p. 128.

34. Elizabeth Cowie, "Women, Representation and the Image", *Screen Education*, # 2-3 (Summer, 1977), pp. 15-23.

35. Benjamin, p. 178.

36. Frederic Jameson, "Postmodernism and Consumer Society", *The Anti-Aesthetic*, p.p. 111-125.

Acknowledgements

I would like to thank Christian Dior for allowing the reproduction of their advertisement.

6

FASHION AND THE CULTURAL LOGIC OF POSTMODERNITY

Gail Faurschou

The Politics of Style[1]

Until recently, the decoration of the body has been a subject confined mostly to the disciplines of sociology[2] and anthropology although literary references to what we might call a 'fashion consciousness' are numerous. I am thinking here specifically of Proust, although Baudelaire and Balzac, among others, were fascinated by the ambiguity surrounding desire, sexuality and style.

If anything can be said about fashion at a general level it is that its history testifies to the fact that the adornment of the body has rarely been a question of strict material or functional necessity. Indeed, as in precapitalist societies, it has constituted a privileged point of departure for inscribing the socius in and through the body and its vestments, the process of recording a memory of alliance, a system of symbolic in-vestment and exchange. Moreover, as with those cultural practices that have persisted throughout all social formations, albeit occupying radically different positions, adorning the body as a form of consuming the social surplus means that here is etched out not only an aesthetic and symbolic but a *political* terrain, an economy that marks and inscribes the most intimate surfaces of our skins. In these designs where the lines of power and desire are drawn, one can trace the fundamental contradictions intrinsic to the history of all societies. Thus bodily decoration becomes a form of cultural production that can simultaneously both limit and enrich symbolic communication, constitute a site of freedom or restriction, submission or rebellion, eroticism or domination, identity or difference. Its intimate relation to the body means it weaves upon it both pleasure and pain, sacrifice and self-indulgence.

As cultural theorists sensitive not only to the subtleties of power in the apparently most insignificant of cultural texts, but also aware of the possibility of complicity with it through moralizing and universalizing judgements, we cannot but approach the subject of fashion with ambivalence. This is not only the ambivalence we face when interpreting past cultural practices of which we are not a part, but the ambivalence that strikes us particularly in evaluating practices in which we participate and, in many cases, enjoy. Like many of the exploratory contributions feminist theory has made to contemporary cultural studies, including the recent debates on sexuality, pornography, and images of women in general, an analysis of fashion must be aware of the intricately entwined relations not only of power and domination, but also of desire and play, however complex and abstract these relations have become in the ever expanding boundaries of the mass society of late capitalism.

There is much work to be done here. Even the initially most simple questions soon prove elusive. What makes up a style, a look? How do shapes and folds of clothing appear aesthetically pleasing or ridiculously old fashioned? How does the play of difference in fashion create a meaningful code and in what sense can we speak of symbolic or expressive communication between subjects — if at all?

While there are many theoretical avenues that one could pursue in relation to fashion, for example, semiotics, psychoanalysis, and deconstruction, I am primarily concerned in what follows with how, on a more general level, we can view fashion and its promotional industries as a point of departure for exploring some of the contradictory tendencies of our present period.

If fashion today appears as the most ephemeral and trivial of leisure pursuits, infinitely distanced from its ritual, mystical, religious, ceremonial, or simply symbolic capacity for communication, surely this makes it all the more an interesting and important area to explore. The fashion-object appears as the most chaotic, fragmented, and elusive of commodities, yet it circulates a pervasive and enveloping logic. I would argue that, for this reason, it constitutes an exemplary site for examining the cultural dislocations and contradictions of the transition from modernity to the late capitalist, new wave, postmodern era. In particular, I will attempt to show that the widely noted tendency toward the abstraction, disembodiment, and even disappearance of the subject is implicit in the very principles of an expanding fashion culture — that if the subject is on the way out, it is going out in style.

II
Modernity: Fashion as a Commodity

Before discussing fashion as a late-capitalist, postmodern phenomenon, a few words need to be said about its development from that initially crucial stage of its origin in modernity. It is, of course, only with the rise of industrial capitalism and the market economy that fashion becomes a commodity produced for the realization of economic exchange value in the division of labour and the separation of production and consumption. In this regard, it is interesting to note that clothing was the first industrialized sector of capitalism and that Marx began his analysis of value equivalence in *Capital* with the example: 10 yards of linen equals one coat[3]. Indeed, the whole rationalization process of capital originated with what would seem to have become the most irrational of commodities. But in the 19th and early 20th century, dress was still a commodity produced according to the existing structure or 'ideology of needs'. As William Leiss, *et al.* point out in their recent study of advertising[4], this production-oriented phase of capitalism marketed its products primarily on the basis of improving, but not changing, one's existing mode of life. The early capitalists emphasized the craftsmanship, traditional values and tastes that were important to the social economy of prestige and class distinction. One can observe this attitude to fashion apparel in the way clothes were marketed in early magazine advertisements and catalogues. Here we find long descriptions of the quality of the material, its impeccable construction, durability, etc. Every effort was made to place these new products in the familiar context of established cultural significations.

It is also interesting to note, in this regard, that it was not until the rise of the market and the bourgeois class that fashion became a notably gendered phenomena. As Elizabeth Wilson points out in her study of modern dress[5], fashion became a way of distinguishing the bourgeois class and its values from the aristocracy and its excessive lifestyle and extravagance. The bourgeois woman was now to become a sign of the conservative family unit: feminine but modest, attractive but frugal.

Similarly, Wilson notes, early feminists' critiques of dress focused on the value of clothing to the body, movement, health, and activity. The Rational Dress Society was only one of the dress reform movements of the 1900's that debated the corset, the introduction of trousers for women, and the return to what they saw as a freer more 'natural' look that was influenced by the art of the pre-Raphaelites. Even many socialist movements took up the issue. But it would be wrong to assume these debates on the use value of clothing excluded the issue of beauty and femininity which was still a foremost concern. In the modern period, beauty as a cultural ideal retained much of its classical importance and allure. That is to say, beauty in early modernity was still thought of as an aesthetic category that bore on some ideal of the ultimate expressiveness of the human soul, specifically one that linked it to its embodied form. Clothing was supposed to assist and accentuate this embodied beauty. Ambiguity and vulnerability, unrefined hints of subjectivity, remained vital aspects of its aesthetic appeal. This is a point to be kept in mind when we turn to our discussion of postmodernity.

In the early 20th century, modernist objects still retained some capacity for symbolic investment, whether that of use value, prestige, or the expression of identity. According to Frederic Jameson, this was possible because commodities still bore traces of the human labour objectified within them. They were not yet the disembodied, free-floating, abstract commodities of the mass consumer market. Jameson argues that surrealism was emblematic of the status of objects in the high modernist period:

> the human origins of the products... their relationship to the work from which they issued — had not yet been fully concealed... what prepares these products to receive the investment of psychic energy characteristic of their use by Surrealism is precisely the halfsketched, uneffaced mark of human labour, of the human gesture, not yet completely separated from subjectivity, which remain therefore potentially as mysterious and as expressive as the human body itself.
>
> ... We need only juxtapose (the object of surrealism), as a symbol with the photographic objects of pop art, (Andy Warhol's) Campbell soup can, pictures of Marilyn Monroe, ... the gasoline stations along American superhighways, the glossy photographs in the magazines, or the cellophane paradise of an American drugstore, in order to realize that the objects of Surrealism are gone without a trace.
>
> Henceforth, in what we may call postindustrial capitalism, the products which we are furnished with are utterly without depth; their plastic content is totally incapable of serving as a conductor of psychic energy... All the libidinal investment in such objects is precluded from the outset, and we may well ask ourselves, if it is true that our object universe is henceforth unable to yield any 'symbol apt at stirring human sensibility,' whether we are not here in the presence of a cultural transformation of signal proportions, a historical break of an unexpectedly absolute kind?[6]

The meaning of this break is also clear for Jean Baudrillard: "The era of function and the signified has revolved, the era of the signifier and the code is beginning."[7] The object of postmodernity has finally become the true object of consumption, Baudrillard argues, when "...released from its psychic determinations as *symbol*; from its functional determinations as *instrument*; from its commercial determinations as *product*; (it) is thus *liberated as a sign* to be recaptured by (the logic of differentiation) the formal logic of fashion."[8]

III
The Postmodern Fashionscape

In contrast to the productivist ethic of industrial modernism, late capitalism is the society of consumption, the society of the mass market and multinational capital, the age of media, information, and electronic reproduction.[9] It is no longer an economy seeking to fulfill the needs of a modernizing society but a society driven to create a perpetual *desire for* need, for novelty, for endless difference and instant satisfaction.

In postmodernity, fashion has become the commodity 'par excellence'. It is fed by all of capitalism's incessant, frantic, reproductive passion and power. Fashion *is* the logic of planned obsolescence — not just the necessity for market survival, but the cycle of desire itself, the endless process through which the body is decoded and recoded, in order to define and inhabit the newest territorialized spaces of capital's expansion.[10] A line of escape at one moment, fashion is recaptured in the network of images the next; frozen in the mirror of the mediascape, we gaze forever at our suspended moment of flight. As Guy Debord says of the "society of the spectacle": "the image has become the final form of commodity reification."[11] This is Baudrillard's world of the hyperreal, and the infinite simulacrum, the abstract, compulsive innovation of signs: arbitrary but perpetual, empty but brilliant. It is Jameson's aesthetic of the euphoric hysterical sublime, the frantic schizophrenic explosion of multiple glossy surfaces without depth, the gleaming hallucinatory splendor of style without substance. Fashion has become our contemporary mode of being in the world — and our contemporary 'mode' of death. Style-speed-seduction-death. We need only think of Hollywood's glamourized version of itself in Warner Brothers' "To Live and Die in L.A.," or its television spin-off, "Miami Vice," or even the increasing popularity of the novels of J.G. Ballard, to realise its imagistic appeal.

Postmodernity then is no longer an age in which bodies produce commodities, but where commodities produce bodies: bodies for aerobics, bodies for sports cars, bodies for vacations, bodies for Pepsi, for Coke, and of course, bodies for fashion, — total bodies, a total look. The colonization and appropriation of the body as its own production/consumption machine in late capitalism is a fundamental theme of contemporary socialization.

> ...monopoly capitalism...not content to exploit the body as labor-power, manages to fragment it, to divide the very expressiveness of the body in labor, in exchange, and in play, recuperating all this as individual needs, hence as productive consummative forces under its control...[12]
> ... the body, beauty, and sexuality are imposed as new universals ... emancipated by abundance and cybernetic

revolution. The deprivation, manipulation, and controlled recycling of the subjective and collective values by the unlimited rival speculation over sign values renders necessary the santification of a glorious agency called the body that will become for each individual an ideological sanctuary, the sanctuary of its own alienation.[13]

For Baudrillard, fashion is the epitome of the cynical survival of capitalism. It is the celebration of a perverse, fetishized passion for the abstract code, at the expense of any collective investment in symbolic exchange. The logic of the commodity multiplies indefinitely in the fascination for objects eviscerated of their substance and history, reduced to the pure state of marking a difference. As Baudrillard writes, "A thousand contradictory definitions of beauty and style are possible [but] one thing is certain: they are never a calculus of signs."[14] Indeed, Baudrillard argues, the very category of beauty is liquidated when the semiological order succeeds the symbolic order.

The disappearance of the beautiful as a sustaining category of precapitalist culture marks an important phase in the eclipse of subjectivity. According to Baudrillard, the forms of beauty were a symbolic play on the ambiguity of the subject. Beauty could be: "an effect of the soul (the spiritualist vision), the natural grace of movement, or countenence with the transparency of truth (the idealist vision), or the inspired genius of the body which can be communicated as effectively by expressive ugliness (the romantic vision)?[15]"

In this juxtaposition of an erstwhile subjective beauty with the postmodern sublime, Baudrillard is not concerned to recall an 'essence', but to draw out the historical supercession of ambivalence and to distinguish this from the substitutive logic of the fashion cycle. In symbolic exchange, the social relations between individuals or groups, as mediated through the gift, the ritual, and writing on the body, are all virtual relations of desire and as such, relations of risk, of unresolved ambivalence, danger, and vulnerability. In this sense, the sign-object of fashion and the symbolic object exist in mutually exclusive cultural forms:

> The sign object is neither given nor exchanged: it is appropriated, withheld, and manipulated by individual subjects as a sign, that is as coded difference. Here lies the object of consumption. And it is always of and from a reified, abolished social relationship that is "signified" in a code.[16]

Opposed to the forever unresolved order of the symbolic stands fashion, an abstract, arbitrary exchange of signs, a system that manifests in its appearance of play and difference the "total constraint of the code."

Replacing the traditional, socially ambiguous forms of beauty, fashion becomes a data base of aesthetic categories. Baudrillard refers to it as a "semio-aesthetic order," one which consists of "an interplay of referrals, of equivalence, of controlled dissonances."[17] This reinscription of the polyvalence of beauty within a homogenous system of endlessly but equally differentiated signs has, Baudrillard argues, as its ultimate goal, closure and perfection, a logical mirage suturing all social contradictions and divisions on the level of the abstract. This is the glamour of fashion, the glamourized body of disembodied perfection. This is *Vogue's* 'total look'; *Cosmopolitan's* 'perfect match'; *Mademoiselle's* 'elegant coordination'. This is the look of envy John Berger speaks of in *Ways of Seeing*. The look of solitary assurance, of impersonal power, a look absent and unfocused precisely because it looks out over the look of envy which sustains it.[18]

These are the images we find as we flip through page after page in fashion magazines. Despotic and total, each confronts us, but only to be overturned in an instant, replaced indefinitely in the continuous oscillation of absolute authority and immediate irrelevance.

Emblematic of this momentary, monthly, seasonal marking of time on the eternally reincarnated youthful body, oblivious to historical recording or wrinkling is *Vogue's* editorial, titled, interestingly enough, "The Last Word", summing up the new look for each issue. Here are a few 'last words' that would seem to exemplify the aesthetic ordering of a semiological culture:

> What works? Lets start with a conclusion. When you're dressing in a small shaped suit or precise dress (and those clothes are some of the stars of this season... and this issue), you're wearing highly finished sorts of clothes. You've a total look; there's not much need to interfere...
>
> In terms of accessories, the modern key to this 'finished' way of dressing may be a certain elimination of things...[19]'
>
> Designers have solved the problem of dressing fast, with wonderfully thought out looks. You'll like these looks best if you enter in, more than somewhat to the equation... In almost any clothes that sense of pureness is one sign of modernity...[20]

For Baudrillard, contemporary fashion is "the generalization of sign exchange value to facial and bodily effects. It is the final disqualification of the body, its subjection to a discipline... The signs are there to make the body into a perfect object."[21] Like Jameson's description of the images of postmodernity, this perfection of the body into an object of glamour "is a feat accomplished through a long and specific labor of sophistication... in which none of its real work (the work of the unconscious or psychic and social labor) can show through. The fascination of this fetishized beauty is the result of this extended process of abstraction, and derives from what it negates and censors through its own character as a system."[22]

Like Berger's "look of envy", this fetishized beauty exercises what Baudrillard calls a "cold seduction." It has nothing to do with pleasure or play or "the illegible ambivalence of desire"[23] In these frozen figures, flawless skins, blank stares, there is no pain, no fear, nothing moves, and nothing could move these invulnerable figures bereft of affect and expression.

But Baudrillard goes even further. He calls this fetishized beauty 'antinature incarnate' and argues that the fascination we hold for this model of reification is the very essence of what desire has become in the postmodern era: the desire for closure and logical perfection, the desire of desire to be ultimately and resolutely sufficient unto itself.[24]

> this kind of beauty is fascinating precisely because it is trapped in models, because it is closed, systematic, ritualized in the ephemeral, without symbolic value. It is the sign in this beauty, the mark (makeup, symmetry, or calculated asymmetry, etc.) which fascinates; it is the artifact that is the object of desire.[25]

Here the aesthetic effect plays on our initial misrecognition of the model for the mannequin and the mannequin for the model. We have to look twice. Yet this 'works,' as the language of *Vogue* would have it — and why shouldn't it? For isn't the reversibility of life and still life, nature and 'nature morte', a kind of epitome of the commodity system itself, a triumph of the principle of substitutibility?

In these inanimate figures, the idea of glamour goes beyond the perfection of the body, its making-up, dressing up, and even cutting up in plastic surgery — toward death itself.

In a recent issue of *Vogue*, Calvin Klein has eliminated the last distinction between the body and its adornment.[26] The body has imploded into
the pure play of surfaces, its outline delineates the imaginary otherness
of the simulacrum, the substance that never was. Beyond the subject as
object, made-up model, idol, mannequin, artifact. Beyond the pure positivity of desire perfected in the object, we now have the equivalent of the
photographic negative. In place of the subject, a shadow, a ghostly absent
presence clothed in angelic white silk. A shadow illuminated in its outline
like the radiated figures of Hiroshima: it haunts us. But, it also seduces us.
The empty abstract black hole of desire... beckons. Sleepwear. Deathwear.
Shrouded in fashion — the ideal logic of late capitalism.

IV
Obsession*

A Scents of Style: Some Thoughts on Calvin Klein's Obsession (four
15 second commercials on Video)

"There are many loves but only Obsession"

"In the kingdom of passion the ruler is Obsession"

"Love is child's play once you've learned Obsession"

"Between love and madness lies Obsession*"

---

* This section was written in collaboration with Charles Levin

Between love and madness lies Obsession. Desire and power spiral interiorized in this zero space of shadows and staircases leading nowhere, mocking all lines of escape. Obsession. All are positioned around it. Everything falls before it. All are reduced "to ashes, all ashes," "abandoned to the wreckage of themselves."

Why Obsession? Why name a perfume after the structure of neurotic inhibition? It appears that in a world so affectless, so sterile, only aggression sustains enough intensity to attract. What is initially most memorable for the viewer of this series of commercials is that in each the sign of the perfume is inserted into an obsessional collection of fetishes, the tokens of destroyed love, of loss, aphanisis, depression. In the first, it is the stolen chess piece, the king; in the second, scattered flower petals, yellow like the Narcissus; in the third, the pathetic child's diary of frustrated Oedipal passion; and in the fourth, the grieving mother's black scarf. In this fourfold cycle, like a Frygian mythos, laughter and love are followed by castration and perversion. The denouement is always an affective metonymy, in which the fragment of a broken bond is liberated as an ironic sign. Each segment transfixes a symbolic relation at its moment of destruction and adds it to the cumulative economy of Obsession. The perfume thus becomes a kind of liquid intensity, a condensation of failed or faded libido.

The phallic, pre-Raphealite woman is the simulacrum of incarnation, an angel, a fever — "all heat and hunger" — "taunting, exquisite creature" — like a wayward Ariel. She begs to be saved, but always escapes. In this sense, Obsession is alchemical, a distillation of the product at the conclusion of each episode, seated in the collection of fetish objects, marks the dynamic mutation of leaden desire into the signifier of charged memory. Each gesture, each touch, each utterance revolves around an absence. "To breathe her innocence was life itself" — a trace.

As in Klein's sleepwear ads, the simulation of 'obsession' produces an absence in order to forestall the death implicit in completion, or semiotic perfection. The 'system' cannot function without its Imaginary other, but this otherness only exists in a relational form, as the abstraction of a sign-object which refers back to a lost body. In the 'Oedipal' sequence featuring the little boy, his diary, and his idealization of the female model, there is a reference to Proust's À la recherche du temps perdu: "the whispers at my bedside, her arms, her mouth..." This maternal projection is "the only woman I'll ever love" — but she steals his fantasies away. "Did I invent her?" the little boy asks.

The sign of obsession is the cynical sign of a purely relational, abstract power, a power which thrives on its own self-hatred. It could be argued that the Obsession commercials interpellate a representation of the social world of late capitalism by recoding desire in Oedipal form, as a despotic signifier which territorializes fantasy as family theatre.[27] But this 'signifier', together with the family organized around it, are no longer credibly interpreted as Oedipal or patriarchal or even phallic. The paternal simulacrum (the narrator in the first episode) is a defeated Prospero, not only stripped of his secular power, but forlorn, unmagical, without spiritual authority. His gold has already turned into lead, his Miranda is a mannequin; and the purloined chesspiece is not a symbol of the procreative possibilities of kingship, but merely a mnemonic ingredient in the nostalgic simulation of coenesthetic seduction, a psychic ruin of bodily attraction.

The Lacanian father no longer has any of his symbolic authority, not even as an ideological constraint on "desire", not even as the progenitor of words. Everywhere and nowhere, language becomes cynical and hollow, evoking a pervasive structure of deauthorization and panic.[28] There is, to be sure, an Oedipal theatre, but it is empty, and the lines of memory echo in its phantom acoustic space like rehearsals for a play the actors know will not be performed.

The grieving mother of the fourth and final sequence surveys a scene in which neither conflict nor repression have any meaning. Sublimation turns out to have been a cruel, patriarchal joke. Like the helpless child, this dark, Trojan woman represents an emotional testimony; but she has witnessed neither struggle, nor death — only the schizoid terror of undifferentiation, the futile will to total consumptive passivity. Obsessional destruction is not final, merely recurrent: it is a repetition compulsion which infects each figure who participates in the concept of the family, and forces him or her to play out destiny in a pattern whose meaning all must pretend not to know, in order to create the illusion of meaning. The signs of absence multiply like the snakes on the Medusa's head, but not because something like the missing phallus is feared and repressed. It is not the phallus which is missing, but the *absence* of the phallus — or in other words, the issue is not absence, but the absence of absence. Not the anxiety of sexual difference, but the depressing apperception of endless sameness. The obsessional meaning-effect overdetermines itself, swallows its own tail in a circle of disembodied power. Every time we grasp a signification, it is substituted by another, which only adds to the collection of objects, but takes us nowhere in time or space. The death instinct, an overpowering odour, beckons.

APPENDIX

[Contract]

CALVIN KLEIN'S
OBSESSION

From the contract between Calvin Klein and model Jose Borain, the "Calvin Klein Girl." Borain appears in advertisements for the designer's fragrance Obsession.

AGREEMENT made as of the 25th day of September 1984 between CALVIN KLEIN INDUSTRIES, INC., a New York corporation (hereinafter called "CK"), and BORAIN ENTERPRISES, LTD., a New York corporation (hereinafter called "Consultant").

In consideration of the mutual covenants contained herein, the parties hereby agree as follows:

I.A. CK hereby retains Consultant and Consultant hereby agrees to be retained by CK and to provide to and for CK the "Services" of its employee, Jose Borain ("Borain"), as a model in all respects which services shall be deemed to include, without limitation, all broadcast advertising, promotion and exploitation (e.g., network, local, cable and closed circuit television, AM & FM radio and cinema), print advertising, promotion and exploitation (e.g., printed hang-tags, labels, containers, packaging, display materials, sales brochures, covers, pictorial, editorial, corporate reports and all other types of promotional print material contained in the media including magazines, newspapers, periodicals and other publications of all kinds), including but not by way of limitation, fashion shows, run-way modeling, retail store trunk shows, individual modeling and other areas of product promotion and exploitation which are or may be considered to be embraced within the concept... of fashion modeling.

4. Consultant shall, and where applicable shall cause Borain to:

A. Keep CK informed of Borain's schedule in the event she travels outside the metropolitain New York area for periods of more than two (2) days consecutively;

B. Maintain Borain's weight, hair style and color and all other features of Borain's physiognomy and physical appearance as they are now or in such other form as CK may, from time to time, reasonably request. Consultant and Borain represent that Borain's current weight level is between 120 and 125 lbs. and CK agrees that Borain's weight up to 130 lbs. will be an acceptable weight pursuant to the provisions hereunder. Illustratively, Borain shall wear hair styles, utilize such make-up and wear such apparel and accessories as CK requests from time to time; use such hair stylists as CK engages or approves; maintain such reasonable physical regimen (including exercise, diet an nutritional programs) as will best enable Borain to perform her Services hereunder; and when requested by CK, consult and comply with the reasonable advice and reasonable recommendations of such physician, exercize coach, hair and make-up stylists and others, etc.;

C. Maintain a personal lifestyle which will, in CK's sole subjective judgment reasonably exercised, be appropriate and most suitable to project an image and persona that reflect the high standards and dignity of the trademark "Calvin Klein" and that do not diminish, impair or in any manner detract from the prestige and reputation of such trademark.

7. A. CK shall pay or cause Consultant to be paid the aggregate sum of one million dollars ($1,000,000) for all of Borain's Services during the three (3) year term hereunder, i.e., the sum of $333,333 per year for each employment year during the term of this Agreement...

13. CK may... terminate this Agreement forthwith by written notice to Consultant upon the occurrence, or upon CK's becoming aware of the occurrence, of any one or more of the following events:

A. In the event of Borain's disfigurement or disability, which shall be deemed to mean any illness, accident or other physical or mental impairment which renders her, in the sole subjective judgment of CK reasonably exercised (except with respect to disfigurement or other change in physical appearance which may be exercised solely based on Mr. Klein's sole aesthetic subjective standards), incapable of performing or unqualified to perform her Services whenever required under this Agreement...

B....If by reason of [Borain's] deliberate or inadvertent action or conduct she shall come into disrepute or her public reputation shall become degraded or discredited so that the Services she is to provide pursuant hereunder shall, in CK's sole subjective judgment reasonably exercised, have become less valuable to CK in projecting the desired image consistent with the dignity and high standards of the CK tradition...

G. Notwithstanding anything to the contrary herein contained, this Agreement shall terminate automatically and forthwith upon the death of Borain, the bankruptcy or insolvency of Consultant, or the dissolution, liquidation, merger or consolidation of Consultant.

Notes

1. An earlier version of this paper was presented in a session sponsored by the C.J.P.S.T., The Canadian Sociology and Anthropology Association and The Winnipeg Art Gallery at the Learned Societies, Winnipeg, 1986.

2. While most sociological literature on fashion has tended to be primarily descriptive or historical rather than theoretical, the exceptions are phenomenologically oriented studies for the obvious reason that they take

the embodied subject as their point of departure. In the introduction to John O'Neill's recent study of contemporary society, (*Five Bodies*: Cornell University Press, 1985) he writes, "We are continuously caught up and engaged in the embodied look of things, especially the look of others and of ourselves. Although philosophers and moralists have decried our attachment to appearances and superficialities, as sociologists we cannot ignore the elaborate social construction of embodied appearances in which we are necessarily engaged as persons... Because *society is never a disembodied spectacle*, we engage in social interaction from the very start on the basis of sensory and aesthetic impression." p. 22.

3. See vol. 1 ch. 1 of Karl Marx's *Capital*. It is also interesting to note in this regard that Adam Smith's archtypic example of the rationality of the division of labour in *The Wealth of Nations* was the manufacture of pins used primarily to secure clothing and cloth in sewing.

4. William Leiss, et al, *Social Communication in Advertising: Persons, Products and Images of Well-Being* (Toronto: Methuen, 1986), See esp. chs. 4 and 5.

5. Elizabeth Wilson, *Adorned in Dreams: Fashion and Modernity* (London: Virago Press, 1985), Ch. 6.

6. Frederic Jameson, *Marxism and Form: Twentieth-Century Dialectical Theories of Literature* (Princeton: Princeton Univ. Press., 1971), p. 106.

7. Jean Baudrillard, *For a Critique of the Political Economy of the Sign*, translated by Charles Levin, (St. Louis: Telos Press, 1981), p. 98.

8. Ibid, p. 67.

9. Frederic Jameson, "Postmodernism and the Cultural Logic of Late Capitalism", *New Left Review*, #146, Fall 1984.

10. Gilles Deluze and Felix Guattari, *Anti-Oedipus, Capitalism and Schizophrenia*, translated by R. Hurley, et al., (New York: The Viking Press, 1977).

11. Guy Debord, *Society of the Spectacle* (Detroit: Black and Red, 1983), p. 11.

12. Baudrillard, p. 97.

13. Ibid., p. 97.

14. Ibid., p. 188.

15. Ibid., p. 94.

16. Ibid., p. 65.

17. Ibid., p. 188.

18. John Berger, *Ways of Seeing*, B.B.C. and Penguin Books, 1979 p. 133.

19. *Vogue*, 'The Last Word', Sept. 1982, p. 568.

20. *Vogue*, 'The Last Word', Feb. 1983, p. 336.

21. Baudrillard, p. 94.

22. Ibid., p. 94.

23. Ibid., p. 188.

24. Ibid., p. 94.

25. Ibid., p. 94.

26. *Vogue,* May, 1986.

27. Gilles Deleuze and Felix Guattari, *Anti-Oedipus: Capitalism and Schizophrenia,* see chapter 4, section 3.

28. Cf. Jean Baudrillard. *L'échange symbolique et la mort* (Paris: Gallimard, 1976), pp. 174-176.

Acknowledgements

The following corporations kindly gave permission for the reproduction of their advertisments: Figure One: Saint Laurent Inc., New York; Figures Two and Three: Calvin Klein Inc. New York.

III

BODY PROBES

Panic Penis/Panic Ovaries

So then, what is it to be? Carnal knowledge of aesthetic states or the body doubled in an endless labyrinth of media images? The local body of the anorexic as a privileged site of resistance against the recuperation of subjectivity itself by the processed world of the simulacrum or the marked body of the AIDS victim as yet another dark sign of the coming fate of the body? Is Foucault's vision of power under the sign of the panoptic gaze finally too conservative for a *fin-de-millenium* culture which is horizoned by Bataille's parodic vision of the solar anus and the pineal eye? Not then, the body as the sacred object of a power which inscribes, but now a whole media carnival of body parts for a contemporary cultural scene where *indifférance* spreads. Thus, body probes of detrital scenes of panic penises, panic ovaries, and panic desire.

Panic Penis

No longer the old male cock as the privileged sign of patriarchal power and certainly not the semiotician's dream of the decentered penis which has, anyway, already vanished into the ideology of the phallus, but the *postmodern penis* which becomes an emblematic sign of sickness, disease and waste. Penis burnout, then, for the end of the world.

And just in time! Because in all of the technologies of sex which make possible a sex without secretions (the computerized phone sex of the Minitel system in Paris; video porn for the language of the gaze: designer bodies; and gene retreading), in all of these technologies of sex, the penis, both as protuberance and ideology, is already a spent force, a residual afterimage surplus to the requirements of telematic society.

Anyway, it was predictable. The male body has always been the privileged object and after-effect of a twofold psychoanalytical colonization: a *psychoanaltyics of reception* which functions, as Lacan insists, by the principle of misrecognition where in the fateful mirror stage the bourgeois infant self substitutes the illusion of substantial unity to be provided by a fictive, abstract ego for concrete identity; and secondly, at the *social* level, where as theorised by Althusser, ideology interpellates individuals as subjects. This may be why, in the end, even Michel Foucault said with resignation that the postmodern self is really about sedimented subjectivity, that is, the constitution of the male self as an afterimage of the moral problematization of pleasure and the torturing procedures of the confessional.

Or maybe it is this and more. Not organic, natural sex any longer and not the discursive sexuality so praised by all the poststructuralists, but a cynical and parodic sex — a *schizoid and hyperreal sex* — for panic bodies. A shizoid sex, therefore, where sado-masochism of the hyperreal kind operates in the language of a liquid power which, no longer belonging as property to the old language of gender divisions (a male masochism? a female sadism?), operates at the more general level of torturer and victim.

When we have already passed beyond the first two orders of sex, beyond sex as nature and beyond sex as discourse, to sex as fascinating only when it is about recklessness, discharge and upheaval — a *parodic* sex, then we have also broken beyond the analytics of sexuality to *excess*; beyond Foucault's language of the "care of the self" to *frenzy*; beyond the "use of pleasure" (Foucault again) with its moral problematization of the ethical subject in relation to its sexual conduct to a little sign-slide between *kitsch and decay*. Not then the nostalgia for an aesthetics of existence today or for a hermeneutics of desire (these are passé and who cares anyway?), but parodic sex as about the free expenditure of a "boundless refuse of activity" (Bataille) pushing human plans; not the coherency of the ethical subject (that has never motivated anyone except in the detrital terms of the subject as a ventilated remainder of death), but the excitation of the subject into a *toxic state*, into a sumptuary site of loss and orgiastic excess. Not, finally, a productive sex, but an *unproductive* sex, a sex without secretions, as the site of the death of seduction as that which makes sex bearable in the postmodern condition.

Bataille was right:

The (pineal) eye at the summit of the skull, opening on the incandescent sun in order to contemplate it in a sinister solitude, is not a product of the understanding, but is instead an immediate existence; it opens and blinds itself like a conflagration, or like a fever that eats the being; or more exactly the *head*. And thus it plays the role of a fire in the house; the head, instead of locking up life as money is locked in a safe, spends it without counting, for at the end of this erotic metamorphosis, the head has received the *electric power of points*. This great burning head is the image and the disagreeable light of the notion of expenditure.

For expenditure is when "life is parodic and lacks an interpretation", that is the excitation of the solar anus. And why not? The pineal eye and the solar anus are also always about an excremental sexuality as the third order of simulation into which sex vanishes after the disappearance of organic and discursive sexuality, and after the fading away of the body itself as yet another afterimage of the postmodern scene.

Panic Ovaries

And what then of women's wombs? Is natural reproduction preserved intact at the end of the world or have we already entered into a darker region of the terror of the simulacrum? Now, more than ever, women's bodies are the inscribed focus of a threefold deployment of relational power. In the postmodern condition, women's bodies are the prime afterimage of a strategy of body invasion which occurs in the inverted and excessive language of *contractual liberalism*.

First, the *medical subordination* of women's bodies which results, whether through *in vitro* fertilization or genetic mixing, in the alienation of the womb. When the ovaries go outside (and with them the privileged language of sexual *différence*), it is also a certain sign of the grisly technological abstraction of alienated labour into the alienation of reproduction itself.

Secondly, the medical inscription of women's bodies is superceded by the subordination of childbirth to the *ideology of law*. For example, in the Baby M case, the natural mother is reduced to the contractual fiction of a "hired womb"; the meaning of the "natural" is inverted into its opposite number (the *actual* mother becomes legally a "surrogate" and the Daddy surrogate — he was always only present as a free-floating seed in a genetic mixing tube — is *juridically* renamed as a real, living father); and, in the end, the entire juridical apparatus is directed towards justifying a new form of legal slavery for women who are poor, powerless, and thus potential victims of the predatory instincts of the ruling elites. A class of professional, middle-class elites, *men and women*, who measure the meaning of the "good" by the standards of petty convenience. Ironically, in the Baby M case, it was only after the natural mother lost custody rights to her baby that the media and the courts began, finally, describing her, not as the "surrogate mother" any longer, but as the *biological* mother. Cynical media and cynical law for a rising class of cynical elites.

Thirdly, panic ovaries are also about all the cases of fetal appropriation where the state intervenes, supposedly on behalf of the rights of the unborn baby, to take *juridical* possession of the body of the mother. A perfect complicity, then, among the *technological* interventions of medicine into the body of the mother (the use of medical technology as an early warning system for detecting birth defects in the fetus); the *juridical* seizure of the fetus as a way of deploying state power against the body of the mother; and the *politics of the new right* which can be so enthusiastic about the jurisprudence of fetal appropriation as a way of investing the contractarian rights of the fetus against the desires of the mother. A whole hypocritical *fetus fetish* by law, by medicine, and by the neo-conservatives as a way of canceling out the will of the natural mother, and of taking possession of the bodies of women. Margaret Atwood's thesis in *The Handmaid's Tale* about the reduction of women to hired wombs is thus disclosed to be less an ominous vision of the future than a historic account of an already past event in the domination of women.

7

CARNAL KNOWLEDGE OF
AESTHETIC STATES[1]

Charles Levin

Part I: The "Fading" of the Body in Postmodern Thought

> I want to speak to the despisers of the body. I would not
> have them learn and teach differently, but merely say fare-
> well to their own bodies — and thus become silent.
> "Body am I, and soul" — thus speaks the child. And why
> should one not speak like children.
> But the awakened and knowing say: body am I entirely,
> and nothing else; and soul is only a word for something
> about the body.

Neitzsche[2]

The Psychology of the Afterimage

We tend to think of images in terms of memory; that is, when we talk
about images, more often than not we are talking about afterimages: the
image as the memory, the trace, the aftereffect, of an experience. This is
the domain of the semiotic. The word, the dream, the picture, the thing
— all these can be thought as if they were decomposable into signifying
elements, or signifiers, which function in systems of *re*presentation.

This conception of the image as afterimage was powerfully reinforced
as one of the forms of social theory by psychoanalysis, in particular through

Freud's model of the psychoanalytical process as *re*construction, the retrieval and retelling of events in childhood, the recovery of childhood experience. This orientation in psychoanalytic thought is reflected in the metaphor of the unconscious as a junkheap, a repository of repressions that resurface as signs, a wastebin of images which fester and ferment and finally foment, in the "return of the repressed." As Deleuze and Guattari have tried to show in the *Anti-Oedipus*, this vision turns the unconscious into a field for the application of power, and psychoanalysis becomes a problematic of control, of neutralization or "reterritorialization."[3] Desire is theorized as the retrospective functioning of a lack, whilst the activity of desire — creative energy or "desiring-production" — is defused, dematerialized. The affirmative desire *for* something gets transposed into the negative desire *of* something, and desire becomes desire of desire itself, or "will to will," a rearguard action against *aphanisis*, the extinction of desire, the exhaustion of the signifying field. It is as if the warmth and light of the mind were nothing but the fading ember of the mind's refuse, signifying both the mind's consumption of psychosocial debris as fuel, and its rejection of life itself.

As Deleuze and Guattari show, it is to Lacan that one must turn to find a theory of passive desire, a completely denatured psychoanalysis. For Lacan, the body exists in biological fragments, it is a shattered *tabula rasa* which must be "granted an image."[4] On this body of absence, Lacan superimposes a quasi-linguistic model of the adapted personality. It is a void (desire) waiting to be filled, a body-without-organs attending the phallic punctuations of signification, a gap subtending the marking operations of power. This discursively positioned subject is the perfect material for a neodisciplinary exterminist society. It is precisely the "volume in perpetual disintegration" which Foucault so gingerly describes, that "inscribed surface of events... traced by language...", a docile receptacle to be "totally imprinted by history."[5]

Lacanian psychoanalytic theory describes the schizoid strategy of the body, in which the body distills itself into the feeling tone of an afterimage, the *déjà vu*. The psyche is theorized as representation, a kind of generalized sign economy which only touches on the physical body at points where it is socially coded, certain primarily genderal *"points de capiton"* relating mainly to the late phases of psychosexual development in classical psychoanalytic theory.[6]

Lacanian thought holds the greatest interest for those who think about culture today precisely because it is a psychology of the afterimage, a hermeneutics of life as lack, castration, and death. The Lacanian "law of the father" is like a second law of psychodynamics, in which the flesh is entropically vapourized by metonymical concatenations of deferral and "infinite referral" — what Derrida once called *différance*. In a way, Baudrillard's "generalized political economy of the sign" (that system of third order abstraction he calls the simulacrum) is a logical extension of

Lacan's externalized and sociologized unconscious (the "discourse of the Other") in which the subject is defined as a "signifier for another signifier." For Lacan, binarism and disembodiment have ontological status. Culture is primordially so: it is a pure system, an unadulterated code. As Baudrillard shows in his critique of the production category in contemporary social thought, even the "material infrastructure" of society is caught up in the process of metonymy, of mirroring and misrecognition, which constitutes the Imaginary.

All of this amounts to saying that there is no cultural "base," or in other words, that there is no foundation of thought in the realm of the living: "Power is dead."[7] In the classical, and more recently, the structuralist opposition between nature and culture, nothing substantial can be placed on the side of culture, or of the human, because sociality is conceived as a superimposition of pure form, code, convention, law. All of culture, including the "forces and relations of production," is thought of as superstructure, an afterimage at play in the field of effects. It is always already a memory, a misremembering, or what acidheads used to call a "flashback."

The Ontology of Postmodernity

The essence of the theory of postmodernism is to interpret Lacanian psycholinguistics as a cultural condition, as a collective way of life. Unfortunately, when Lacanian thought is explicated at the level of the postmodern socius, its presuppositions still function to achieve an epistemological closure. These presuppositions have been developed into their purest form in the contemporary theory of textuality. Lacanian feminism, for example, always reproduces the "phallus" as an occult principle, because in its attempt to erase the phallus, it not only furthers the Lacanian project of translating the body into an algorithmic language, but deepens the phallic logic of inscription itself. As for the politics of desire, its deep-seated epistemology of the signifier usually evades the question of desire by starting from the play of formal differences at the level of "effects," and then deriving from this a formal model of desire as a generalized principle of direct investment, of "plugging in."[8] Even deconstruction, in all the purity of its self-effacing operations, gets caught up in the Lacanian circle: an endless oscillation of phallus and hole, presence and absence, trace and space, mark and blank, form and (non) substance, signification and "force" — in short, the epistemological circle of inscription and "writing:" the logic of the separation of the symbolic and the physical, the metaphorical split between "culture and nature."

The structuralism latent in postmodernist theory — the vision of culture as an autotelic system of signs — compels the intellect to think the *Anti-System*. But the Anti-System is a conception as ideal as the signifying *System* it opposes. The Anti-System usually appears as an alloy of classical substance and modern force: an unmediated desire, an absolute unconscious, a pristine nonmeaning, a pure power, a negative being, a non-entity. The Anti-System thinks the body as a completely closed and dimensionless, unruptured surface "without organs." This nonpresence is not so much "nature in the raw" as nature in fine filigree. The concept of matter and energy without extension or sensible qualities becomes the new infrastructure (in the politics of desire) and the new referent (in deconstructive philosophy). Everything is defined as a manifestation — an *effect* — of power, desire, *différance*. Thus, the post-structuralist negation (e.g., the critique of Levi-Strauss and Lacan: the subversion of the "system of signs" and the "symbolic *order*") emerges as a paradoxical revival of nineteenth century models of base and superstructure, ranging from Marx's "forces of production" to Freud's "libidinal economy" and various "secondary drive" theories of "socialization." As in the behaviourist paradigm, nature functions as a kind of nonspecific base, while human behaviour counts only as a reflex. According to Deleuze, for example, Nietzsche was concerned "with forces [on the one hand], and [with] forms of general semiology [on the other]. Phenomena, things, organisms, societies, consciousness and spirits are signs, or rather symptoms, and themselves reflect states of forces."[9] In Deleuze's *Logique du sens*, the relation between the Anti-System and the System is one of pure cause and effect.[10] Everything in the alleged System is conceived as an effect of the Anti-System, or the Will-to-Power (which is also necessarily the purest expression of the System). But the Anti-System is just chaos (in the sense of disembodied formlessness): it is nothing more than the abstract negation of Plato's Doctrine of Ideas — its mirror image. The "logic" of sense of which Deleuze writes exists only within the cut-off and castrated realm of effects, so that when the System is deconstructed, nothing is left over but the unsullied negativity of the Anti-System: a world without sensible being, a desire without objects, a force without energy.

The Body and the Sign

There is an intimate connection between our ability to conceive what we call postmodernity and the deconstruction of the sign. The latter plays on the appearance of logical regression set up by the temporalization of the sign's metaphysical constituents (signifier, signified, and referent). The diachronic relation between sign and sign destroys the trinitarian unity of signification, so that the constitutents of a completed meaning are volatilized in the protensional void of an infinite referral process. The conception of society as sign and simulacrum, which is ideologically contemporaneous with Plato's Idea and Pythagoras' *ratio* of discrete harmonic relations, is revived in the crisis of the sign's dissolution. And this deconstructive moment of history imposes upon the mind a heightened consciousness both of history and of the futility of remembrance, such as Nietzsche explored in *The Use and Abuse of History*. If meaning is composed by a sign, and if it exists by virtue of a system, as our rationalist and schizoid ego impulse would lead us to believe, and even to wish, then the temporalization of the sign, and consequent failure of the ideal, traps the meaning of being-alive-now in the scrutiny of the screen memory of the signifier. We become fascinated by the mystery of the signifier's presence, the enigma of the forces and sequences which must have carried the signifier hither. The signifier, or screen memory, condenses an absence that compels us, and we are hypnotized by the prospect of a personal significance in the apparently random constellations of effects before us. Life becomes a kind of obsession with fate which Freud would have linked to the subterfuges of a perverse superego, and which Nietzsche would have read as the nihilism of *ressentiment* itself.

The theory of postmodernity translates deconstruction — as exemplified in the thought of Lacan and Derrida — back into the field of the "referential illusion" which deconstruction has systematically evaded. An example of this is provided by Baudrillard, who simply takes Derrida or Kristeva or the early Deleuze and reads them directly into social experience. In effect, Baudrillard says: "Let us take these exalted theorists of language at their word: there is no such thing as metatheory, metaphysics, or epistemology — everything they appear to be saying about the philosophy of meaning is nothing more than a mediated description of what they feel like being alive in the world today." In other words, we live in a world of afterimages, of ghosts, signifiers, and simulacra.

Reflecting on this relationship between philosophical deconstruction and postmodern social theory, one cannot fail to be impressed by the fact that no attempt to deconstruct the signifier itself has ever been carried off successfully in this era of the linguistic turn, and that both philosophy and cultural science are themselves caught up in the mesmerism of the signifier. This is because the strategy of temporalizing the sign, though it may dissolve the scientific pretensions of structuralism, is itself implicated in the metaphysics of Rationalism. Deconstruction depends on the technical procedure of reduction to the discrete which constitutes the metaphysical problem of the sign in the first place.[11] The regression released by the deconstructive technique cannot begin without taking the constituted and historically constructed existence of the signifier as a given. The signifier is the formal starting point of rationalist thought: it is the discrete manipulable segment which makes analysis, abstraction, and substitution possible, and thus enables the construction of models for the independent organization of thought. Deconstruction merely plays with such potentialities, without really questioning the concealment of the signifier's origin in an operational reduction. Once the signifier has been granted this ontological status, it takes only a slight shift in perspective from traditional (i.e., realistic) rationalism, to arrive at a skeptical version of rationalism in which the entire and unfathomable state of irretrievability and regression to which it gives rise, ceases to look like the consequence of formal segmentation. Instead, it presents itself as a kind of negative causality which leads inexorably to the signifier itself, producing the signifier's discrete and closed effect as a necessity, an already totalized and inescapaable world of screen memories and sourceless effects, the timeless aftermath of the postmodern condition.

Deconstruction finds that we must begin with "writing," and that we are properly directed toward the formal and formalizable status of the word, and not toward the body which speaks and writes it. Of course, the deconstruction of the sign engages us in a discourse of the body. But this is the Lacanian body of *points de capiton*, discrete markers, and decoupage. Deconstruction invokes the death of the body against the living word, the furrowed "ground" against the dancing figure (the phallus, the signifier). But it can only accomplish this corporeal referentiality as an inversion, a moment of extinction, the exhaustion of a formal regression which cannot begin without its priveleged moment within the sign, the formal or phallic moment, which is already a reductive cancellation of the body. Deconstruction theorizes the body, to be sure, but only as a kind of negative theology or temporal mystery. The body becomes the unlocalizable antecedent of the sign — an absence lurking behind the dense significance of the signifier: merely the site of a future depletion.

Postmortemism and Ultramodernism

The argument of this paper links together the classical conception of psychoanalysis as reconstruction (of a forgotten or obscure past), the deconstructive paradox of the temporalized sign, and "postmodern experience" itself. The connection implies that contemporary social experience and the dominant academic theories about it are overdetermined by the rationalist wish for historical recovery and completion, the revealed impossibility of such recovery, and the paradoxical nature of any attempt to think meaning and the image as the traces of a determinate reality. Since the rationalist effort at reconstruction always fails, and always for perfectly rationalist reasons, the rumour has started to go round that perhaps there is no body to be reckoned with; that there are only the abstractions, the shifters, and codings that mark out the spaces where the body might have been.

The theory of postmodernism may therefore best be described as a social theory of the afterimage, a theory of collective life as an aftermath. In short, postmodernism is really a kind of *"postmortemism."* There is an ontogenetic analogy here with the way a person may grow up into a being organized around the introjected core of the parents' unconscious grief or sense of failure. This is something like the situation of the most radical contemporary social theory. Yet, in a way, postmortemism is a healthy maladaptation — an Adornoesque refusal of the potential terrorism of all instrumentalizable thought. Postmortemism sees contemporary history largely as it is: a juggernaut of operationalized rationalism (the celebrated "unity of theory and practice," from dialectical materialism to the semio-cybernetics of urban space). Contestation becomes inconceivable, except as living on the fringe and testing the limits of contradictory experience. Postmodernists think and write about aesthetics, artworks, art practices, textuality, indexicality, and death. As witness of intellectual history, the post-modern mind is paralysed by the devastations wrought by modern social and technological science.

But postmortemism has the unfortunate result of reducing everything that is happening now to a mnemic effect of what went before. It forces us into the mode of reconstruction and the logic of bases and superstructures. In fact, postmortemism posits a chain of such mnemic effects, reaching back indefinitely in historical time. One only has to read such dystopic reconstructions as *Dialectic of Enlightenment* to realize that the seed of Fascism, if it is to be conceived as the culmination of an historical process, is irretrievable in time.

Freud talked about screen memories, those condensed and highly-charged doubles that mask the prehistories of the psyche. What was the pre-history of the social body that is masked and condensed in the "runes" of the postmodern aftermath? Was it modernism? Or was modernism it-self just the sliding signifier of the classical world, the play of afterimages in the wake of sinking civilizations — what Marx called the "childhood" of humanity? Derrida has shown that, in principle, the logic of the af-terimage, the logic of the signifier, is an infinite regress.

And yet, perhaps the problematic of the sign can be pinned down to certain historical determinations. As Arthur Kroker has argued, there is reason to believe that the theory of institutionalized Christianity, particularly as preserved in the work of Augustine, may be pivotal for comprehension of the deep structures of modern experience.[12] The church father worked with a concept of the signifier, its imaginary double, and the mediation of a vanishing point in experience (signifier, signified, referent?). There are a variety of such trinities in Western thought, all of which revolve around the paradox of mentality and its relation to earth. What is new about such an interpretation is that it depends on the Freudian concept of idealiza-tion (and its underlying Nietzschean conception of *ressentiment*). And it is significant for our understanding of both postmodernism and poststruc-turalism that all of this psychology of idealizing defence finds perfect ex-pression in Lacan's theory of the phallus as the structural principle of signification.

Popular intellectual historians like Bertrand Russell and Kenneth Clark have depicted Jean-Jacques Rousseau as the first modern thinker, with good reason; but Augustine wrote a much earlier "Confessions;" and it was perhaps Augustine who fully grasped the reflections of the ego, the self-less recounting of deeply-felt compromise, as an emblem of the human condition and as a model for a new theory of socialization. For the thoroughly modern individual, to tell a story, to recount, is actually to re-cant: to confess, as Foucault has argued.[13]

Kroker has also proposed that the theory of postmodernism be aban-doned in favour of a new kind of critical radicalism coalescing around the concept of the "ultramodern." This term should suggest neither the tor-tured aftermath of modernism nor a primitivistic short-circuiting of cul-tural history, but rather the dissolution of modernist consciousness itself, as it lives on in the postmodern taste for linguistic and collective models of being.

Modernism contemplated the history of Spirit, Idea, Mind, Convention, and Sign, and defined progress as faith in a kind of thickening skin of such idealizations. By returning to Nietzsche and Freud, postmodernism as crit-ical theory notes the absurdity of such an encrusted barrier against the real — not by returning us to 'reality,' but by trying to demonstrate the nullity of the real itself through the paradox of the temporality of the sign. Thus, postmodern skepticism does not so much defeat modernist ideal-ism, as take over its duties. Postmodernist theory tends simply to reverse the meaning of the rationalist equation of idealization with knowledge. The failure of the Ideal becomes the failure of all activity. It is as if, having condemned the hypocrisy of pure Reason, we then throw ourselves into the abyss with it, in order to retain one last link with it, and thus remain pure ourselves.

Nietzsche was prone, like Freud, to interpret psychological defences like projection and splitting as cognitive barriers; he anticipated Freud's discovery that the Ideal can serve as a defence against fantasies of (good and) evil. An intelligent reading of Nietzsche might reveal that the cogni-tive problem of reference (or lack of reference — the "transcendental sig-nified"), and in particular, the existential problem of the difference between human constructions on the one hand and natural formations on the other (the great epistemological and sociological issues of modernity), are emo-tional in origin: universal predicaments, but not constitutive of thought in themselves. Of course, as a young professor, Nietzsche made an influen-tial (and unfortunately somewhat moral) distinction between the preten-sions of human knowledge ("wretched... shadowy and flighty... aimless and arbitrary"), and the vast realms of real nature beyond human cogni-tion and control.[14] But this kind of ironic distinction, typical of poststruc-turalist thought, in which the sheer poverty and impertinence of human Reason and Language have become a kind of status symbol setting history and society apart from the nonhuman 'eternities' of nature, is no longer possible once Creationism has been forfeited. There are no grounds for believing that anything that humans might ever do (however linguistic, ra-tional, or ridiculous) is any *less* a significant part of "nature" than other phenomena. The relativity of culture and the "arbitrariness of the sign" are no substitutes for divine favour. If God is dead, his *absence* must also cease to be significant for our interpretation of the world. This, Freud grasped better than Nietzsche. We no longer have the theological luxury of demonstrating that our own thought unaided leads nowhere. We cannot return to something else, or produce it later. Neither fusion nor transcendence is either past or future, neither nature nor spirit is merely lost or pending. We are already as much "it" as anything else, because the past and the future exist only as potential intensities of the present. Real nature bumbles along, and our bodies with it.

A farewell to the rationalism of modernism and its sequel in postmortemism requires, in addition to the usual Nietzschean reading of Freud, a Freudian reading of Nietzsche. The referential aporias of the temporalized sign nearly always turn out to be questions of the physical body in relation to other physical bodies, informed only secondarily and uninterestingly by the celebrated "arbitrariness" of the linguistic "construction of reality" which we have a tendency to read back into the outlooks of Nietzsche and Freud.

The "reality" of the body will have to be explored much more deeply if 'ultramodernism' is to be more than another version of postmodernism, i.e., another face of modernism itself. The idea of the ultramodern would then no longer participate so blindly in the Lacanian cosmos of ontological lack, the ascetic suction of a protensional void, of which the theory of textual deconstruction, of displacement as a kind of romanticized death instinct, has lately served as such a fine example. The prefix 'ultra' implies a kind of concentrated and cohesive madness, perhaps even the implosion of the signifier itself into the fulness of an immediate physical relationship — an extremism which will be presented in this paper as the perfectly ordinary, but thoroughly underrated and unlikely psychosomatic reality of the infantile body.

Part II: The Aesthetic Substance of the Infantile Body

The mind does not know itself, except in so far as it perceives the ideas of the modifications of the body.

Spinoza[15]

Psychoanalysis has rarely concerned itself with the problem of reference or the normativity of theories of reality because the reconstruction of the past is in a way merely a tangent of the psychoanalytic process. The process itself has more to do with the adumbration of psychosomatic states through dreams, talk, and the negotiation of a peculiar but highly specific relationship. Remembrance takes place, of course; but the fact that every narrativization recedes eventually into temporal oblivion worries few who have been impressed by the intensity, immediacy, and increasing explicitness of bodily states. In dreams, every variety of sophistication is expressed as a situation of the body, its relations, states, and parts.

The fact of being a body is inescapable, it cannot be deferred, lost in a chain of reference, or divided into signifier and signified. Neither *différance*, nor indeterminacy, nor the ideological constitution of the subject, nor the social or linguistic construction of reality, can succeed in disguising the biological status of our existence.

One does not have to be a body without organs in order to undo the order of representation (Deleuze), any more than one has to build up sensorimotor schemas in order to be able to match the gestures of others (Piaget).[16] Psychoanalysis discovers that the body is not just an obscure relation to its afterimages, but a being which is an immediate image of itself; and that the transference is not only repetition, but the physical difference of bodies in the present. The body *is* the symbol; and while the relationship between what constitutes meaning and the functioning of the body can be separated out and arranged in the discrete markers of temporal sequence, its actuality is never exhausted by this or any other variation of linguistic modelling.

When psychoanalysis breaks out of the logic of reconstruction and the conundrum of the afterimage (signifier), it encounters the fact that the infantile body knows nothing of political systems or family systems, nothing about signs and machines. Theodor Adorno defined the whole as the untrue; psychoanalysis would add that the body is the truth of the unwhole — that it cannot be synthesized with its totalizations and investments.

The popular image, in *Anti-Oedipus* and other poststructuralist works, of a prodigious infrastructure of instinctual nature ("desiring-production") is in many ways an evasion of the question of the body. One of the great psychoanalytic contributions to general knowledge was to show that nobody really knows where the "inside" of the body ends and the "outside" begins. The body inevitably generates a kind of "hermeneutic circle," but it hardly follows from this that the inside and the outside may simply be translated into one another, or that the "internal world" can be evacuated, through the plugs and ducts of some libidinal machinery of discharge, directly into the socio-political field. The insight that desire is never merely a "lack," or a sort of ineffable excess of fixed structures (as Deleuze and Guattari correctly point out), does not turn desire into a virile apparatus of production. The ideology of structuralism is not overcome simply by adding the concept of flows and currents to the paratactic chains and metonymical networks of the linguistic model. The desiring substance of energy is just as much an abstraction of the body as the formalism of a linguistically-structured concept of the symbolic.

The infantile body is saturated with fantastic meaning, which can never be entirely discharged through "linkages" of "production" or "investment" (cathexis). But this does not mean that the infant is "blind," a "narcissis-

tic" bundle of nerves, or a "blooming, buzzing confusion." The infantile
body already knows that it is in a predicament, dependent on an ecology
which evades complete understanding and fantasies of control. The infantile body knows that there are holes in itself, that you can put things in
and force things out, that it is a body in a physical world of bodies with
ambiguous boundaries, entrances and exits; that bodies fold in on themselves and unravel, that they may contain each other and things, or be contained, that there are emotions, that these are powerful, ecstatic,
annihilating, unmanageable without help. This is one of the things that
a very small body already knows: that it cannot go it alone or, at least,
that going it alone is only a hypothesis, depending on whether those other
bodies that *seem* to be able to go it alone really can. This is what psychoanalysis is about: not the paradoxes of linguistic communication or the
aporias of reconstruction, but the question of how people live through
the situation of being a neotenous body, the strategies of being in a world
of bodies and things, and their various consequences.

* * * * * * * * * * * * * * * * * * * *

In 1913, Sandor Ferenczi wrote of how the child's "attention is arrested above all by those objects and processes of the outer world that on
the ground of ever so distant a resemblance, remind him of his dearest
experiences." (One might add, of course, the child's least dear experiences
as well.) Ferenczi had in mind

> those intimate connections, which remain throughout life,
> between the human body and the objective world that
> we call *symbolic*. On the one hand the child in this stage
> sees in the world nothing but images of his own corporeal-
> ity, on the other he learns to represent by means of his
> body the whole multifariousness of the outer world.[17]

Here, Ferenczi emphasizes the basic psychoanalytic intuition that the
bodily imagination is the substratum of all our "models." But there are some
problems with the way he thinks this through. In Ferenczi's days, for the
most part, psychoanalysts tended to think of the baby as proceeding by
analogy, animistically, identifying everything with its own pleasurable functioning. Freud's "hungry baby" in *The Interpretation of Dreams* cannot
tell the difference between its hallucinatory afterimage of the mother's
breast and an actual feeding. Freud's baby will only achieve this distinction between the internal production of imagery and the external object
by means of the reality principle, which will gradually evolve out of the
frustrating experience of the image.

The philosophical behaviourist and empiricist assumption that the neonate is a narcissistic and autoerotic isolate has led to an overemphasis in

psychoanalytic theory, particularly in North America and France, on the problem of psychological differentiation, what Freud called the "reality principle" and Lacan called "language," or "le nom (non) du pere." The father is supposed to be the one who is responsible for rupturing the "narcissistic" closure of nature (mother-child dyad) by introducing language, culture, deferral, displacement, the signifier, and the Law. But the foregoing is largely a social scientific and culturalist myth.

We privilege the ego-function of abstraction and decoupage, and thus set up a hierarchy in which the signifier or "word-presentation" has authority and priority over the symbolic process or "thing-presentation." But there is a further degree of abstraction involved: the immediacy of the internal world (what the Romantics called Imagination) is reduced, in theory, to the status of hallucination, which will eventually be trained through frustration to become the ego function of memory. The symbolic activities of the infantile body are viewed as a kind of mnemic anarchy, a play of afterimages yet to be subjected to the governance of a temporal order and the order of rationality. The pleasure of imagining is reduced to the pressure of need, which has no object, but only an aim of gratification — or in other words, abeyance, blankness. (This aspect of Freud's early instinctual theorizing has been spun out into a vast generalization of Thanatos by Lacan and his followers: the imagination is toward death, the symbolic is the dead father, living is castration, etc.). In this way, the infantile body is fitted into the temporal logic of the signifier, psychic life and even dreaming are comprehended one-sidedly as a play of afterimages, and the body without language is condemned to the status of false consciousness (the Imaginary), and replaced with the false empiricism of the body without organs.

This whole approach hinges on the half-truth that the difference between the inner and the outer, the dream and the object, is alien to the organism, a secondary acquisition imposed by the harsh lesson of necessity. The infant is supposed to know no outside of itself, only so that it can eventually learn that in principle, there is no inside either, except by virtue of blind instinct and ideological delusion. But the clinical and experimental evidence no longer supports this generalization. The difference between the imagination and the external object is always relative, never either wholly absent or complete. The cognitive distinction between the self and other is not actually learned from scratch; it is built in to the organismic structures of perception at birth, gradually refined, lost in affective retreat, exaggerated in self-defence, practiced according to a cultural code. But it is always there. Difference is a very difficult experience, but its existence rests on more than the reality principle, or the therapeutic discoveries of linguistic philosophy. The problem for the infantile body is not to cognize difference as a first principle under the reign of necessity, but what to make of difference emotionally. And what one *makes* of this cognition is always symbolic — always a state of the body. It cannot be reduced to a series of discoveries about "external reality" (ego psychology) or "language" (Lacan, deconstruction). It is an active creation of new images, a way of being; and not just a progressive differentiation between memory and perception, signifier and signified.

Long before language and Oedipal sophistication, the infantile body has discovered that its own subjectivity shifts with each displacement of the object. If the symbolic substitution of the object creates a third term, the body becomes a fourth term in relation to a fifth, producing a sixth, and so the baby discovers that it can lose itself. Triangulation and displacement are, along with splitting, incorporation, and projection, the basic forms of symbolization, they are inherent to the human body. Melanie Klein theorized all these goings on as the deferral of object anxiety. In her view, symbolization is "the foundation of all fantasy and sublimation but, more than that, it is the basis of the subject's relation to the outside world and to reality."[18] This, in 1930, still sounds like Ferenczi, but there is a subtle shift. The infant is still narcissistic and autoerotic, but no longer an isolate ignorant of the existential fact of otherness, as Lacanians and ego psychologists claim. Babies differentiate their bodies from others', and people from things, and they do all this without benefit of language. The neonate quickly discovers that it can get outside of itself and into other bodies, and that it can destroy other bodies and their organs or take them inside itself. Klein already understood deeply through the analytic process what the most recent experimental psychology of neonate cognition is only just beginning to discern.[19]

There is another way of looking at symbolization which might be described as epiphanic, because it involves a joyful dissolution of boundaries, and is less driven by object-anxiety. There are times for lucky people when desire is in a manically omnipotent and playful phase, and just then another person will come along and present this manic fantasy back to the infantile body in the form of a real external object. This kind of experience has several consequences, one of which might be called aesthetic experience.[20] Such coincidences increase the capacity of the infantile body to acknowledge and contain its own pain without recourse to defensive splitting and projection. (The body is, after all, both "a pleasure palace and a torture chamber.") But this kind of experience also inclines one to feel eternally grateful for the existence of other bodies. One acquires a certain faith that bodies and fantasies can intermingle without destroying each other's internal worlds, that bodies can get in and out of each other and intensify each other's pleasure without too great a risk of destruction.

Considerations such as these eventually lead to the idea of the "mental image" of the body, or in other words, the *body image*, which has just been taken up as a special theme in the most recent issue of *Psychology Today*.[21] Apparently, the body image is something that people have and can learn to manipulate. The body image appears, in other words, as an afterimage, something to do with Oedipal codings and adolescence. This is true so far as it goes, but it does not take us very far. In fact, the body's image of itself is not an afterimage (or in other words, a signifier): the body *is* its image of itself. As Nietzsche wrote: "In the tremendous multiplicity of events within an organism, the part which becomes conscious to us is a mere means: and the little bit of "virtue," "selflessness," and similar fictions are refuted radically by the total balance of events." And Nietzsche added: "We should study our organism in all its immorality."[22]

In his classic psychoanalytic study of the image and appearance of the body, Paul Schilder argued that we must dispose of "the idea that there are [sense] impressions which are independent from actions. Seeing with an unmoved eye when inner and outer eye muscles are out of function would not be real seeing, and would not be seeing at all, if the body were completely immobilized at the same time." He continues: "The perception is always our own mode of seeing... we are emotional beings... Our knowledge will be dependent on the erotic currents flowing through our body and will also influence them... The postural model of the body is in perpetual inner self-construction and self-destruction."[23] In other words, perception of other bodies is immediately proprioception, and self-perception is immediately perception of other bodies. The activity of sensory experience cannot be analytically extracted from the basic levels of fantasy. Signifiers are not necessarily involved. The infantile body is like an Aladin's lamp containing the genie of the whole world — it's skin is already psyche, for the epiderm is saturated with nervous fibre — and all you have to do is rub it.

The body image, or body schema, as some call it,[24] is profoundly unconscious, but it is not closed onto itself, as we consciously think of it; like Rabelais' grotesque, which is so beautifully described by Bakhtin,[25] the unconscious body is inside out and upside down, full of orifices, studded with protrusions, great big bellies and pointy heads, ears like vortexes, spilling out organs, exploding into pieces, drowning the world in urine, piling up turds and making them into space invaders or babies, swallowing the whole cosmos, constantly in the throes of death and rebirth.

The body is its own postural, kinesic, proxemic, temporal model. The body in relation to other bodies is the substratum of the imagination, the psyche is nothing if not the body's own image of itself, and its elaborations of this.

The psyche-soma can think of itself as split between body-machine as extension and mind-spirit as time, or as desiring-production versus coding and signs; but this is only another way the body imagines itself, this split image is then the body. It is not a signifier and signified, running away in time from a referent. Bodies interact directly. Pure mind is a particular kind of physiological state; the schizoid who feels that he exists hundreds of feet up in the air, above his body, attached to it only by an umbilical string, is living entirely within his body, this is the way that the schizoid body is actually functioning, it *is* this image of itself in the world.

* * * * * * * * * * * * * * * * * * * *

For a long time, Freud thought that repression was the central structuring agency of the psychesoma. Dreams could be explained by the way the ego ideal performed a few clever manouevres across a horizontal threshold called the repression barrier. The explanatory power of this elegant model made it possible to think of all the complicated actions of the bodily imagination in terms of the two broad and very general categories of fusion and division — or "condensation" and "displacement."

Freud's explorations of repression revealed the psychosomatic origins of the ontotheological split between "mind" and "body." Yet the tendency to interpret the concept of defence as an essentially horizontal split suggests that traditional spiritualist dualism has retained its influence. The persistence of the 'above' and 'below' model of psychic organization has severely limited our conception of what primary symbolization may be like. In fact, the body can divide itself up in numerous ways, as Freud was well aware. The early work with Breuer on hysteria was concerned also with *vertical* splits, and other forms of "defense." But it was not until later in Freud's career that attention returned to problems of splitting, projection, and identification.

Unfortunately, the dominant image of what Freud left behind remains an oversimplification: there is consciousness (an afterimage which only appears to exist in the "here and now"), and then there is that "andere Schauplatz" (the "other scene"). In this version of Freud, the unconscious is also divided from the body: it straddles the region *between* the body (as a kind of given), and the blandishments of the external world. In practice, this model usually corresponds to the traditional commonsense division between a natural core of needs, drives, and schedules on the one hand, and a complex of externally imposed psychic contents on the other. In short, it tends to be assumed, even in psychoanalytically informed cultural theory, that the body is a kind of biological given which can be cancelled out of the equation or simply held constant; whereas the matter to be studied and understood is rather what society pumps into the body (or "writes" onto it). In this light, it appears as if Freud was really concerned with the (semiotic?) *rules* (metaphor and metonymy?) according to which "what society (the Creator?) pumps in" (i.e., a Soul or a Culture) is further sorted into what is conscious and what is repressed. In this way, even the psychoanalytic conception of the psyche can be held theoretically apart from the empirical body, and the old division between meaning and its husk of matter can, in spite of impressive anti-Cartesian rhetoric to the contrary, be effectively maintained.

Theoretical aesthetics and socio-cultural thought can no longer get by with a simplified model of the psyche in the body as a process of mediation between drives and codes. The theory of culture cannot rely solely on the linguistically-oriented study of mnemic images and signifiers, while leaving the rest to a sociology of conventions and structures. The view of the body as a kind of libidinal *tabula rasa* just waiting for entire systems of culture and politics to impose their repressions and taboos was liberating and useful in its time, and led to some interesting developments in social theory; but as a way of understanding the potentialities and activities of the body (or as a way of grasping what psychoanalysis is about), it is anachronistic and inadequate.

The question remains: what kinds of experiences do those who are only *potential* members of society have, and how significant are they? Social thought needs to develop a clearer appreciation of the difference between the social intuitions of the infantile body and the process of "socialization" (which really ought to be called "societalization"). If babies are already social before they are socialized (i.e., societalized), and continue to be so as they grow up, then our whole concept of what it means to talk about 'society' and 'culture' needs to be revised.

There is today a growing realization that the body has already undergone several revolutions before it reaches the Oedipal or phallic phase of development, and that the social orientation of the body at the age of less than two (which may already be blown apart) is going to be decisive for the way the body, as potential member of society, will react to the societal codes, and the gender issue, which will be introduced to it and generally imposed upon it with increasing assiduity in the ensuing years. Moreover, as Freud was perhaps beginning to recognize, the infantile body is not only pleasure-seeking (or pain-avoiding); it is something more like an organismic intensity, oscillating at times wildly between ecstatic totalizations (the "oceanic feeling") and abject annihilation (the "death instinct"). The infant is not only functionally dependent on its caretaker, and otherwise blissfully ignorant (the pleasure-pain axis); but threatened with psychic death in the prolonged absence of an object, and groping for the internal worlds, the life experience, of others (the self-object axis). This is not just a matter of pleasure through gratification, followed by discharge or repression, all of which will be secretly revived in the adult social world of signs and rituals (the consumer society hypothesis); it also has to do with identifications, projections, splits, incorporations, destructions, massive creations, tragic atonements, an ideal love matched only by moments of abyssal hatred — all of this well before there is any question of repression and socialization in the classical sense. The issue is that not just instinctual — but also emotional life — is pre-societal. In other words, the infantile body has already constructed a whole cosmos entirely out of the corporeal aesthetics of a few interpersonal relationships well before its surface is even tickled, let alone "traced" (as Foucault would say) by language. The body will survive a multiplicity of extinctions before it becomes that socio-cultural or epistemic "volume in desintegration" which Foucault describes.

* * * * * * * * * * * * * * * * * * * *

It may seem simpler, but in the long run it is misleading, to make hard and fast distinctions between states of the body and processes of symbolization, however susceptible to semiotic formalization symbolization (the Symbolic!) may appear to be.

The great literary student of symbolic process Kenneth Burke was one of the first to explore the implications of the fact that meaning is not just a matter of *systems* of signs, but of inchoate bodily states and fluxes of interaction. Burke developed a theory of *substance* which is based on the ambiguity of the word 'substance' itself.[26] The substance of a thing is taken to mean what a thing *is*, in its most essential "inner being." Yet, in a sense, the "essence" of a thing is really what stands *under* the thing and holds it in its being: the *sub-stance* of the thing. Thus, the substance of something is, in a curious kind of way, precisely something other than the thing — something under, or behind, or perhaps even *after* it. And if the substance comes "after," this might be because it is a kind of "symbolic exchange," or in other words, an emergent property or "equifinality," which cannot be derived from a "ground" or initial condition of the "system." (The concept of the "simulacrum" would be appropriate here, if it were not for the word's Christian connotations of diabolism.)

At any rate, Burke's point is not that substance is a linguistic category mistake to be banished for its metaphysical or theological overtones — although he would admit that it is hardly anything solid. Substance is indeed a kind of illusion, like the relation of the infantile body to its objects: it is both inside and outside, subjective and objective, as in the chance coincidence of a fantasy and the external world. Like the infantile body, substance is a fundamentally contradictory and paradoxical process, slipping and sliding, refusing to remain still. Its world is an elaboration, without an original or final point of reference which can be codified. Yet it has a certain kind of inevitability about it. No society can completely abstract this "substance" without destroying itself, no historical process can supercede the infantile body and determine it in its essential being, or reduce it completely to a signifier or an afterimage.

All of this amounts to saying that the body is not reducible to the structures and conventions of its "invaders," that there is something about the body, which I have tried to define in terms of its infantile dynamics, which is indestructible so long as it remains biologically viable. In other words, there *is* a kind of "animal substance." In the age of sophisticated theory and the linguistic turn, such a claim will seem outlandishly naive and absurd, but that is precisely the effect it should have. If the infantile body were not absurd, it would have no critical or aesthetic value whatsoever — it would just be a subject for various "materialisms" and "idealisms."

The issue for the theory of postmodernism is not that the body has been evacuated and absorbed by the cultural system, but that the body, the unconscious, the infantile, the grotesque, the aesthetic — or whatever we choose to call it — seems to have become *irrelevant*, especially for theory. There are two likely reasons for this. On the one hand, there is the supervention of a certain kind of techno-logic, or instrumental reason, with its problematic of *simulation*; and on the other hand, there is the academic hegemony of rationalism in cultural thought, which is epitomized by the rise of the language paradigm in critical philosophy and social science. The latter has an uncanny tendency to recapitulate the epistemological assumptions of the former, as Baudrillard has demonstrated in various books.[27] So the carnal knowledge of aesthetic states (the infantile body) seems to have become now virtually meaningless and irrelevant on both counts. Yet, it is probably when the aesthetic dimension becomes sociologically irrelevant that it is most radical and interesting, which is not irrelevant at all.

Notes

1. A shorter version of this paper was presented to the graduate seminar on "Postmodernism and Aesthetics" at Concordia University, Montreal, April, 1986. I would like to thank the members of that seminar for their engaging response; also Marty Allor, Loretta Czernis, Michael Dorland, Bruce Ferguson, Arthur Kroker, Elspeth Probyn, and Beth Seaton for their conversation, comments and encouragement in connection with this particular piece of work; and A.T.

2. Friedrich Nietzsche, *Thus Spoke Zarathustra* in *The Portable Nietzsche*, trans. Walter Kaufmann (New York: Viking, 1954), p. 146.

3. Gilles Deleuze and Felix Guattari, *Anti-Oedipus: Capitalism and Schizophrenia*, trans. Robert Hurley, et. al. (New York: Viking, 1977).

4. Jacqueline Rose, "Introduction-II," in *Feminine Sexuality*, eds. Juliet Mitchell and Jacqueline Rose (New York: Norton, 1982), p. 30.

5. Michel Foucault, "Nietzsche, Genealogy, History," in *Language, Counter-Memory, Practice*, trans. Donald Bouchard and Sherry Simon (Ithaca: Cornell University Press, 1977), p. 148.

6. For a discussion of Lacan's "points de capitons," see Anthony Wilden's commentary in Jacques Lacan, *The Language of the Self: The Function of Language in Psychoanalysis* (New York: Delta, 1968).

7. Jean Baudrillard, *Oublier Foucault* (Paris: Editions Galilee, 1977).

8. See Deleuze and Guattari, *Anti-Oedipus*, p. 1ff; p. 29: "... libido has no need of any mediation... in order to invade and invest... *there is only desire and the social, and nothing else*;" p. 166: "... the individual in the family, however young, directly invests a social, historical, economic, and political field that is not reducible to any mental structure or affective constellation."

9. Gilles Deleuze, *Nietzsche and Philosophy*, trans. Hugh Tomlinson (New York: Columbia University Press, 1983), p.x.

10. Gilles Deleuze, *Logique du sens* (Paris: Les Editions de Minuit, 1969).

11. For further discussion of these points, see my "La Greffe du Zele: Derrida and the Cupidity of the Text," in *The Structural Allegory: Reconstructive Encounters with the New French Thought*, ed. John Fekete (Minneapolis: University of Minnesota Press, 1984), pp. 201-227.

12. See Arthur Kroker's reflections on the psychohistory of the sign in "Augustine as the Founder of Modern Experience: The Legacy of Charles Norris Cochrane," *Canadian Journal of Political and Social Theory*, Vol. 6, No. 3 (Fall, 1982), 79-119.
    See also Arthur Kroker and David Cook, *The Postmodern Scene: Excremental Culture and Hyper-Aesthetics* (Montreal: Oxford/New World Perspectives, 1986).

    Kroker's hypothesis of the "fictitious unity of the Western episteme" is based, in part, on his discovery of an internal pattern of experiential inversions and structural reversals, reaction formations and denials, which links early Christian thought symbolically (as a condensation of the historical impasse in classical culture) with the central themes of the philosophical and aesthetic canon of modernity and its aftermath.

    In *Symbols That Stand for Themselves* (Chicago: University of Chicago Press, 1986), the anthropologist Roy Wagner has worked out an interesting formal model of the internal dynamic connecting medieval Christian culture with modernity. Wagner traces a "process of figurative expansion" and "obviation" (reversal), in which symbolic strategies for organizing experience, beginning with Augustine's theory of the sacrament, exhaust and recapitulate themselves in a succession of permutational registers. According to Wagner (p. 121), "the medieval and modern core symbols have developed in relation to each other through a holographic process of figure-ground reversal." In his view, "our contemporary epoch realizes the third and final cancellation of the modern cycle."

    Kroker's work is focussed intensively on the details of contemporary experience, at the James Joycean level of the hermeneutics of quotidian epiphany; yet the framework of his analysis implies a theoretical supervention in the whole discussion of postmodernity. Where Foucault, as the major representative of the "new French thought," suggests an "epistemological break," Kroker discovers the lineaments of a significant continuity, which itself must be overcome.

13. Michel Foucault, *The History of Sexuality. Volume 1: An Introduction*, trans. Robert Hurley (New York: Pantheon, 1978).

14. "On Truth and Lie in an Extra-Moral Sense," in *The Portable Nietzsche*, trans. Walter Kaufmann (New York: Viking, 1954), pp. 42-47

15. Benedict de Spinoza, *The Ethics*, trans. R.H.M. Elwes (New York: Dover, 1955), Part 2, Prop XXIII.

16. See A.N. Metlzoff and M.K. Moore, "Imitation of facial and manual gestures by human neonates," *Science.* 198, 75-8.

17. Sandor Ferenczi, "Stages in the Development of the Sense of Reality," in *Sex in Psychoanalysis*, trans. Ernest Jones (New York: Brunner, 1950), p. 228.

18. Melanie Klein, "The Importance of Symbol-Formation in the Development of the Ego," in *Love, Guilt and Reparation & Other Works, 1921-1945* (New York: Delta, 1975), p. 221.

19. For some standard neonatological references, see Margaret Bullowa, ed., *Before Speech: The Beginnings of Human Communication* (Cambridge: Cambridge University Press, 1979); George Butterworth, ed., *Infancy and Epistemology: An Evaluation of Piaget's Theory* (New York: St. Martin's Press, 1982); and Edward Tronick, ed., *Social Interchange in Infancy: Affect, Cognition, and Communication* (Baltimore: University Park, 1982). For the most recent attempt at synthesis, see Daniel Stern, *The Interpersonal World of the Infant: A View from Psychoanalysis and Developmental Psychology* (New York: Basic Books, 1985).

    From the point of view of any cultural reality principle, the problem may be less whether the baby will learn to perceive the distinction between bodily fantasy and external objects, than whether it can be persuaded to continue doing so. In fact, there is some clinical evidence that the only basis upon which such a distinction (between self and object) can be securely maintained by the ego is, paradoxically, an unconscious *identification* of self and object. Melanie Klein called this the "internalization of the good object." To put the whole matter in a different set of terms, one might say that the schizoid is consciously and manifestly narcissistic because he is, in a sense, unconsciously *too* realistic, i.e., too *deeply* detached for existential comfort.

20. See W.R.D. Fairbairn, "The Ultimate Basis of Aesthetics," in *The British Journal of Psychology, 29*, Pt. 2 (1938), 167-181. See also D.W. Winnicott's discussions of the transitional object, in *Playing and Reality* (Harmondsworth, Middlesex: Pelican, 1971), and his discussion of Schechehaye's concept of "symbolic realization" in *The Maturational Processes and the Facilitating Environment* (New York: International Universities Press, 1965), p. 60.

21. *Psychology Today*, April, 1986.

22. Friedrich Nietzsche, *The Will to Power* (New York: Vintage, 1967), p. 355, *674.

23. Paul Schilder, *The Image and Appearance of the Human Body: Studies in the Constructive Energies of the Psyche* (New York: International Universities Press, 1950), pp. 15-16.

24. W.C.M. Scott, "The Body-Scheme in Psycho-Therapy," *Brit. J. of Med. Psychol.*, Vol. XXII, 1949.

25. Mikhail Bakhtin, *Rabelais and his World*, trans. Helen Iswolsky (Cambridge, Mass.: MIT Press, 1968), pp. 303-367.

26. Kenneth Burke, *A Grammar of Motives* (Berkeley: University of California Press, 1969), pp. 21-58.

27. See Jean Baudrillard, *For a Critique of the Political Economy of the Sign*, trans. Charles Levin (St. Louis: Telos Press, 1981); and *L'echange symbolique et la mort* (Paris: Gallimard, 1976).

8

BODY SHOPS
THE DEATH OF GEORGES BATAILLE

Andrew Haase

Jürgen Habermas, the primary spokesperson for modernity, concludes his lecture *Between Eroticism and General Economics: Georges Bataille*, with the following determination:

> But philosophy cannot in the same way break out of the universe of language: "It deploys language in such a fashion that silence never follows. So that the supreme moment necessarily transcends the philosophical problematic." With this statement, however, Bataille undercuts his own efforts to carry out the radical critique of reason with the tools of theory.[1]

Having thus dealt a death blow to Bataille's "critique," Habermas is free to develop his own theoretical architectonic (*The Theory of Communicative Action*)[2] and aid the flailing "project of modernity." Unfortunately for Habermas, the death of Georges Bataille,[3] like the death of God, leaves a corpse slumped in a corner; a corpse silently decomposing, emitting an insidious effluvium, a deadly nerve gas, that crawls along the floorboards and slips (too quickly?) into our nostrils. Bataille's carcass, his refuse, non-disposable, continues to obsess Habermas. Finally, Habermas's own project, as it recoils in the face of an emerging postmodern society, serves to reaffirm Bataille's conception of the heterogeneous and to open a space for the exercise of sovereign *dépense*.

In order to approach that which is contained under the rubric of heterogeneity, it is necessary to examine the modernist concept of "the gift" and its relation to Bataille's critique. Marcel Mauss's text, "Essai sur le don," (1923-24) and its analysis of the gift as a "total social fact" which provides a mechanism for exchange within societies, is the ethnographic reference point from which Bataille's critique begins. For Mauss, a reciprocal structure provides the undergirding for all gift-giving activity. In other words, all offerings imply a transaction "based on obligation and economic self-interest."[4] The possible forms of remuneration which may be received in exchange for a gift, however, have been enlarged beyond simple property to include intangibles such as "symbolic satisfaction" and "recognition." This portrait of the gift as a "pledge," a "loan," a "trust," is "intended to shake the utilitarian prejudices of classical economic theory."[5] Yet it is Mauss's re-inscription of gift-giving within the causal, binary oppositions of the economic and social structures of modernity, which inspires Bataille's unrestrained attack.

This new expanded sphere of modernity, in which *homo oecomomicus* may operate, continues to be analyzed today, according to structuralist models of exchange derived from Mauss. For Habermas, all speech acts may thus be categorized by intersubjective exchanges occurring between competent actors. Ideal speech situations (and less than ideal speech situations) must occur within structures of language and can be assessed according to their immanent validity claims. This *economy*, to which Habermas assigns the term "Universal Pragmatics," attempts to exclude any phenomena which does not conform to his portrait of linguistic exchange.[6] A paranoiac obsession to conform to particular modes of thought and limited representational systems, clouds Habermas's modern utopia and simultaneously provides a ripe target for Bataille. And it is these clouds which hold up heavy over the Combat zone, the red light district, Chinatown, and the river. Finding a space to park on a Saturday afternoon in the rain is impossible. Yet David knows these spaces: the back roads and blind spots that circle Tufts University Medical school and the buildings under construction. And Karen knows this place from her last visit. Then we pull up behind an abandoned Cadillac. A church faces the entrance. Karen flicks her cigarette into a puddle as we cross the street.

David holds the door for us. "I'll check you in," he says. The security guard rolls up his sleeves and turns back to the video monitors without a question. This building, immense from outside, concrete, a modern facility, closes down quickly. And for this contraction perhaps the temperature should be a bit cooler. "This way." Three rubber gloves protrude from David's back pocket. They slap at one another as he walks. His jeans are tight. Stairs to the basement, the hallways lined with foot lockers, exposed piping and ventilation equipment; a machine room hums louder and the paint is dull.

> We'd better change out here. The smell gets into your
> clothes. Sometimes I feel like I'm falling asleep and wak-

ing up, both to the scent of...Karen, you can change in
front of me. I'm a doctor, remember?[7]

Stripped to the waist, I slip on a green surgeon's shirt. David approves my
doctorly appearance and we hide our street clothes in an empty locker.
The starch of the shirt is hard; forcing the fabric away from my skin, forcing air to circulate, it billows. "Now please," David says, "don't make too
much noise" and, I am perfectly calm, "try to be... just don't go crazy."
"Don't worry about it," Karen says. "Alright. Alright. And if you want," perfectly calm, "to leave just, just say so." Karen nods. I nod. The sign on
the door says "Morgue."

And suddenly the door swung open at us, at us, at us, at us, and a
Chinese student runs past clutching some specimen which must be fascinating because of the speed with which she propels herself down the
length of the corridor her laboratory smock waving, and in her wake formaldehyde snaps up my nose, snaps shut my mouth, my tongue inside,
and my body takes one giant step forward. Steel lights (too bright for medical reasons?) pinch my eyes and I am blind. The florescent sun squeezes
my head. The deaf door swings closed behind us. This is Bataille's sun:
effective anesthesia, parodic, an expenditure of electricity beyond the demands of any utilitarian project. And this is Bataille's night:

> Love, then, screams in my own throat; I am the Jesuve,
> the filthy parody of the torrid and blinding sun.
> I want to have my throat slashed while violating the
> girl to whom I will have been able to say: you are the night.
> The Sun exclusively loves the Night and directs its lu-
> minous violence, its ignoble shaft, toward the earth, but
> it finds itself incapable of reaching the gaze or the night,
> even though the nocturnal terrestrial expanses head con-
> tinuously toward the indecency of the solar ray.
>
> The *solar annulus* is the intact anus of her body at
> eighteen years old to which nothing sufficiently blinding
> can be compared except the sun, even though the *anus*
> is the *night*.[8]

The image of the sun for Bataille is both creative and destructive. As the
day the *solar annulus* nourishes and creates. However, when perceived
directly the sun castrates vision, annihilates the day and reveals the black
night. This "castration" immanently connects to a transgressive violence
which unveils the realm of the heterogeneous.

The question is raised: "how, within contemporary culture, the heterogeneous can be acknowledged and even mobilized to counter the deleterious effects of homogeneity?"[9] For Bataille, homogeneity orders a social

organization which manipulates power to continuously assert its own hegemony via rationalism, abstraction, specialization, and fragmentation. In addition, homogeneity insists on the commensurability of elements and spheres of experience, and reduces possible actions to fixed rules culled from well-defined situations.[10]

Preservation of homogeneous factors within society mandates the "reduction of human character to an abstract and interchangeable entity."[11] This is the modern project. Bataille states:

> What is novel about modern rationalism is its increasingly insistent claim that it has discovered the *principle* which connects up all phenomena which in nature and society are found to confront [human]kind.[12]

With the development of "Universal" pragmatics and *The Theory of Communicative Action*, Habermas has formulated an effective mechanism for excluding all experience not conforming to his linguistic schemata.[13] Indeed, it is imperative that homogeneous systems purge or repress heterogeneous power.

In the face of a voracious desire for homogeneity, heterogeneous elements nevertheless, continue to assert themselves as

> all that homogeneous society rejects, either as detritus or superior transcendent value. These include the excremental products of the human body and certain analogous materials; those parts of the body, persona, words or acts possessing an erotic charge; the diverse unconscious processes such as dreams and neuroses, the numerous elements or social forms which the homogeneous sector is incapable of assimilating...[14]

It is a mistaken belief that "one can dispose of the heterogeneous by demoting it to the status of excrement"[15] for it is that very status from which heterogeneity derives its power.

Bataille's conception of the individual identities of homogeneity and heterogeneity raises the question of their interdependence. Heterogeneity is initially conceived as a limited economy (within the dualistic economy of homogeneous/heterogeneous forces) through its expulsion and subsequent repression by homogeneity. For Bataille, the relationship between homogeneous and heterogeneous elements are characterized by distinctness, by difference, by otherness, and not by unity. The "refusal of a higher synthesis through discourse...does not seek to dispel its anguish over time" but to position each component so that each can manifest its own inherent, subversive power.[16] Nevertheless, as this limited economy becomes a homogeneous whole, heterogeneity's status as *tout autre* (wholly other) is realized. This second manifestation of heterogeneity continually elides appropriation by modern economism and infinitely encodes itself as *other.*

> Base matter is external and foreign to ideal human aspirations, and it refuses to allow itself to be reduced to the great ontological machines resulting from these aspirations.[17]

Bataille is able to avoid idealist pitfalls which can only result in a perverse and nostalgic desire for some romantic utopianism, while affirming the cycle of seizure and excretion.

In opposition to Bataille, Habermas desires to stagnate the process of creation/destruction (homogeneity/heterogeneity) and enforce a cryogenised rationalism within its own rearticulation of hierarchical and fascistic principles. Habermas's quest to perform a quiet relinking of the three life spheres of experience and to fulfill the project of modernity, is evidence of his orientation to the *future* rather than to the *immediate* violence of the heterogeneous present. Furthermore, Habermas, the consummate politician, protects his own position from criticism; the insistence upon rationality's "higher" position as opposed to irrationality or non-rationality is not deconstructed, and the desire to implement models of "communicative action" through "instrumental action" is never exposed. It is impossible to communicate rationally with a terrorist poised to slice your jugular. Thus, it is in vain for Habermas or David, when inside the "body shop," to suggest; "O.K., just stand here a while to let your eyes adjust, just look around a while. Check things out." For David's statement doesn't register since the screaming of the light, as it bounces and recoils off stainless steel, jumps and re-jumps itself, a mighty fulguration, deafens and echoes off clean tile and I look down at my shoes, down at my shoes. "O.K." Slowly my eyes begin to pan up.

Pan up to a jungle of coasters. Thin steel tubes. A jungle of tables. Hundreds of tables. Thousands of tables. "O.R. 8." and "Terms of Endearment," automatic anamnesis, Beth Israel Hospital, Saint Francis Hospital, L.I. Jewish Hospital. "General Hospital." Pan up to tables which reveal nothing. Curved lids trapped together, slapped together, and equipped with locks and latches when Karen says, "Look over there." She points to the left. To a table to the left, to the steel curtains unhooked. Where the steel curtains dangle underneath, where the body of a human being lies recumbent, a brownish mass, feet sticking ignobly upward, pointing at the overhanging lights. And a sign on the wall says, "No Food or Beverages Please!"

Near the back of the room three Chinese medical students stand close and whisper around their work. They wear white laboratory coats. They wear white laboratory coats. Slowly, one takes a hammer and chisel to the cadaver's skull. Its head rests in a wooden block and the bone breaks easily. David walks over and lays his hands on the edge of another table. "Well, there it is." He snaps on his gloves and removes a probe from his back pocket but does not bother removing the bit of cheesecloth which conceals the face, the face of this corpse. Instead he peels the breast plate off and tosses it between the legs. The lungs pink, grey, the heart, liver, tinged eggplants, spleen; sown deeper the kidneys, furrowed intestine, lubricious, collapsed and thinly folded; reddish-brown muscle wired with tendons, bifurcation of veins and ventricles.

> ...and here's the carotid artery. Follow it down. Just like in the anatomy books. The bifurcation of...oh, last month when I was working in here, some guy had removed all the organs from the chest cavity of a woman searching for a kidney infection, and then, then, as he was leaning over the body, he just passed out. Out cold...his head fell right into the old woman![18]

David's hands move quickly through the maneuvers, tearing away organs.[19] Flesh sticks off the body, tough sheets of parchment, of horse hide; bits of eraser rubbings litter the table, bits of rubbery muscle.

And throughout this procession of terminology I, a reasonable man, am completely calm. David's voice transfixes my gaze; circulating sentences, parodic catch-phrases, rebuses from a modern Haruspex, and I do not see the procession of parts. And I do not know where Karen has gone, and I do not know where David has gone. But I look into this chasm, this eviscerated thing: a tomb, a sacrifice, heterogeneous refuse. I look into black cavity and I begin a white, vertiginous spin. Down in Maniae's sanctuary, perhaps I am capable of other actions:

> In my view this is a surname of the Eumenides; in fact they say that it was here that madness overtook Orestes as punishment for shedding his mother's blood. Not far from the sanctuary is a mound of earth, of no great size, surmounted by a finger made of stone; the name, indeed, of the mound is the Tomb of the Finger. Here, it is said, Orestes on losing his wits bit off one finger of one of his hands.[20]

And again:

> On the morning of December 11, he [Gaston F., age 30] was walking on the Boulevard de Ménilmontant, and having arrived at the Pére-Lachaise cemetery, *he stared at the sun, and, receiving from its rays the imperative order to tear off his finger,* without hesitation, without feeling any

> pain, he seized between his teeth his left index finger, suc-
> cessively broke through the skin, the flexor and extensor
> tendons, and the articular ligaments at the level of the
> phalangeal articulation; using his right hand, he then twist-
> ed the extremity of the dilacerated left index finger, sever-
> ing it completely.[21]

And from these people, being blind, I look away. For "human eyes can sustain the view of neither the sun, nor a cadaver, nor darkness...."[22] Thus, auto-mutilation (or the dissection of bodies) becomes re-ritualized for David, Karen and I by Tufts Medical School. Shall we forgive this institution "for it knows not what it does"? Or is the inscription of death within this sanctuary a bit of "modern" prestidigitation? Regardless, the violent transgressions of cadavers cannot be contained within the walls of the hospital. Death, qua heterogeneous, cuts through the "unity of modernity."

Furthermore, although heterogeneity may be extreme, it does not imply *privilege*. Bataille sets out, as a first step, to transgress (and thereby deconstruct) the illusory position of autonomy which the "high" term continues to insist upon, and replaces it with the "low."[23] In this sense, heterogeneity's power qua transgressive becomes apparent; death disrupts dialectic, death disrupts rationalism, death disrupts discourse. A modern *utopia*, on the other hand, demands a hierarchical ordering of masteries (low/high, subordination/domination, slavery/freedom, homogeneous reason/heterogeneous refuse) so that it may transgress (and thereby reaffirm) that order.

Bataille's first step suggests developing a space for the exercise of transgression between homogeneous and heterogeneous realms. Philosophy has historically dismissed transgressions thereby obeying the limitations of discursive reality. Habermas's "systematic denial of the other is the outcome of a pathological attitude that has lost a sense of its own violence."[24] In the same breath there is an insistence on dualism and a call for an inversion of traditional labeling techniques, a deconstruction of hierarchy for equality, and a transgression of boundaries which cuts across, cuts through, cuts away.

Nevertheless, Bataille's notion of transgression is not a longing for transcendence. Dualisms of all types (light/dark, sacred/profane, evil/good, masculine/feminine, passion/reason, original/copy) must be realized as dual, and the delusion of *aufhebung* undermined. There is no difference between thesis and antithesis. Habermas's pedestal, upon which rational discourse reclines, is undercut. Transgressive explosions force the equal positioning of reason and non-reason yet does not reveal any absolute "Truth" beneath material phenomenon;[25] rather, the power of transgression lies in its ability to de-center, to open human experience up to heterogeneity and the voice of the other.

The process of transgression, however, as well as the realm of the heterogeneous, is profoundly ambivalent. Bataille notes, for example, that the exterior beauty of flowers is besmirched by hideous yet central sex organs which, when uncovered, reveal themselves as rather sordid tufts.[26] With the metaphor of an orchid's erect stamen, attraction and repulsion are prevalent. Both an uncontrollable bodily fear and a simultaneous desire for experiences of decentering, must be acknowledged.

> In this respect, the eye could be related to the cutting edge, whose appearance provokes both bitter and contradictory reactions; this is what the makers of the *Un Chien Andalou* must have hideously and obscurely experienced when, among the first images of the film, they determined the bloody loves of these two beings. That a razor would cut open the dazzling eye of a young and charming woman—[27]

The exaltation of transgression is fused to the terror of loss; as transgression interferes with a modern service to the utilitarian, "useful, reasonable operations of life," the possibility for "play" becomes actualized.

Within a modern understanding of power, transgressive acts are primarily conservative, re-affirming the necessity for law and reason. Indeed, within the economism of gift-giving, heterogeneous transgressions stabilize the homogeneous "order of things." Nevertheless, Bataille identifies literature's power to "expose the *game* of the transgression of the law without which the law would have no meaning independent of an order to be created."[28] It is possible for Bataille to transgress the homogeneous order and write:

> The curse (terrifying only to those who utter it) leads them to vegetate as far as possible from the slaughterhouse, to exile themselves, out of propriety, to a flabby world in which nothing fearful remains and in which, subject to the ineradicable obsession of shame, they are reduced to eating cheese.[29]

Bataille's writings themselves embody an implementation of transgression. They are heterogeneous detritus which deconstruct — and call into question — homogenizing labels. Attempts at generalization serve only to reveal the inadequacies of homogeneous groupings.[30] Bataille's body of work is no-body. "Nobody I know." And quickly David slams the steel curtains shut around this body and moves to another table, to another. But I am transfixed by this immovable feast. "Look at this," David says. "Look at his cock! It's all black!" Karen says. David grabs the half-hard cock and begins waving it around, gesticulating, jerking it off. It is thick and stiff, and David laughs, "The formaldehyde didn't reach here. Want to crawl on top?" Karen is hysterical, "I wonder how many people come here at night? Or perhaps we could steal...." But the cock is too big and it is growing. It fills the room, pressing me to the walls, pink veins, a stallion's erection. This *Homo erectus*, a black tree trunk, or perhaps it is an avatar of some other tumescence? The noise of its growth is wrenching. And David spits out a burst of laughter.

> One night at a party, Danny, another medical student and I arrived with a friend in a wheelchair. We called him "George." George. It was late; people were drunk and dancing around, screaming music, a wild dance. At first no one noticed us. Then, this girl Diane realized George was dead. We expected her to go crazy, or faint, or something. Instead she started wheeling, wheeling, George around the room, screaming, faster and faster, making giant circles. The blanket we had covered his lower body with blew off.... Diane let go of the chair and it went sailing across the room past dancers, past bowls of popcorn, glasses of wine and beer on tables. Well, George slammed into the wall so hard, I thought he'd go right through. Instead he just stopped. A painting fell off the wall, glass was everywhere. Diane's mouth was bleeding. She had bit her tongue....[31]

"You guys are sick! Totally sick!" Karen laughs and says, "And so is that girl Diane!" But I cannot laugh. I cannot breath.

The Chinese students still hammer at the face of their corpse. A low thumping. When David uncovers the head of our corpse, I see the face is sliced vertically down the middle, split open, split chicken breasts. David takes one half of the face and pries it to the side. He points out the nasal passages, the too big tongue, mouth, teeth. The brain has been removed and placed in a plastic bag near the skull. But even David winces as he examines it; a brain reduced to liquid, an abscess implosion, pale grey slime.

"Now that's disgusting," Karen says. She walks away. Walks to specimen jars. Jars of nascent fetuses, waving, mini-astronauts, mouths flung open without speech. She spins them around. Suspended in the water, sheets of white membrane dangle, remnants of aborted fecundity. She mixes up the jar's order; three months after six months, four after seven. She has them face each other and turned on their heads. "Now didn't I tell you that dead babies are not allowed to do headstands! Sit up straight!" Her vituperations become more furtive and then suddenly, her face changes, a smooth metamorphosis, and she laughs without reserve.

David returns his attention to the body's face. The eyeballs protrude as the thin lids are stretched open. David's two fingers grasp this eye and easily pop it out. He laughs and calls to Karen, calls to Karen to look. "Look at that." But what I see once again binds me. And I multiply an isomorphic eye: a cannibal delicacy, the eye of conscience, seductive, obsessive, lugubrious, the eye with which we see the enucleation of the matador's eye.[32]

> Granero was thrown back by the bull and wedged against the balustrade: the horns struck the balustrade three times at full speed: at the third blow, one horn plunged into the right eye and through the head. A shriek of unmeasured horror coincided with a brief orgasm for Simone, who was lifted up from the stone seat only to be flung back with a bleeding nose, under a blinding sun; men instantly rushed over to haul away Granero's body, the right eye dangling from the head.[33]

Then David quickly slips the eye back in place; this eye which looks at me, this eye which looks at me, of which I become its object. So I maintain silence. I maintain my face. But even as I look at David working I must ask, what is this face? What is the screen upon which it projects itself and upon which I visualize this "thing"? My quiet shrieks as, "the nondiscursive violence of eroticism remains silent."[34] David says, "Hey, let's go look at the animals, the animal lab." However, this doctor-to-be's attempt at placating anxiety is impotent. And Bataille identifies this impotence in the face of a force which repudiates conservative transgression — the transgressive, active, nihilism of *parody*.

And thus I find the pleasure of dual-surveillance; where the "network" has replaced the "panopticon's"[35] mutually affirming identities, master equals slave, the restrictions of bi-polararity, the pleasure of a perfect heterogeneity, neither rationality nor irrationality and a non-reciprocal[36] yet circular[37] sadism. This is the prison of postmodernity. This is the prison which reduces all signification to parody.

Thus, for Bataille, the *eye is* the *anus*. And the innocence of vision is rejected for a vision which orders excrement. A vision which simultaneously consumes and expels feces. The eye which sticks out from the face is directly connected, by some tubular derma, to the bronze eye. This is what the science of modernity is incapable of enacting. And its delusion is that it does not play in dejecta.

> What science cannot do — which is to establish the exceptional signification, the expressive value of an excremental orifice emerging from a hairy body like a live coal, as when, in a lavatory, a human rear end comes out of a pair of pants —[38]

For as the eye opens up to the emasculating sun, it shits tears. And a different model of liquid, incandecent power spurts out. The material body strips away the veil of modern reality, and reveals itself (and the "order of things") as parodic. But a parody of what? Some "original" body which exists somewhere, repressed and forlorn, which must be regained? Rather a parody of a parody, where no original, and no copy, no absolute and no relative, is possible. Modernism is over. This is the postmodern condition.[39] Our condition.

The project of modernity however, is stubborn. It provides evidence of a repugnant desire for some lost order where the simulatory aspect of the world could be assessed with respect to a "real" world. Regardless, we live in a civilization where images form a whirlwind of non-sense, where signifiers have become unleashed from their signified, where "reader and author are mutually annulled, reciprocally effacing each other so that finally only the Verb exists."[40] The Verb, the *copula*, ("which is no less irritating than the *copulation* of bodies"[41]) is the text; "the author is only a link among many different readings [VI, 408]."[42]

Even Bataille's transgressions are co-opted and commodified, forclosing the potential for "empowered" heterogeneous elements.

> The very definition of the real becomes: *that of which it is possible to give an equivalent reproduction.* This is contemporaneous with a science that postulates that a process can be perfectly reproduced in a set of given conditions, and also with the industrial rationality that postulates a universal system of equivalency (classical representation is not equivalence, it is transcription, interpretation, commentary). At the limit of this process of reproductibility, the real is not only what can be reproduced, but *that which is always already reproduced.* The hyperreal.[43]

Postmodern society solidifies homogeneity as heterogeneity and vice versa. The reduction to pure *différance*[44] is complete. Transgression functions as "that which reaffirms the re-reproduction and circulation of the hyperreal." The influence of hyperreality is stretched from language and semiotics, across consciousness and into the realm of the body.

Today it is possible to eat, drink, shit, and make love only in parody, in simulation. Cultural images dictate bodily functions. When I make love I do so as a movie. My orgasm is a parody of Paul's simulated paroxysms (since now Marlon Brando cannot exist as real) on some floor in Paris as images dance à "Last Tango." In a postmodern society there is no more "natural" intercourse. There is no more desire. "Deprived of symbolic substance, it [desire] doubles back upon itself," as we search for some "desire of desire," some hyperreal desire or "simulated Oedipus."[45] The "unconscious itself, the discourse of the unconscious becomes unfindable—."[46]

Bataille's awareness of conservative transgression (whose ramifications may be felt in an encroaching postmodern society) inspired him to conceive a model of power which could not be appropriated. His liquid challenge becomes solidified in the non-paradigm of sovereignty, which, as *dépense*, is incommensurable with atrophied modernism or commodified, postmodern power relations. Bataille opens a space for another type of action modeled after (but not identical to) sovereignty, which confronts the reduction to economies, the "otherwise inaccessible unconscious of Western culture,"[47] and the individual's colonized body. A body which has been cold-frozen. A body which hangs from overhead hooks, slabs of fresh meat, whole animal carcasses. These bodies which await dissection by veterinary students.

Yet, the cold air clings to my skin, inside this giant refrigerator where dead cows hang upside-down, where dead dogs are shelved alphabetically, shelved according to student names, in wooden shelves which stretched up, in shelves which stretched up too high to reach. This is not David's turf and he closes the door behind me. "Pretty cold in here...check out these dogs, eh?" The light is filtered through water vapor. Instead of speaking I blow smoke from my mouth.

On a small steel table, off to one side of the room, a Great Dane lies on its side. The legs splay open; rigid sawhorse legs. The mouth is caught in a snapshot grin. Its blotched fur is still. And Bataille writes: "Man, despite appearances, must know that when he talks of human dignity in the presence of animals, he lies like a dog."[48] David grabs one of the paws to turn the body over but its bulk, unbalanced already, falls to the ground. A low thud on the iced tiles resounds, rebounds, reflects. "Shit!" David says. He takes the animal by both paws and hoists it back onto its perch. "He didn't even feel it," he laughs,

> ...but look at all these horses. See, now *this* grosses me
> out. I don't know where they get them all. Where *do* they
> get them all? All these...I mean, are so many horses dying
> each day and leaving their bodies to science?[49]

David pats the flank of the bloodless carcass. Formaldehyde has replaced blood. Blood has replace formaldehyde. For in our time "the slaughterhouse is cursed and quarantined like a plague-ridden ship."[50] And the body of a dozen or more horses swing on pulleys screwed into the ceiling; memorabilia of some other theatre and some other curtain call. Swinging in another singles scene, in another playground. But this is our playground and David gives the body a powerful shove. The horse careens into other horses, into other horses, a plethora of horses, and stops at the wall with a jerk.

Behind me, I hear the door of the chamber opening slowly and my body takes one giant step forward. Karen says, "What are you guys doing in here?" She shuts the door behind her and I watch for her reaction. To the left, amputated horse legs jut out of a laundry basket willy-nilly; fleshy pick-up-sticks awaiting the first movement. Karen shakes her head and says, "Jesus Christ it's cold." And suddenly I am cold. Too cold. The room closes down, becomes darker. The taste of meat coagulates in my nostrils, stuffs them up. Meat stuffed higher into nasal passages, stuffed higher into nasal cavities.

Then quickly I cross the room. "Let's go," David says. So I leave the refrigerator, its wet walls, I leave the hanging carcasses. And my body is numb from the cold. And as David smiles, a white miasma follows me out of the room. But Bataille also notes my metamorphosis:

> A man in an apartment, for example, will set to groveling before those around him and eat dog food. There is, in every man, an animal thus imprisoned, like a galley slave, and there is a gate, and if we open the gate, the animal will rush out, like the slave finding his way to escape. The man falls dead, and the beast acts as a beast, with no care for the poetic wonder of the dead man.[51]

It is this beast which Bataille wishes to unleash. Thus, "potlatch,"[52] as a paradigmatic case of *dépense*, cuts across Mauss's (and Habermas's) desire to assimilate all gifts into a generic, homogeneous formula of prestations. This homogeneity is violated by a giving without the goal of a return — giving qua potlatch is destroying. "The Principle of Loss" which describes potlatch, cannot be conceived of as a gain (or as a loss which is a gain). Bataille finds in our everyday experience,

> unproductive expenditures: luxury, mourning, war, cults, the construction of sumptuary monuments, games, spec- tacles, arts, perverse sexual activities (i.e., deflected from genital finality) — all these represent activities which...have no end beyond themselves.[53]

Periodic instances of "potlatch" disrupt the established order of things (whatever that order happens to be) by refusing the quantification of clas- sical economics and the constraints of rational discourse. The hierarchy of gift-giver/gift-receiver in Maussian gift exchange leads to a stagnating equilibrium; continually reaffirming the same ordered hierarchy. The powerful "will to loss" forces another recognition; *dépense* has no utility, it cannot be put to use. Within a lifeworld wholly devoted to production and gain, within a lifeworld which excludes a model of gift-giving without view to compensation, activities of *dépense* (such as potlatch) refuse to die out.

Interpretations, for example, which would inscribe *dépense* under the dominant hermeneutics of logocentrism, (the recreation of "no-thing" as "thing"[54]) occur *a posteriori* with respect to the event in question.[55] This *inscription* is a modern blind spot and necessitates an obsessive appropriation which encodes all "giving" as "taking." Whatever events of gift-giving cannot be subsumed by society as "taking," are immediately subject to repressive action. Traditional modes of *dépense* are rejected as archaic, as latent nostalgia or, as incompatible with the goals of a *modern* civilization. This form of domination however is never totalizing. It is thus necessary to consider *dépense* as cutting across structures of language and the limits of the rational order of exchange.[56]

After a radical "breaking" of the Hegelian master/slave model which informs a modern, closed systematization has been completed, after postmodernity has unmasked itself as the absolute equality of all dualisms and all *différance*, sovereignty is envisaged as an ability to enact *dépense*. Sovereign action does not accord to the "physics of power" upon which the project of *modernity* insists. Since no particular logic governs; logic is an interpretation and reinterpretation is simulated repetition.[57] A space (an operation) for a simulation of death/*dépense*, indistinguishable from "real death," and therefore embodying experiences of "deleterious and blind joy" as well as "danger," is opened up.[58] Is there not the danger here of the appropriation of even this "sovereign model of action" to another modern dialectic? Bataille's inclusion of the double negation forecloses this possiblity.

In the redoubling of negativity (the redoubling of death), sovereignty plays a game of murder, then murders murder.

> Rather than act as building blocks to construct a solid argument, one cluster of thoughts appears to cancel the next; the poet is playing dice, and at every page he has thrown a new game: "Each one of my sentences reflects the acceptance of the game, until the one where I finally reject it." (III, 536).[59]

The game, which attempts to escape the constraints of a completely socialized language, provides a space for a "willed determination to sacrifice all that language adds to the world."[60] Derrida notes: "...we must redouble language and have recourse to ruses, to stratagems, to simulacra."[61] Poetry as sovereign communication maintains itself as ambivalent: affirming the game of craps and negating the possibility of play. As a simulation, poetry is able to invoke sensations and permit the reader to experience rather than reason.

It is the unveiled body, the stiff, which is a negation of my body and which forces the double negation of my body.

> It is the human world which, within the negation of ani-
> mality or the negation of nature (formed by work), negates
> *itself* and, in this *second negation*, goes beyond itself
> *without ever returning to that which it originally negat-
> ed"* (*L'Erotisme*, 94, emphasis added).[62]

The double negation of the body is the double negation of language. Thus, Bataille is free to attack Saussurean models of semiotics.[63] The one-to-one correspondence between signifier and signified is called into question by permitting multiple signifiers to represent a particular signified, by considering possible signifiers which cannot be adequately signified, and by promoting signifiers which signify nothing and no-thing.[64] Bataille is proposing a *free*-association where, after many years of servility to *higher* demands of rationality and logocentrism, "an alternative expression of energy not exclusively concentrated in the head" could be possible.[65] Modern civilization's refusal to accept the multi-dimensionality of contemporary discourse, disorder and non-order of signification, or freedom from "origi-nary" communicative rationality, freedom from this "ruse of reason,"[66] necessitates the generation of "intellectual mechanisms" both empty of meaning and destructive of meaning.

For instance, the metaphor of the sun (as ambivalent) is employed by Bataille to refer to homogeneous production of philosophic rationality[67] as well as heterogeneous combustion and subsequent ejaculation of waste products (ie.: light, heat, Ultra-"violent" rays.)

> The distinction between order and disorder clarifies the
> juxtaposition of two suns. One, the elevated representa-
> tive of philosophy, reason and logic, symbolizes the good,
> true, and beautiful. It is the ideal sun of the father and
> source of the spoken word. The other is the material, base,
> sexual, sweating, urinating, anal, pineal sun of *dépense* and
> disorder. It provides understanding of a qualitatively differ-
> ent order opposed to the castrated knowledge of those
> who fear to laugh in the face of the first. The two suns
> meet, collide with and rebound off each other, playing in
> one another's shadow. Their mutual presence and uncom-
> fortable cohabitation is necessary within the transgressive
> universe in which they orbit.[68]

Bataille frequently employs the metaphor of the sun ("...the eternal exem-plar of a munificent outpouring of energy which gives without demand-ing a return."[69]) to speak about events of *dépense*, castration, immolation. The sun's overpouring is without a view to return; a self-sacrifice which "in certain instances can have no other result than death."[70] Yet when the sun is hidden by the clouds of "reason" its vengeance is a fulmination.

The inclusion of multiple signification furthermore, precludes the possibility for a *Theory of Communicative Action*, and opens up a space for a signification of chance. The labyrinth, in Bataille's symbol of the Acéphale, is an impure difference: an earth sign, an "all-encompassing signifier," embracing every (single and multiple) contradiction and possibility "from the chaotic to the structured, the aleatoric to the necessary, the sacred to the profane, and from life to death."[71] This is the absorption of all possible signifiers and symbols which offers nothing in return and nothing in exchange.

> The symbolic collapses under the weight of the totality of the signifieds which it assumes, destroying willful intentionality and announcing intensive libidinality.[72]

One particular signification is no more "normal" or "correct" than the next.

The concept of "normativity," upon which Habermas's *philosophy of language* rests, is condemned by Bataille as ridiculous, puerile, and dangerous. The very attempt to formulate a norm reveals the absence of any "common measure." For instance, "public opinion" is both *formed by* and *formed from* localized, non-autonomous sample groups molded by a barrage of cultural messages and imagery. The "norm" refers only to a simulacrum of normativity, a normativity that has become not "unreal" but "*hyperreal* — a fantastic hyperreality that lives only off montage and test-manipulation."[73] Habermas's desire for normative abstractions is typical of the modern nostalgia for a mastery long ago repudiated by poetry, laughter, death, and eroticism. Existence itself "no longer resembles a neatly defined itinerary from one practical sign to another, but a sickly incandescence, a durable orgasm."[74] Thus, as I stare at a legless cow, hideously held erect by a dozen wooden posts, or the emasculated and dissected cock of a bull, even the meaning of destruction is destroyed. And the veterinary students who busy themselves around a horse's chest don't notice us. David says,

> ...and it's even more difficult than med. school. After graduation, next week, a lot of med. students are going... I'll go to Greece, God damn it! ...and just sleep for a year, a whole year. Perhaps...I think we should leave; we're not supposed to be here. We're not supposed to be here. Since I'm a med. student...where's Karen? Did she go back to the other lab? Is she outside? Where the fuck...[75]

But Karen is standing in the hall having a cigarette; preferring the smell of tobacco to that of formaldehyde. "Karen, you can't smoke in here." She says, "Fuck it," and draws heavily on the butt. Then she throws it down and grinds into the floor with a shoe. They look at each other. And the narrator of the *Story of the Eye* writes with naïve reciprocity: "I realized that her feelings at seeing me were the same as mine...."[76] David looks up at the ceiling, the piping, the video cameras, the walls, the hall lights, dimmed. He says, "Alright, wait here and I'll go close up the bodies in the lab." I go with him as Karen goes into the bathroom to change into street clothes.

Slowly, a janitor shuffles down the hallway, moves in and out of shadows and light. He pulls a plastic garbage can behind him. He wears a too-big grey uniform with a name tag I cannot read. David has gone into the lab already but I, desiring to see this image, still stand still. As he approaches, the janitor smiles. The janitor smiles and I am surprised. A brown rag is draped over the broom's head which he pushes down the corridor picking up lint and Karen's mashed cigarette.

And this time as I enter the morgue the lights do not seem so bright although the formaldehyde still chokes my throat. David calls, "Over here." I quietly step through the labyrinth of steel tables and David says, "Sometimes...I just don't understand her." He raises grey lungs and replaces them in the chest cavity. He holds intestines high in the air and lets it slip back in place, strands of linguine falling back on his plate, falling by gravity, falling with gravity. His terror is a visible terror. But Bataille writes of an-other encoding of the women he calls "Dirty":

> In terror the servants saw that water was trickling across the chair and down the legs of their beautiful guest. While the urine was gathering into a puddle that spread over the carpet, a noise of slackening bowels made itself ponderously evident beneath the young woman's dress — Beet-red, her eyes twisted upwards, she was squirming on her chair like a pig under the knife.[77]

Beet-red, her eyes twisted upwards, she was squirming on her chair like a pig under the knife.[78] And I look over at the Chinese students; the hammer still falling and rising, slipping in and out of the dead man's head. One holds a scissor over the body; her hand shakes a bit. Then I think of a childhood game: scissor, paper, stone, scissor, paper, stone.

David grips one of the metallic curtains and pulls it up over the body. He walks around to the other side and raises the second curtain. And the cadaver disappears inside its cave, inside its cage. Traces of our intrusion are erased while the Chinese medical students continue to ruminate over their body and David forgets (as he might forget an umbrella in the corner of some Cambridge restaurant) to secure the flimsy latch which should hold the curtains closed. Thus, as we leave, some slight vibration in the building, some shifting earth or some human being who moves across the floor above, or perhaps the performance of an aged ghost, upsets the metal casket. And as the curtains drop down around the mutilated body, a shotgun sound opens up, spins my head back with electric reflex. David says nothing as we turn to leave, as we leave the corpse exposed to air. For this sound creates a poetic vacuum which implodes — "poetry murders words."[79] And we, as poetic communicators, by adopting poetic speech, become murderers (or sovereigns) ourselves.

Bataille's communication is itself poetic. Yet, with undaunted perspicacity, Michele Richman's exegesis, *Reading Georges Bataille*, utilizes the concept of a "general economy" in an attempt to apply a policy of containment (of closure) to Bataille's work. This goal is in vain. The issue is not that of attainment of a goal for Bataille but the escape from the traps which goals represent.[80] Richman, in fact, quotes Bataille himself, noting that his writing

> is the movement of a thought which, losing all possibility of arrest, easily falls prey to criticism that believes it can stop it from without, since criticism itself is not caught within this movement.[81]

Again Bataille anticipates Richman's desire for "coherence":

> And in this place of gathering, where violence reigns at the limit of that which escapes coherence, the one who reflects within coherence perceives that there is no longer a place for him.[82]

Throughout Richman's work she insists on corralling Bataille's concepts within the homogeneous. Why does Richman continually appeal to the *consistency* of a "general economy"? What is her desire for a masterful,[83] phallocratic[84] encapsulation of Bataille's thought? Clearly, Richman is still stuck within a *modern* paradigm. She ignores that the form of *Reading Georges Bataille* is its content. Her rational exposé is an exemplary deconstruction but refuses to deconstruct itself. Situated within the bi-polar atrophy of homogeneity/heterogeneity, her reading proves fundamentally conservative. Richman fails to realize the transgressive power of inconsistency and ambivalence[85] as well as Bataille's conception of a non-economic (as opposed to an anti-economic) sovereign power.[86]

Eroticism, for example, as a form of sovereign *dépense* and therefore inextricably linked to death and poetry,[87] refuses Richman's economics. Bataille makes an important distinction between sexuality and eroticism: sexuality lies within the positive model of gift-giving and the dualistic visions of modernity, while eroticism embraces sovereign *dépense*. "Eroticism is assenting to life to the point of death."[88] Bataille's erotic novels simultaneously provide a polemical challenge to prevailing interpretations of "modern love" and, a formulation of philosophical and bodily limits.

Bataille recognizes that models of *dépense* which may be implemented within society can only maintain a parodic relationship to (their material counterpart) death. All action is limited by the body. The body, as "guarantor" of its own sacrifice is thrown back upon itself.[89] For example, Bataille identifies the ability of laughter qua heterogeneous (like eroticism) to first deconstruct the rational discourse taking place within modern models of exchange.

> *As soon as the effort at rational comprehension ends in contradiction, the practice of intellectual scatology requires the excretion of unassimilable elements*, which is another way of stating vulgarly that a burst of laughter is the only imaginable and definitively terminal result — and not the means — of philosophical speculation.[90]

Second, laughter doubly reveals its parodic relationship to death. Third, laughter takes up its position, qua sovereignty, "by dint of its impersonal force engaging energy into any experience of *dépense....*"[91]

The materialism of the body is, in addition, the limit of philosophy of consciousness and philosophy of language. Bataille's philosophy comes to be represented by an image of the Acéphale:

> irreducible to idealizing, intellective operations; headless, it lacks identity, and thus reveals its universality in a negative manner, where all identity is false identity, mere fiction; and, headless, it is also speechless, and so escapes the ontotheological rule of Logos.[92]

Bataille suggests the inclusion of acts within society which provide complete parodies of death, perfect simulations. Bataille's conception of the purely parodic nature of the world is clear: "each thing seen is the parody of another, or the same thing in a deceptive form."[93] Sovereign acts of *dépense* cut through the unremitting censure of modernity and the pure heterogeneous edifice of postmodernity. And it is from this edifice which David, Karen and I emerge laughing. For we ran past the security guard's station forgetting to "sign out," and David left his curved probe buried inside the bowels of some unsuspecting corpse, for some unsuspecting medical student to find, and experience, the unexpected.

But we are outside; busy with breathing in the cool air, the ionization in the wake of an electrical storm. And we trod quickly past the concrete of Tufts Medical School, around corners thick with Saturday shoppers, down Chinatown streets, past windows, the last batch of diners still relax in Szechuan restaurants, picking at kumquats in syrup, fortune cookies, cold tea. Past neon moviehouse displays. Past neon moviehouse displays which brandish *Deep Throat* and *Flesh XXX*. Past neon moviehouse displays. Behind me I hear David stumble and catch himself. Karen lights a cigarette and smiles. Our hair smells of formaldehyde.

And as we traverse a construction site, I see the car waiting; florescent orange paper sticks out from under the wiper blade, the handiwork of some noble law officer. "Shit!" David says, "I got a ticket!" Karen laughs and throws the summons on the pavement.

> No. Pick that up. Last year my brother got a ticket and, and did that, and the cops traced him, and the cops traced him, through his bank account and credit cards, and they came and towed, they towed his car, and he had to pay a hundred and fifty bucks to get it back (and the whole left side was, the paint was all stripped off).[94]

Karen doesn't move. "Come on." David walks around the car, grabs the ticket, and stuffs it into his breast pocket.

Later, as we drive along Route 9, as David's humming accompanies the radio, Karen stares at the houses running past. And I, exhausted, sleep. Perhaps I dreamt

> I was in a desolate landscape of factories, railroad bridges, and empty lots. I was waiting for the explosion that would, with a single blast, upheave from end to end the dilapidated building out of which I had emerged. I had got clear of it. I went toward a bridge.[95]

Or perhaps I dreamt "I'm something like three years old my legs naked on my father's knees and my penis bloody like the sun."[96] But when Karen wakes me, I do not remember these dreams. And I leave a patch of drool on David's car seat.

The sun burns through the last reluctant clouds. But even this sun (the sun of reason and the sun of sovereignty) is parodic. The project of modernity finds no footholds here. Acts of transgressive violence have upset the hegemonic position reason has previously enjoyed. In postmodernity Habermas can only play a parody of himself. "Gold, water, the equator, or crime can each be put forward as the principle of things."[97] Furthermore, since modernist philosophy refuses to critique and deconstruct itself reflexively, since it continues to abhor models of power which do not correspond to its own theoretical formulations, it can never break out of its own narcissistic trap. Reason, rather than safeguarding humankind, feeds the postmodern minotaur. As postmodernity continues to invade, continues to colonize, all areas of experience, Habermas's obsessive desire for "sanity" becomes unhinged. The production of "Communicative Action," Habermas's prescription for salvation, is doomed to be shelved with the other canned goods in a perfectly commodified system. Production has been replaced by (re)production. In our system, in our condition, there are only parodies of parodies, simulations of simulations — the hyperreal. Yet Bataille is willing to look at the face of heterogeneity.

Visions of excess are visions of the body and visions of death. Bataille's paradigms of sovereign *dépense* possess the ability to go directly to the limits of the body. Sovereignty parodies death and then parodies parody. The Sun exclusively loves the Night and directs its luminous violence, its ignoble shaft, toward the earth, but it finds itself incapable of reaching the gaze or the night, even though the nocturnal terrestrial expanses head continuously toward the indecency of the solar ray.[98] And I, an aberration of postmodernity, turn instead to receive the gaze of another solar anus. And I, an aberration of postmodernity, turn instead to receive the gaze of another solar anus. The Sun exclusively loves the Night and directs its luminous violence, its ignoble shaft, toward the earth, but it finds itself incapable of reaching the gaze or the night, even though the nocturnal terrestrial expanses head continuously toward the indecency of the solar ray, sovereignty parodies death and then parodies parody Bataille's paradigms of sovereign *dépense* possess an ability to go directly to the limits of the body visions of excess are visions of the body and visions of death visions of the body and visions of the body and visions of the body, and parodies of of the bodythe parody of parody of body of fo and the body shop, and the shopping body body which body which chops and chops and chops stopchop chop chop shop chopping the body body bodifixes abody6 which cuts a body andf cuts to paste the paste taste and cuts and past3e shape pastes the past paste which cuts and cuts then copy cop cope but body butts mope and cops shop the cut s and issues an edit c of cuts to pastecutvisions[99] visions visions a a body vision bodyof vis a a vis of fo the bod bod vis whichbody and thevis is si but bo vs a b v w x y is lif;a;a;lfdjw3h$\Sigma\infty$grk.rew'lwrxd;oz;ohrvo8hr'irj'ohvoigv;ogoipwzfr0809 gf'pxgr0r39efhv;oxr0ervsrfg'hfv'0gfgp9r.ohfvnm-fa-fryo0e4fo0h4ecn[100]mçbnbmfbssear;fwjfrohefrqvibrv56358¢3hy8r54yh g438hs450y894308r543wfjohdfrcoihfroihfroifr09wr409r408i43084308 fr5408wq4t08qwf4to8ifr08wqfr40iqghf4309i3wt09faxzgfs0ikxzgfimkxz fwwe'w[101]efwegf98efr4t08iqfgt084gzfregfsretiujmfc.............................
....

Notes

1. Jürgen Habermas, *The Philosophical Discourse of Modernity*, trans. Frederick Lawrence, (Cambridge: The MIT Press, 1987), p. 356.

2. Habermas, *The Theory of Communicative Action*, (Vol. 1), trans. Thomas McCarthy, (Boston: Beacon Press, 1984).

3. Habermas, *Philosophical Discourse*, p. 317. This is the point from which Habermas begins his dismissal of Bataille: "After Bataille's death in 1962...." Ironically, it is precisely Bataille's death which Habermas's *communicative rationality* cannot compute. Furthermore, by labeling Bataille's body as dead, the incommensurability and continual production of the heterogeneous is affirmed. Habermas has already conceded his position (qua homogeneous) with respect to Bataille and has formulated a "policy of exclusion" consistent with the fascistic tendencies of modern power paradigms.

4. Michele H. Richman, *Reading Georges Bataille: Beyond the Gift*, (Baltimore: The Johns Hopkins University Press, 1982), p. 10. Within the spaces modernity provides, there is no room for altruism.

5. Ibid., p. 11 and p. 13. "...because economic structures are no longer integrated into the ensemble of social structures but have achieved autonomy, it would be virtually impossible for contemporary readers to fulfill the project [Mauss] devised...." p.15. This modern desire for "integration" is commensurate with Habermas's reductive demand for a "relinking" of scientific, moral, and aesthetic lifeworlds. See Habermas, *The Theory of Communicative Action*, p. 70-72, 82, 337, etc. A parallel may also be drawn between Habermas's insistence on a communicative rationality which suppresses the erotic and Mauss's hope that "the feverish intensity of archaic festivities, capable of suddenly veering 'from a feast to a battle' (80), has been replaced with the progressive stabilization of contracts and the triumph of reason...." p. 16. In another context, a Maussian structuralism encompasses the circulation of all goods which could be inscribed within the "symbolic order." See also Jacques Lacan, *Speech and Language in Psychoanalysis*, pp. 249-261.

6. Habermas, *Communication and the Evolution of Society*, trans. Thomas McCarthy, (Boston: Beacon Press, 1979), pp. 1-69. Furthermore, the possibility of non-linguistic action, which Bataille would contend clearly exists, is completely discounted by Habermas.

7. David X., Tufts Medical School, April 25, 1987.

8. Bataille, *Visions of Excess: Selected Writings, 1927-1939*, trans. Allan Stoekl, (Minneapolis: University of Minnesota, 1985), "The Solar Anus," p. 9.

9. Richman, *Reading Georges Bataille*, p. 40.

10. Ibid.

11. Ibid., p. 41.

12. Ibid., p. 43.

13. Ibid., p. 40. Bataille often highlights the exclusion of ritualized violence from society as symptomatic of homogeneity in operation. In another context, the editors of *The Nation*, May 30, 1987, p. 706, recently noted: "The fundamentalists are right when they argue that schools are places of indoctrination and socialization. They are wrong when they demand that schools indoctrinate fundamentalist values and socialize authoritarian attitudes in the pupils. By the same token, liberals who fight against the right's agenda for the public schools are now forced to describe, compare and contrast their own ideological program with the cultish prudery and creationist superstitions that

have been foisted on their children." Thus, reason's position as a ground must be called into question. Is Habermas's inquisition a less violent "socialization"? A less fascistic "indoctrination"?

14. Bataille, [I, 346], Quoted in Richman, *Reading Georges Bataille*, p. 46-7. Heterogeneous facts are foils to the thrusts of homogeneous colonization by the project of modernity. p. 57.

15. Richman, *Reading Georges Bataille*, p. 53. This is the same critique Bataille launches against the surrealists. Stylistically however, Bataille and the surrealists were concerned with disorienting and disrupting the intellect which has been stupefied by scientific rationalism. p. 57.

16. Ibid., p. 30 and p. 67. In contrast to Hegel's notion of *aufhebung*, Bataille is concerned with a transgression between thesis and antithesis which does not result in synthesis. (One apple plus one apple does not synthesize into a single entity known as "two apples" but remains one apple and one apple.) *Aufhebung* is perceived as an "unnatural unity" which "...so reconciles the tension between opposing forces as to impose on the cycle an ahistorical, eternal status, rendering it impossible to grasp its practical effects." Ibid., p. 54. (See p. 58. for a discussion of the specific rejection of Hegelian phenomenology.) In psychological terms, the heterogeneous, in so far as it is repressed by the homogeneous, dominant ideology of the Law, maintains its potential for disputing, deconstructing, and repudiating the Law while reaffirming the dualism which constituted its difference.

17. Bataille, *Visions of Excess*, "Base Materialism and Gnosticism," p. 51.

18. David X., Tufts Medical School, April 25, 1987.

19. "The basin he left on the ground, and the delighted Don Quixote observed that the pagan had acted most prudently in imitation of the beaver, who, when hard pressed by the hunters, with his own teeth bites off what he knows by his natural instinct to be the object of the chase." Miguel de Cervantes Saavedra, *Don Quixote*, trans. J. M. Cohen, (New York: Penguin Classics), p. 162.

20. Bataille, *Visions of Excess*, "Sacrificial Mutilation and the Severed Ear of Vincent Van Gogh," p. 69.

21. Ibid., p. 61.

22. Richman, *Reading Georges Bataille*, p. 91.

23. Ibid., p. 61. The double dependence of the master and the slave: the master is dependent on the slave for recognition of superiority and the goods consumed, and the slave is dependent upon the master for protection and identity.

24. Ibid., p. 103. For example, Bataille centers the power to awaken modern society from its lethargy (to a consciousness of what it excludes) within a transgression of sacred and profane categories.

25. Transgression does not, as Judeo-Christian religions describe and many Eastern religions suggest, provide a mystical experience which strips away the scrims of maya thus allowing the "real" oneness of the universe/God to be perceived.

26. Bataille, *Visions of Excess*, "The Language of Flowers," p. 12.

27. Ibid., p. 17.

28. Bataille in Richman, *Reading Georges Bataille*, p. 106.

29. Bataille, *October*, "Slaughterhouse," p. 11.

30. For example, a title such as "The Writing of Georges Bataille," when considered in the light of the texts, proves amorphous. Similarly, statements which seek to establish homogeneity based upon norms, (which this statement does not) reveal the irrelevant nature of the norm.

31. David X., Tufts Medical School, April 25, 1987.

32. Bataille, *Visions of Excess*, "Eye," p. 17.

33. Bataille, *Story of the Eye*, trans. Joachim Neugroschal, (London: Marion Boyars Publishers Ltd., 1979), p. 53.

34. Richman, *Reading Georges Bataille*, p. 107.

35. Michel Foucault, *Discipline and Punish*, trans. Alan Sheridan, (New York: Vintage Books,1979), p. 306-07. The cogito also is reduced by Bataille to a "relation," a "network of communications, existing within time." See Richman, *Reading Georges Bataille*, p. 130.

36. Sartre, in his critique of Bataille, notes that "Bataille's provocations refuse the judgement of the reader and pre-empt those of the critic; however, his communication is 'without reciprocity.'" (Richman, *Reading Georges Bataille*, p. 113.) Bataille fails, Sartre's phenomenology argues, when he moves beyond "internal discoveries" (ie. solipsism) to inductive conclusions regarding the "external world." (This is also the Sartrean critique of sociology. Ibid., p. 115.) "Sartre's position is unambiguous: the subject cannot leave the domain of the *expérience intérieure* to examine itself from without." (Ibid., p. 114.) Bataille's response first centers around situating phenomenology itself within language; second, raising the body's materiality as the limit to philosophical epistemology; and third, proposing a paradigm of sovereign *dépense* which confounds Sarte's analytical position.

37. Jacques Lacan in *The Four Fundamental Concepts of Psycho-Analysis*, trans. Alan Sheridan, (New York: W. W. Norton & Company, 1977), pp. 206-209, identifies the structure of desire in the relationship between the subject and the Other as circular but not reciprocal. Thus, in their non-reciprocity, Bataille's texts reveal the desire for an *illusionary* reciprocity and its impossibility. Allen S. Weiss also notes in "Impossible Sovereignty: Between *The Will to Power and The Will to Chance*," October 36, p. 145: "the homogeneity of the ego dissimulates the heterogeneity of the body; the ego, a function of language, organizes the cathexis, manifestations and expressions of the libido." Thus, the order of the ego and the body, as individual entities, may be transgressed; however, this difference is to be maintained. In postmodern society, (where the terms "ego" and "body" lose their meanings and separations via deconstruction) actions from within and without the individual reformulate each other reciprocally.

38. Bataille, *Visions*, "The Pineal Eye," p. 87.

39. See Jean-François Lyotard, *The Postmodern Condition: A Report on Knowledge*, trans. Geoff Bennington and Brian Massumi, (Minneapolis: University of Minnesota, 1984).

40. Richman, *Reading Georges Bataille*, p. 129.

41. Bataille, *Visions*, "The Solar Anus," p. 5.

42. Richman, *Reading Georges Bataille*, p. 130.

43. Baudrillard, *Simulations*, trans. Paul Foss, Paul Patton and Philip Beitchman, (New York: Semiotext(e), 1983), p. 146.

44. For Bataille, Derridian *différance* is the maintenance of thesis and antithesis, and implies the ability for perfect transmutation of terms. An infinite defraction of difference which ultimately serves a regulatory role. A flat line on the oscilloscope. Cardiac arrest.

45. Baudrillard, *Simulations*, footnote, p. 155.

46. Ibid., p. 157.

47. Richman, *Reading Georges Bataille*, p. 126.

48. Bataille, *October 36*, "Metamorphosis," p. 23.

49. David X., Tufts Medical School, April 25, 1987.

50. Bataille, "Slaughterhouse," *October 36*, p. 11.

51. Ibid., p. 23.

52. Richman, *Reading Georges Bataille*, p. 17. "Practiced among the American Indian tribes of the Pacific Northwest, potlatch ceremonies consist in *the sacrifice of vast quantities of amassed goods,* usually blankets and copper blazons..." (emphasis added).

53. Georges Bataille, *Visions of Excess*, p. 118.

54. Richman, in *Reading Georges Bataille*, p. 20, notes Bataille's "preoccupation with *les choses*" and his recognition of their "inevitable role in identity formation." This is one avatar of the modernity vs. postmodernity debate. Must "nothing" invariably be regarded as a "thing"? Bataille's work attempts to provide a space wherein "nothing" can enact its power.

55. Ibid., p. 142, Richman notes the insistence by Occidental thought, on a "white mythology" of (a metaphoric) rationalism which functions as a "figure of domination, the instrument of repression, the means whereby one triumphs over many...."

56. Ibid., p. 30. To term *dépense* "irrational action" would also be misleading since it is necessary to assume the referent "rational action."

57. Derrida, *Writing and Difference*, trans. Alan Bass, (Chicago: The University of Chicago Press, 1978), p. 260.

58. Richman, *Reading Georges Bataille*, p. 68-69. Derrida, in *Writing and Difference*, p. 257, notes that sovereignty "mimes through sacrifice the absolute risk of death. Through this mime it simultaneously produces the risk of absolute death, the feint through which this risk can be lived...."

59. Richman, *Reading Georges Bataille*, p. 74. "If you wish to burn all, you must also consume the conflagration...." p. 146. Thus, Derrida further notes in *Writing and Difference*, p. 259, that sovereignty can "no longer be called negative precisely because it has no reserved underside, because it can no longer permit itself to be converted into positivity, because it can no longer *collaborate* with the continuous linking-up of meaning...."

60. Richman, *Reading Georges Bataille*, p. 125.

61. Derrida, p. 263.

62. Richman, *Reading Georges Bataille*, p. 109.

63. See Ferdinand de Saussure, *Course in General Linguistics*, trans. Wade Baskin, (New York: McGraw-Hill Book Company, 1959).

64. Bataille, *Story of the Eye*, p.42. For example, the terms "eye," "sun," "testicle," "egg," are all interchangable signifiers within the text. "I stretched out in the grass, my skull on a large, flat rock and my eyes staring straight up at the Milky Way, that strange breach of astral sperm and heavenly urine across the cranial vault formed by the ring of constellations: that open crack at the summit of the sky, ...a broken egg, a broken eye, or my own dazzled skull weighing down the rock, bouncing symmetrical images back to infinity." Richman in *Reading Georges Bataille*, p. 90, notes: "Their common denominator is a challenge to the rationality that has dictated commodity exchanges since the advent of market economies."

65. Richman, *Reading Georges Bataille*, p. 93.

66. Derrida, *Writing and Difference*, p. 252. Furthermore, Derrida notes: "Through a ruse of life, that is, of reason, life has thus stayed alive. Another concept of life had been surreptitiously put in its place, to remain there, never to be exceeded, and more than reason is ever exceeded (for, says *L'erotisme*, 'by definition, the excess is outside reason')." p. 255.

67. Bataille (VII, 189) quoted in Richman, *Reading Georges Bataille*, p. 96. "For the popular consciousness, the sun is the image of glory. Light for the naive [Hu]man is the symbol of divine existence. It possesses splendor and brilliance...."

68. Ibid., p. 98.

69. Ibid., p. 17. See also Bataille, *Visions of Excess*, "The Solar Anus," p. 5-9, and, "Sacrificial Mutilation and the Severed Ear of Vincent Van Gogh" p. 62-72. I would suggest the love a mother gives to a child as another example of dépense. In fact, Richman, *Reading Georges Bataille*, p. 20, notes, "the etymology of potlatch may be traced from the verbs to nourish...." There seems to be great potential for a feminist theory of dépense.

70. Richman, *Reading Georges Bataille*, p. 34.

71. Allen S. Weiss, "Impossible Sovereignty," p. 133.

72. Ibid.

73. Baudrillard, *Simulations*, p. 122. (Emphasis added.)

74. Bataille, *Visions of Excess*, "The Pineal Eye," p. 82.

75. David X., Tufts Medical School, April 25, 1987.

76. Bataille, *Story of the Eye*, p. 10.

77. Bataille, *Blue of Noon*, trans. Harry Mathews, (New York: Marion Boyars, 1957), p.17. Yet one must question the culpability of both David X. and Bataille with respect to what Alice A. Jardine *Gynesis: Configurations of Woman and Modernity*, (Ithaca, N.Y.: Cornell University Press, 1985), p. 25, terms: *gynesis* — "the putting into discourse of 'woman' as that *process* diagnosed in France as intrinsic to the condition of modernity; indeed, the valorization of the feminine, woman, and her obligatory, that is, historical connotations, as somehow intrinsic to new and necessary modes of thinking, writing, speaking."

78. Ibid.

79. Richman, *Reading Georges Bataille*, p. 69.

80. "Autobiographical Note," *October 36*, p. 110.

81. Bataille (VI, 199) quoted in Richman, *Reading Georges Bataille*, p. 128.

82. Ibid., p. 154.

83. Weiss argues for a conception of Bataille's self-mastery under the heading of sovereignty. However, since sovereignty deconstructs its own position, it is not masterful. Weiss neglects the importance of double negation so that he may squeeze Bataille's work into a Nietzschean mold. See Weiss, "Impossible Sovereignty," p. 138-139.

84. Luce Irigaray, *This Sex Which is Not One*, trans. Catherine Porter, (Ithaca, N.Y.: Cornell University Press, 1985), p. 143. "In this 'phallocratic' power, man loses something too: in particular, the pleasure of his own body."

85. I would further note that Richman, in her introduction, admits to attempting an interpretation "irrespective of genre or chronology." Richman, *Reading Georges Bataille*, p. 6. Thus, she refuses to acknowledge the development of Bataille's thought or its/his position in history. Ironically, Richman, when writing of her own text, reveals her fear of *misinterpretation* when she warns the reader: "It should be noted that no one chapter is conceived as a self-contained unit: issues raised in one often reappear in a later section." p. 6. See also, "Betrayal in the Later Bataille" in Allan Stoekl, *Politics, Writing, Mutilation; The Cases of Bataille, Blanchot, Roussel, Leris, and, Ponge,* (Minneapolis: University of Minnesota, 1985), p. 100-101.

86. Throughout Haase's work he insists on corralling Bataille's concepts within the homogeneous. Why does Haase continually appeal to the consistency of a "general economy"? What is his desire for a masterful, phallocratic encapsulation of Bataille's thought? Clearly, Haase is still stuck within a *modern* paradigm. He ignores that the form of *Reading Georges Bataille* is its content. His rational exposé is an exemplary deconstruction but refuses to deconstruct itself. Situated within the bi-polar atrophy of homogeneity/heterogeneity, his reading proves fundamentally conservative. Thus, Haase fails to realize the transgressive power of inconsistency and ambivalence as well as Bataille's conception of a non-economic (as opposed to an anti-economic) sovereign power.

87. Richman, *Reading Georges Bataille*, p. 78. The sexual fusion of sperm and egg cells (the two "donor" cells must die) to create the zygote, present a powerful metaphor for Bataille.

88. Ibid., p. 89. Furthermore, sexual organs embody the attraction/repulsion ambivalence which is characteristic of heterogeneity. Stoekl, on the other hand, understands Bataille's eroticism as a response to the failures of political action. Allan Stoekl, *Politics, Writing, Mutilation*, p. 26. However, Stoekl's political bias binds him to a duel conception of society where philosophy is *opposed* politics; the lacuna separating political action and literature (praxis and ideology) is both wide and deep. (p. xviii.) Yet in our postmodern society: politics is philosophy, philosophy is politics, literature is action, action is literature. Stoekl realizes the transgressive power of Bataille's eroticism but he fails to note eroticism's parodic nature and the role it plays in formulating another paradigm of power.

89. Allen S. Weiss, "Impossible Sovereignty," p. 132. Derrida will also note that sovereignty "must simulate, after a fashion, the absolute risk, and it must laugh at this simulacrum...in the comedy that it thereby plays for itself...." Derrida, *Writing and Difference*, p. 256.

90. Bataille, *Visions of Excess*, "The Use Value of D. A. F. De Sade," p. 99. Allen S. Weiss, "Impossible Sovereignty," notes: Laughter is "scatological even though it is a nonmaterial, and thus ideological, mode of excretion...a mode of nonknowledge, the adequate but meaningless sign...." p. 140.

91. Richman, *Reading Georges Bataille*, p. 151. Furthermore, Sartrean phenomenology cannot appreciate this form of sovereignty since, as dépense, laughter is inaccessible from within. (Richman, p. 150.)

92. Allen S. Weiss, "Impossible Sovereignty," p. 130.

93. Bataille, *Visions of Excess*, "The Solar Anus," p. 5. The actual experience of death (a termination and forclosure of the possibility of experiencing death) is an unacceptable paradigm for acts of dépense.

94. David X., Tufts Medical School, April 25, 1987.

95. Bataille, *Blue of Noon*, p. 118.

96. Bataille, *Visions of Excess*, "[Dream]," p. 4.

97. Ibid., "The Solar Anus," p. 5.

98.

99.

100.

101.

Selected Bibliography

Bataille, Georges. *Blue of Noon*. Translated by Harry Mathews. New York: Marion Boyars, 1957.

_____.*Erotism: Death and Sensuality.* Translated by Mary Dalwood. San Francisco: City Lights Books, 1986.

_____.*Story of the Eye.* Translated by Joachim Neugroschal. New York: Viking Penguin, 1982.

_____.*Visions of Excess: Selected Writings, 1927-1939.* Edited by Allan Stoekl. Translated by Allan Stoekl, with Carl R. Lovitt and Donald M. Leslie, Jr. Minneapolis: University of Minnesota Press, 1985.

_____."Writings on Laughter, Sacrifice, Nietzsche, Un-Knowing." Translated by Annette Michelson. *October 36.* (Spring 1986).

Baudrillard, Jean. *Simulations.* Translated by Paul Foss, Paul Patton and Philip Beitchman. New York: Semiotext(e), 1983.

_____.*Forget Foucault.* Translated by Nicole Dufresne, Phil Beitchman, Lee Hildreth and Mark Polizzotti. New York: Semiotext(e), 1987.

Baynes, Kenneth., Bohman, James., and McCarthy, Thomas., ed. *After Philosophy: End or Transformation?* Cambridge, MA.: The MIT Press, 1987.

Bernstein, Richard J., ed. *Habermas and Modernity.* Cambridge, MA.: The MIT Press, 1985.

Derrida, Jacques. *Writing and Difference.* Translated by Alan Bass. Chicago: The University of Chicago Press, 1978.

Dreyfus, Hubert L., and Rabinow, Paul. *Michel Foucault: Beyond Structuralism and Hermeneutics.* Chicago: University of Chicago Press, 1982.

Foucault, Michel. *Discipline and Punish: The Birth of the Prison.* Translated by Alan Sheridan. New York: Vintage Books, 1977.

_____.*Madness and Civilization: A History of Insanity in the Age of Reason.* Translated by Richard Howard. New York: Vintage Books, 1965.

_____.*This is Not a Pipe.* Translated and edited by James Harkness. Los Angeles: University of California Press, 1983.

Habermas, Jürgen. *Communication and the Evolution of Society.* Translated by Thomas McCarthy. Boston: Beacon Press, 1979.

_____.*Knowledge and Human Interests.* Translated by Jeremy J. Shapiro. Boston: Beacon Press, 1968.

_____.*Legitimation Crisis,* Translated by Thomas McCarthy. Boston: Beacon Press, 1973.

_____.*Philosophical Discourse of Modernity: Twelve Lectures.* Translated by Frederick Lawrence. Cambridge, MA.: The MIT Press, 1987.

_____.*Philosophical-Political Profiles.* Translated by Frederick G. Lawrence. Cambridge, MA.: The MIT Press, 1983.

_____."Questions and Counter-Questions." *Praxis International 4.* (Oct. 1984) : 229-249.

_____.*The Theory of Communicative Action,* Translated by Thomas McCarthy. Boston: Beacon Press, 1981.

Held, David., and Thompson, John B., ed. *Habermas: Critical Debates*, Cambridge, MA.: The MIT Press, 1982.

Irigaray, Luce. *This Sex Which is Not One*. Translated by Catherine Porter. Ithaca, NY.: Cornell University Press, 1985.

Jardine, Alice A. *Gynesis: Configurations of Woman and Modernity*. Ithaca, NY.: Cornell University Press, 1985.

Lacan, Jacques. *Écrits: A Selection*. Translated by Alan Sheridan. New York: W. W. Norton and Company, 1977.

The Four Fundamental Concepts of Psycho-Analysis. Translated by Alan Sheridan. New York: W. W. Norton and Company, 1977.

Lyotard, Jean-François. *The Postmodern Condition: A Report on Knowledge*. Translated by Geoff Bennington and Brian Massumi. Minneapolis: University of Minnesota Press, 1984.

Richman, Michele. *Reading Georges Bataille: Beyond the Gift*. Baltimore: Johns Hopkins University Press, 1982.

Saussure, Ferdinand de. *Course in General Linguistics*, Translated by Wade Baskin. New York: McGraw-Hill Book Company, 1959.

Stoekl, Allan. *Politics, Writing, Mutilation: The Cases of Bataille, Blanchot, Roussel, Leiris, and Ponge*. Minneapolis: University of Minnesota Press, 1985.

Weiss, Allan. "Impossible Sovereignty: Between The Will to Power and The Will to Chance." *October 36*. (Spring 1986): 129-146.

9

THE PORNOGRAPHIC BODY DOUBLE: TRANSGRESSION IS THE LAW

Berkeley Kaite

The Body Double: Transgressive and Sexual Effects

The pornographic body knows no textual limitations. The uneasy (unfixed, androgynous) gender identity of the (female) model is evident in soft-core, 'straight' versions of the genre (e.g. *Playboy, Penthouse, Hustler*, etc.). Various transgressions appear on the body textual of the model(s) and in the interplay between reader and photograph. For example, in the descriptive paragraphs which accompany photographic spreads, the models speak their desires (literally).[1] That is, the semiotics of self-referencing[2] attends to the 'speaking voice' of the models' — or their representational stand-in — which disturbs the silent exchange between image and reader: a "model" clamouring to be heard.[3] Frequently the fantasy lovers of the models are described as, and implored to be, "big and hard"; "a real tiger in bed". The perfect lover possesses a sexual technique, unspecified beyond the ability (and appeal) to perform endlessly for the model to the point of her satiation. And her desire is to be so sated, often in pursuit of auto-erotic pleasure to the diegetic exclusion of the viewer. Some examples: Robin likes "regular sexual workouts" with her boyfriend. "He really makes me sweat"; Claudia "thrive(s) on pushing (her) body to its limits, and beyond. I can be... in bed with a man, so long as I end up totally exhausted. If I'm not sound asleep 20 seconds after sex, my partner's somehow failed me"; "Tina prefers nonstop lovemaking"; Kate wants "to made love all day long." These statements challenge the privileged masculine position within sexual discourse by imposing sexual demands, unsettling, certainly, to even the most confident of readers. That is, instabilities

Photo: Bob Guccione
Penthouse, August 1985.
Centrefold without staples.

around male sexual identity, performance and "equipment" are given space in a discourse which purports to empower men and give full range to their sexual expression. This disturbs the claims that pornography "silences" women, and it *can* be argued that pornographic machinery speaks, in the Foucauldian sense ("What is so perilous, then, in the fact that people speak, and that their speech proliferates? Where is the danger in that?")[4], of women's sexuality and the fetishization/masculinization of the body. This speech exposes the body as a history of discourses and, in this case, drawing upon perhaps not the "already-said" but a "never-said", an unwritten text, "a writing that is merely the hollow of its own mark".[5] If "everything that is formulated in discourse was already articulated in that semi-silence that precedes it...",[6] these women are speaking the unspeakable, their representations bearing male quotations. These women transgress what Heath calls the "sexual fix" (as all women do): that inscription into "the happy family of sexually confirmed individuals"[7]. Similarly, in "TV" porn, an acronym for 'transvestite' in which the hermaphroditic/transsexual body is adorned as a 'woman' through erotic accoutrements, the most popular model is "Sulka", the "most erotically unusual" 'she-man'; in hard-core, the transsexual model has "buns... itching for some wild fucking excitement"; fingers "inching towards his military anus"; "her own tiny prick grew hard from the jabs". This latter phrase exposes a male signifier of desire (the "tiny prick grew hard"), an unmistakable masculine projection. These are seductive transgressions for the reader, pleasures dependent on "prohibition and fear".[8]

Technologies of Ocular Penetration

The discursive space of 'foreplayed' androgyny and transgression of the 'sexual fix' is fleshed out on the textual *body* as well, beyond the literal narrative. Specular identification is central to the workings of visual imaginaries but the axes or twinned oppositions of seeing/being seen and male/female[9] do not represent antinomies when applied to the gaze or look within pornographic genres for it (the look) is contradictory and oscillating. The look is possessed by *both* the reader and the subject of the representation; thus subject positions of male/female are only as good as their discourses: i.e., when talking of the power of the gaze, designations of masculine/feminine do not represent a picture of unity but are themselves unstable, shifting and rife with cross-currents. Paul Willemen posits the "fourth look",[10] a negotiation of "looks" and enunciations which organize the field of vision of camera, viewer and "direct address" of the "object or scene", the "light-in-the-eyes" of the pornographic model. He writes: "When the scopic drive is brought into focus, then the viewer also runs the risk of becoming the object of the look".[11]

Or as Bataille notes of the seductive power and fear of the eye: "...extreme seductiveness is probably at the boundary of horror... the eye could be related to the cutting edge".[12]

I want to open the case on penetration in pornographic discourse, which is to say I want to open the case on eyes. The visual moment in any medium (and one might argue this is especially so with pornography) is a courtship between image and looking, the vehicle of which is the eyes, those (of the model and the viewer) which manage the look. In pornographic photographs we have models looking, who solicit a series of looks from the reader; this solicitation involves an exchange of looks which circulate within libidinal economies. The investment is in a sexual discourse privileging a commerce and penetrating exchange which are by definition ocular (not carnal). To speak then of ocular penetration is to penetrate the workings of this visual imaginary. To speak of the gaze is to invoke the metaphysics of staring: the gaze is not a glance but a stare, the "gaze gone hard... a will to penetrate, to pierce, to fix in order to discover the permanent under the changing appearances... implies a certain anxiety in the relation between spectator and object seen".[13]

The eye, at the summit of the skull... opens and blinds itself like a conflagration... the head has received the electric power of points. *This great burning head is the image and the disagreeable light of the* notion of expenditure...[14]

Bataille, "The Pineal Eye"

The eye is an orifice, the window to the bodily soul, an opening which takes in the perceptible world. It is the body's peep-hole; an "eye-opener", after all, is that which shocks and surprises, a revelation, to have seen the light, an act of revealing to view, an enlightening disclosure. A hollow organ, the eyeball is penetrable, e.g. the eye of the needle, that through which thread passes. The eye is also Bataille's agent of illumination, a provider of light, an orifice of projection. To "cast an eye on", "lay an eye on", to "have eyes for", to "look into something": the eyes are active agents of capture, possession, penetration. The eyes do not just receive; they take in and they do this through the light they shed. In this way, the figurative eye is both feminine and masculine: like the eye of the camera, it is an aperture which admits light; as a metaphor for looking, however, it is aligned with a masculine trajectory and the ability to extend vision to the spectacular. Ocular penetration offers up documentation of the perceptible world, hence in-sight; a visible inventory which is nonetheless partisan (like the 'reality' captured before the camera lens). Beauty is in the eye of the beholder; and this signifies an aesthetic or intellectual perception or appreciation. To "have an eye for" is to submit a point of view or judgement. In this predatory way, there is power in the workings of the gaze.

*... her gaze demands that you be patient ... that you allow her to call
the shots ... She holds the torch for no one, and yet her eyes suggest a flame,
fathoms deep, that is both mysterious and inextinguishable.*

Penthouse (August 1985)

There is a bisexual potential to the eye and its inscription in the gaze
such that power resides in the eye of the beholder and in this case is shared
by the model who is often the subject doing the looking. This is clearly
visible in the pornographic photograph which organizes the eyes around
the workings of desire as they permit a reciprocity between both masculine and feminine possessions, i.e. one possesses at the same time as one
is being possessed.

The most notable opposition in all genres is that between opened and
closed eyes. Opened eyes operationalize the code of power: they resem-
ble beady eyes: small, round, sinfully 'shiny with interest or greed'. A bead
is also a "small knob in the front sight of a gun"; therefore to "draw a bead
on" is to take aim at something. These eyes in focus are taking careful aim
at their object. The model bears the marks of masculinity in her eyes/look.
The eyes of her desire are a masculine projection, an erection in front of
the male viewer: they are penetrating. Beady eyes do not provide the most
candid view (they are not wide open to all possibilities). The less-than-
candid model acknowledges the illicit exchange of sexual glances (with
a photograph, with a stranger), and threatens the fiction of stability of both
subjects (the subject of the representation, she who desires to be looked
at and in so doing carries the mark of *his* — the Other's — desire; and
the subject who is reading the representation, who is enlisted in his "feminine" surrender to penetration). The less-than-candid glances expose the
non-spontaneity of the profilmic event, its reproduction (simulation) for
the camera.

We may say, then, that this desiring female subject is looking, casting
an eye at the "apple of her eye", that highly cherished object. The "apple"
of her eye can also refer to the pupil, the eyeball, the object of one's desire,
and, in slang (Partridge's *Historical Slang*), 'testicles'. The apple of her eye
is the cherished object of her heart's desire: that sexualized core of the
reader's masculinity. And there is a symbolic rapport between the eyes and
testicles which invites their sexual affinity even further. Both are associated with "light" (the eyes take it in and throw light on, eyes "see the light";
the testicles are the apple of the eye and provide the seed or the light of
life, they emit fluids of seminal light), and both are claims to "truthfulness":
the "eyewitness" is the one who bears testimony based on his own observation. 'Testicle' is derivative of the Latin 'testis' or *witness* and is thus related to 'testimony' and 'testify', both referring to the provision of evidence,
demonstrable proof, a declaration, confession or affirmation based on the
"truth". To give evidence, to testify, to bear witness: she is witness to his

virility, calls upon him to provide evidence of it and offers up her body as testimony to his virility/masculine desire.

The slightly shut eyes, focussed intently on the unsuspecting viewer (the beady eyes), are not eyes wide open. Again, from Partridge, to "have one's eyes opened" is to be robbed; hence the "eye-opener" is the lesson learned, instruction for the uninitiated. The model in question however is already "in the know" but savvy enough to only give away her desire once she sees evidence of his (the reader's). This she demands; nothing can be taken from her. It can be argued that the hard-core genre is the "eye-popper"; that is, the reader is privy to the graphic "exposing to view certain acts or anatomies"[15], and is voyeuristically ensconced at the peep-hole. *His* projection is also a visual one: his eyes "pop out of his head" in shock, fascination, narcissistic identification and overwhelming desire. At the same time he is also emasculated (she's got him by the eyeball). To have eyes "pop out of the head" would be to lose one's eyesight; in collo-quial terms to "nearly lose one's eyesight" is to obtain an unexpected and very intimate view of a member of the opposite sex (Partridge). Is it not perhaps then the viewer who is robbed, who eyes are opened in the act of gazing, who surrenders to the penetrating gaze of the model, who is disempowered (disembodied), rendered sight-less by the model who is an "eye-popper"? Also, blindness is associated with the Oedipal drama: guilt and castration.

Thus, the look can take an active or passive stance. The model in this case 'looks' as a projection of the reader's desires; she also desires to be looked at and thus solicits a visual rapport from her desiring reader (or makes a visual pass at him). But unspeakable longings are in the air, i.e. the reader's desire to be dispossessed of his bodily properties, to be, as it were, stripped.

The viewer is engaged in the pleasurable fantasy of the satisfaction of his desire (and, to paraphrase Chevalier,[16] his inadmissible desire to be dis-possessed or desire for castration). This involves the visible expression of the model's desire, projections which masculinize her subjectivity/femi-ninity, and it involves the masculinization of her body, its 'positions' and its symbolic adornment. The opened eyes are the window by which this desire is read, entered. But the eyes opened (and ready for business) emit more than they take in, are beady. Beads are often sacred relics, icons of religious ritual (rosary beads); beads are also jewels. The beady eyes in this case are fixated and focussed on the 'apple' of the model's eye, that is, the 'apple' of the reader: his testicles/balls or (colloquially) the "family jewels". The look is "eyeball to eyeball": an intense gaze, a "close confrontation". But the look is also 'eyeball to cherished object', from eye/ball to 'apple of the eye'/ball, bead/jewel to ball/family jewels. The beady eyes are the eyes of desire, engaging the desire of the Other; *and* the beady eyes are ambi-sexual: possessed by a woman who longs to be possessed by a man (the real apple) and in so doing incites his desire. However, in so doing she possesses the family jewels with her insightful (and lustfully inciteful) gaze; and the gaze penetrates the 'apple'/testicles of the/her 'eye'/ball.

So the eyes can be a projection of desire and the "eye-popping" effect of the sexually explicit and illicit robs the reader (he with the open eyes) of stability and the sole power of the gaze. And, as the saying goes, to "have someone by the balls" is to have someone utterly in one's power, especially of women over men (Partridge).

Ocular penetration is an important motif of pornographic photographs but its diegetic absence does not signify a lack of penetrating potential. The closed eyes which accompany a display of auto-eroticism, for example, do not simply denote the creation of a passive spectacle. Eyes closed in simulated pleasure or ecstasy follow, in the photographic spread, the look which has already confronted the reader: there isn't a singular or un-problematic eye. The closed eyes prevent ocular penetration of that orifice. However, although the eyes may be closed, covered by lids, sunglasses or the brim of a hat, they are viewed in conjunction with parts of the *body* that are offered for penetration. That is, closed eyes consort with differ-ent parts of the body, and its symbolic adornment, which are masculinized to the point of erotic entry themselves. For example, "Kathy" is lying on a small coffee-table, head at one end, rear-end resting at the other, her legs bent to balance her pointed toes on the floor. The view we have of her is from the side, a long-shot. This is what we see: her back is arched, her head tilted back on the table (eyes closed), her chin is in the air, and her breasts are protruding with fully erect nipples. "Kathy" is sporting white lace finger-less gloves, her hands are resting just above her breasts on her collar bone; stockings studded with small shiny beads, and ballet slippers encasing feet similarly arched to point the toes, elongate the feet, legs and support the upward-arching of the back. Two areas of her body are "high-lighted", interestingly, through the use of beams of light which appear to enter from an unseen window. Each beam points to, and highlights, both the breasts and the pubic area such that both are shiny and glowing. The former are erect and looking to penetrate — in slang, her "highbeams"; the latter, the pleasure zone which is highlighted for penetration. The model in this picture does not possess the incisive gaze but her body is no pas-sive spectacle/receptacle either.

Similarly, we have "Susan" who "loves to flirt with strange, unsuspect-ing men by turning them on only with her beautiful brown eyes." She shades her eyes with sunglasses while she spreads her legs, bent at the knees, to reveal wider possibilities; at the same time *her* breasts are in the path of a light-beam (the "eye-beam" of the reader). "Susan's" hair may also partially occlude her vision; she then sports a man's tie whose tip ends at her most feminine point of entry. Her long, blood-red fingernails, in the closed-eye shots, are placed on the pubic or anal area, signalling again points of entry, as well as the body's simulated protrusions. The heel of her shoe serves the same visual and phallic function as she contorts her body to aim it (the spike heel) directly at the vaginal orifice.

This is the masculinization of the model's desire to satisfy the viewer's desire. The closure of the model's eyes does not simply mean that she is looked at because in fact she *is* doing something: desire is written on her body and thus her self-containment (the apparent exclusion of the viewer) is still an active solicitation of the interests or desire of the reader. The model knows she is being looked at — she has already engaged the reader through the previous exchange of looks and glances. However, she is not merely reduced to an orifice (she has put the lid on that orifice which invites ocular penetration, or phallic insight) as her body bears the simulated marks of masculinization, masculine insight: it carries, for example, its own projections, erections, protuberances (the breasts — or 'headlights' — are prominent and thrusting outwards either in their placement in the photograph or the nipples are fully erect), and excrescences (the anus is a favourite offering/invasion). This is the simulated world of sex, the "delirious surround" of the spectacular, the consumption of meaning which defies representation.[17] That is, the display is not the latter half of the real/representation juxtaposition but is itself a simulated world of signs which anticipate and shape the real: how do you represent desire, that which is only ever the desire of an Other, which only exists in a non-referential exchange and is not the property of One? In this case it is written on the body in a series of simulated codes; and this body only shows up simulation as the 'real as reproduction'.[18] The masculinized body of the woman has no referent but is a composite of signs which only refers to signs of masculinity anyway: it is hard, taut, turgid with desire and bearing protuberances which aim for penetration, the desirous be·longings of an androgynous commerce (fingers, finger-nails, spike heels, the positioning of limbs, etc.).

In soft core, the model's gaze penetrates when her eyes are open. The open eyes are a prelude to what will follow: eyes closed, the model engaged in auto-erotic activity, the body offered up for ocular penetration. This may explain why the reader would relinquish the privilege of the power of looking and allow himself to be penetrated/castrated by her gaze. Although the reader may long for ocular penetration, his power in gazing is partially restored when the model surrenders hers. The closed eyes present a picture of simulated possession of desire (as mentioned above, the body in a discursive arrangement which "speaks" projections or, from Chevalier, longings of desire),[19] the foreplay which precedes the 'real' thing yet to come. And what is to come (although the real possession never comes), penetration of her, is signified by her body simulated with the possessive marks of her desire to be penetrated. This is pronounced and visible when she relinquishes the power behind her looking, when she, at the same time, puts closure on her "eye-hole" and the option of being penetrated *there*.

This dynamic interplay of looks is much more than a "mere parody of the male look", or a look, powerful in its "dark" and "smouldering" vision, as simply a prelude to women's impending victimization or fantasization of her masochistic desires.[20] It *does* suggest that the woman looks, knows she is being looked at, and in so doing encounters her double who is already inscribed in his own drama involving the "pleasure of passivity, of subject-ion".[21] If woman is castration, and the female model carries the marks of both pleasure *and* penetration; if her look is a formal elaboration of voyeurism and identification (she controls the gaze and is a self-conscious display), then perhaps the viewer enthralls in being "cut" (a re-enactment of that penetrating rupture by which subjects are formed) at the moment when he meets, "eyeball to eyeball", his stand-in, in a "sutured discourse".[22] No parody of the male look, but a model with phallic insight.

The Mutilated Body Double: Transvestite ("TV") Porn

This visual imaginary is a libidinal investment circulating among an exchange of glances and unfixed sexual identities. A particularly vicious collapse of the discursive and the real is found in representations of the transsexual adorned as 'female' in transvesite ("TV") pornography (these photos are inserted into mainstream, straight soft-core magazine; as well, there is a genre composed solely of the "TV" hard-core narrative). The spectacular moment contains a body in excess of normative and pleasurable transgressions. The 'body double' in "TV" pornography, in its symbolic, sexual and feminine masquerade, is a body that doubles as its other. Linda Williams investigates the structure of the female "look" in the horror film, thus upsetting the cliche that men look while women exist only to be looked at.[23] Her focus is the visual encounter between the female heroine (the "silent screen vamp") and the monster or Phantom, prompting the question: what happens when the woman in the text tries to look, and actually sees? And what does she see? Williams argues that the woman and the monster share an affinity "within patriarchal structures of seeing" such that "when the woman looks" she sees herself in the mutilated body of the monster: she encounters her double and is inscribed in a masochistic drama. What would happen, then, when the pornographic ("TV") model (Williams' freak, the monster body) looks at 'her reader' and what is s·he looking at? And, where does the reader fit into this exchange of looks, i.e. what of *his* dramatic scenario as *he* encounters the 'freak'? What does *he* see? There is (I conjecture) pleasurable (yet unspeakable) surrender, on the part of the (male) reader, to the "cut", that incisive moment formed around loss and pleasure; that is, at the moment of "reading" the subject is reaffirmed as subject/other, a position originally formed in reflection, opposition, otherness. Also, borrowing from Williams, I suggest that the "freak" in the representation encounters the freakish and mu-

tilated ("cut") body of the viewer. In "TV", each meets the double of the other, in a body which doubles as its other, which bears the marks of a simulated adrogynous writing. That is, categories of sexual difference collapse around a law which prescribes transgression of the 'sexual fix' such that there is potency in that "different kind of sexuality" (Williams) but this is a desirable transaction, not totally threatening. In "TV" porn, potency resides in the 'body double', weighted with meaning in a non-aligned sexuality, and transgresses the sexual fix. The 'apparent' feminine body, read thus through its erotic accoutrements, is restored to masculinity through (not only) its *biological* adornment. It is also masculinized beyond the fleshy configuration which always threatens to emerge: discursively, psychoanalytically, symbolically, sartorially and literally – the penis/phallus is never "out of sight." That is, the surplus of clothing which marks the masquerade also carries the possessive marks of masculine desire. Thus the 'androgyne' bears the marks of simulation (the erotic clothing), a writing of what might never take place: simulation as incomplete synthesis, which is why the body is written on top of its androgynous properties. In other words, the 'androgyne', far from being a unity of opposites (or the desirable, lost, original union), is 'jouissance', that which cannot achieve closure, and plays on the open seam of the "cut" through its simulation (clothing).

Men Are Men and So Are Women

This seemingly perverse pornographic moment carries more (hidden) subversive elements which coalesce *not* around a 'body' which is rendered feminine and therefore a spectacle *but* a 'body' read as feminine but at the same time restored to masculinity through its *biological* adornment and masculine vocabulary. *In this genre the men are men so are the women.* A close reading of all pornographic genres reveals that penetrating exchanges are initiated and carried by the 'feminine' model. Masculine projections: heels, a penetrating gaze, fetish objects, carry the marks of (phallic) desire and pleasure. These are his be · longings on the female body; this erotic theft surely speaks to the 'flesh of the unconscious", the unsettling body double where the laws of transgression speak the unspeakable, where women in fact are allowed to be men and encounter a reader who, in his fixation on the androgynous model, transgresses his own apparent 'sexual fix'. He lends his vision to a 'she-male' — s. he costumed as 'female' but only as a masquerade against a surplus of masculine identification.

There are two versions of "TV" porn, "soft" and "hard." Soft core depictions are of the "ultimate she-male", sole occupant of the diegetic space. The view of the body is fully frontal or at least a rear view positioned to show the genital zone. This is an androgynous display whose text must somehow bear the weight of desire (and hence of lack: the 'real' thing which never comes), for the legs are spread to reveal a flaccid penis – no turgidity of desire here. Hard core contains a sexual narrative: the graphic unveiling of a sexual encounter (chance, spontaneous and between strangers) in which the "body double" transgresses the 'sexual fix' and sets in play a circuit of simulated desire based on longing, possession and lack.

The "look" in "TV" porn (both 'soft' and 'hard') once again engages a "freak." She possesses the gaze, sharp and penetrating: s.he has phallic insight. This look of critical perception accompanies a body which is a discursive play of transgressive sexual positions and which competes with the look of the model for the reader's attention. What *of* the reader's confrontation of the "horror version" of his own body?[24] The freakishness of the "TV" body is its phallic protrusion; and indeed, in hard core the pleasurable narrative is a simulated model of men who, in a reciprocal play of desire, desire masculinized women. This is a perverse challenge to the *social* construction of gender identity; a celebration of the postmodern "death of the social" through the representation of subjects who, in desiring what the other desires, enter into sexual arrangements which continually threaten the *apparent* 'sexual fix'. This is, in Williams' phrase, the "extreme excitement and surplus danger when the monster and the woman get together."[25] The freakishness of the "TV" display is the "TV" façade always slipping away to reveal the "TS" (transsexual) underneath. To be totally stripped, however, would be the death of language (Pacteau: "Discussions of androgyny... come up against a resistance... from language itself... Any attempt to *define* androgyny... takes us to the limits of language... such definitions ask for their own *dépassement*")[26] and the death of desire. The vestmentary code anchors meaning to what appears to be the ultimate transgression, although androgyny may still mean the longing for a lack.

The "TV" hard-core narrative begins with an exchange of looks between models, a chance encounter between a transsexual/hermaphrodite, whose "true" identity is concealed by clothing, and an unsuspecting yet persistently willing male. The story unfolds as the model gradually reveals her hermaphroditic body through the shedding of clothing (and the male, although surprised, is no less desirous). And there is a range of possible looks. One is the look of genital fascination in which one or both of the models engages the penis/phallus during penetration (intercourse) or with auto-erotic enthrallment. In the case of an ambi-sexual and a male model, the fascination with looking (read on their faces as well as on the part of the viewer) appears to take on the voyeur's aim of looking outside himself: he is again implicated in the highly illicit consumption of 'public sex' (clearly antithetical to Western traditions of "taboos regulating the sight of bare flesh"[27]). And sexual pathologization doubly heightens curiosity: the body/subject so discursively arranged is not just displayed in acts which should be consumed in private but is, as Mort notes, the morally unhygienic body (it subverts a system of difference based on binary opposites) and once again non-normative.[28] However what cannot be overlooked is the narcissistic component of the look or how the reader sees himself in this scopic moment. Penises, anal entry, *and* the literal phallus (the transsexual playing with a dildo in mock sexual ecstasy) are key signifiers: the common shot is of the "female" model spreading her buttocks to display 'rear entry' (s.he in the "dominant" position, sitting on top of him); or in a view from the front s.he covers her genitals either in mock-masturbation or to hide her hermaphroditism. But can that knowledge be suspended? In a curious way we have men looking at men; and men in circuits of desire *vis à vis* MEN.

The *look of pleasure* accompanies intercourse and is signified by closed eyes, head tilted back, open mouth often with a protruding tongue or tongue licking the lips in sexual or oral readiness. It is a look of pleasure at, it must be acknowledged, anal penetration. Freud on anal eroticism:

An invitation to a caress of the anal zone is... used... to express defiance or defiant scorn, and thus in reality signifies an act of tenderness that has been overtaken by repression. An exposure of the buttocks represents a softening down of this spoken invitation into a gesture... both words and gestures are introduced at the most appropriate point as an expression of defiance.[29]

So the viewer takes pleasure in looking at bodily configurations which visually privilege the anal-erotic. The fe.male model, however, is the one with the "defiant" offering (*he* is never anally penetrated) and her boldness (not to mention her "filthy" offering)[30] would challenge any vulgar reading of "male domination" in this case. The vulgarity may lie, however, in the challenges which are put to fictive male subjective coherence. Also, there is the overlapping of voyeurism and narcissistic identification as phallic signification abounds.

Direct Address is the look (of the transsexual; 'men' never look at the camera) which meets the gaze of the reader but is not often "straight on." That is, the model looks over her shoulder, while offering a "rear view" of penetration, or shifts her head, in a reclining position, to partially face the camera; however, her eyes directly meet those of the reader. It is a look which talks, as if to say either: "Are you watching me?" or "Caught you!" or both — the reader is caught in the act of watching. Both model and reader are complicit in the act; in that way the gap between image and spectator, the "absent field, the place of a character who is put there by the viewer's imaginary"[31], is only partially sutured by the look.

Contrary to the idea of the putative impulse behind voyeurism, the woman's look in transvestite pornography is not punished but is empowered with phallic insight and is subversive in its potential to penetrate the castrated viewer: the model is dressed up, the reader/viewer stripped. It is precisely in the pornographic moment where women are allowed to be men; this discourse thus speaks the unspeakable, is the flesh of the un-conscious. All of which is not to say that the reader enlists in total annihi-lation in front of the monster/hermaphrodite, but that he surrenders to *la petite mort*, the pleasure of his simulated death. He sees himself in the distorting mirror which is the unity of the voyeur and exhibitionist; his own mutilated form repeatedly "cut" at the visual moment. The look which mocks the reader and the display of the dildo/phallus enjoys the partial surrender of the reader to the "distorted mirror-reflection of (his) own puta-tive lack in the eyes of..." (Williams is talking here of women's self- recog-nition in encountering the monster, *her* lack in the "eyes of patriarchy"; I would say that in this instance it is *his* lack in the "eyes" of desire). Her clarity of vision is *precisely* phallic and she gazes at the mutilated body of the viewer who meets himself in the mirror of the (dressed up) an-drogynous model who carries the marks of his desire.

"A Cross-Dressing ... On the Body Itself..."

Do clothes make the wo·man? This "cross-dressing inscribed on the body itself"[32] is more than a play on transvestism or the masquerade. In this case, the "feminine" writing on the body is a joke (the laugh being, of course, on the reader) as it cannot disguise the fleshy masculine extremi-ty. As well, anal invasions are the common property of all "female" models; the sadistic component to anal fantasies as well as the "anal penis" or anal projections is not to be overlooked.

Female models (in all genres) also wear spike heels which not only phal-licize the legs but also signify masculinity: men are 'heels', women are not. And to be under the heels of another is to be "under control or subjec-tion". The body's limbs are elongated for penetrating potential; high heels are sharp projections, erections on the female body. Similarly, fingernails are long, hard. The model contorts her body to position the 'heel' for mock phallic entry, frequently anal; similarly the hands and finger nails placed at vaginal and anal openings expose the 'normally-hidden' and point to penetrating possibilities written on the body itself. This is an erotic theft, a masculinization which points to the textual body as the site to anchor sexual difference.

Pacteau characterizes androgyny as that which eludes a semantic an-chor; that is, it is easy enough to identify the androgynous body in phys-iological terms, but the lines of demarcation between the subject and its object of desire (the androgyne which fascinates) are continually oscillat-ing.[33] However, in "trying to organize a meaning for androgyny," she ar-gues that the concept represents a repression of desire, that the nature of ambiguous sexual appearance and identity is the specular image of an "un-canny double": nostalgia for the imaginary space during whose reign "desire is unobstructed".[34] That is, this desire — a resurrection of the original plenitude, merging, a disavowal of 'otherness' — is repressed within the laws of sexual difference. But I would argue that sexual mutations are not simply a "disavowal of sexual difference" upon observation, a "pleasurable perception"[35]; but that *transgressions* are the law behind the deviations of the 'sexual fix' and the desire for repression (not the repression of desire) is part of the (simulated) androgynous union. And the androgynous textual body is a possessive site of desire, the embodiment of the partial belongings of the other. In the case of "TV" porn, the body masculinized is in simulated possession of the desirous be · longings of the masculine viewer. Transgressions are the norm, an eroticized "dialogue of lovers",[36] representing desires, in the case of the male reader, for women to be more like men. The feminine enunciation may then be a phallicization for the reader, a discursive drama of his desire to be possessed by the powerfully penetrating subject of the photograph.

"The androgynous figure has to do with *seduction...* before undressing...".[37] It is not so clear that the "fashionable discourse" is the effete prerogative of women, at least within the codes of the dominant representational *doxa*: i.e., the male reader lends his eyes to the image, a highly exhibitionist one at that. Within the contemporary ideological framework men *are* charged with negotiating the "look", and seeing themselves as "the ones who look at women".[38] But normative transactions within specular economies invite transgression of the boundaries around an apparent fixity of sexual identity and desire. However, there are limits to this cultural lawbreaking: misrecognition, suspension and disbelief (that the reader is looking at a man, himself, "cut" at the moment of his inscription into sexual difference) are anchored on the textual body in the sumptous display of the transsexual/transvestite model.

At the same time, identification involves visual projection, a loss and surrender. In this case the visual object oscillates between the 'feminine' and the 'masculine'. I would argue this represents more than the (repressed) pleasurable wish for a reunion with the original plenitude. That would be the death of the subject (Bataille: "... human beings are only united with each other through rents or wounds..."). The pleasurable spectacle is the body which has annihilated difference and which at the same time cannot disguise the masculinity, apparently renounced by the surplus of ("feminine", fetish) signifiers on the model's body. Does the fetish disavow difference? In "TV", as with all porn, it bestows a virility on the body making it a body poised to penetrate and invade. Desire is not opposed to its correlative threat but may itself be threatening, involving as it does, subjection and death (*"la petite mort"*). But why speak of a fetish, a stand-in, when the 'real thing' is so unabashedly visible (and "semantically overdetermined")?[39] It may be that the fascination with looking at the androgyne (the 'freak') does not contain the lustful search for a lost 'wholeness' but the seductiveness of the image promises a "representation of moments of separation and loss which captivates us more than the

promise of plenitude".[40] It is the *mutilated*, "cut" body which stands before ("under the heels of") the body double, always threatening to cancel
out the 'other'.

"A Certain Refusal of Difference" or, There's Still "Trouble in the Text"[41]

In pornography, sexual configurations appear, at first glance, as a "site
of realism", the immediately visible and prehensible bodies "in evidence"
of possession of feminine or masculine identities.[42] But the pornographic genre, *apparently* the most revealing (and apocalyptic) of all fleshy discourses, that which "with semiology... cannot bear the sight of
modesty"[43], provides entry into a discovery of the body and the normative transgression of desire such that what appears as obvious biological
and discursive difference is really the simulation of androgyny on the
body's text. This is the masculine identification of the masculinized body
of the woman; men desiring, not men — as that would be the literal
homosexualization of desire — but, women with men's desire, the 'semiotics of other-referencing'. To a point. And this is amply demonstrated in
"TV" porn where the masculinized body is 'dressed-up' as feminine. This
is femininity "with a vengeance, suggest(ing) the power of taking it off."[44]
The naked body is not desirable; it must be posed, poised, dressed, written, spoken — and fetishized — to be desirable and only then within a
discourse of others.

A close, synchronic reading of the pornographic moment (and a
paradigmatic discussion of the 'penetrating eye') reveals a powerful ambiguity of the gaze. If pornographic negotiations position the (male) reader to be mastered by the image (or to surrender pleasurably to the castrating
potential of the model); if pornography is that representational discourse
where the 'female' model is masculinized and transgressions are the norm,
then it is not so much an anchor for Heath's "sexual story" but a lawful
transgression of it: it unpins both the 'pin-up' and the reader of their 'sexual fix' thus disrupting the safe world of sexual difference. Endowing the
'female' model with the fetish(es) does not invite the ineluctable search
for the lost phallus (a closing in on lack), but is a simulated representation
of the desire for lack, for repression.[45] Pornography's 'oeuvre' is a surplus
of phallic investment on the body; a textual disinvestment of the body's
essential power and the management of sexual difference; ultimately, a
pathetic exposure of the representational nature of desire, the fetishiza-
tion of the spectacular, the phallus and 'otherness'.

The Politics of Ambivalence

Representation's self-fulfillment and transcendence into simulation is
the sign-work that stands at the eye of the social maelstrom. Discursive
bodies have surpassed real bodies and what remains is an ambivalent and

representational inflation, a fetishism of objects complemented by a fetishism for subjects. This postmodern moment is a radical play on 'otherness', the stand-in, what's 'gone missing', and, in which the (ubiquitous) fetish represents a twofold manoeuvre: it manages the threat of separation/otherness as it courts 'present absence'; but the threat is once again activated, a rather pathetic attempt to cover up the flaw of the 'real' (and the flaws — the 'trouble', what unsettles — in the text). Fetishistic negotiations thus cut both ways: they contain *and* represent the threat/desire of otherness — a postmodern (ambi)valence.

Notes

* "Transgression is the law", "be·longings", the idea of dispossession, among others, are renditions of Jacques Chevalier's. Many of the central ideaas contained here are borrowed from conversations with him and his forthcoming, *Schemanalysis: Daughter of the New Wor·ld*. I thank Ian Taylor, Graham Knight, Arthur and Marilouise Kroker and two anonymous reviewers for comments on an earlier draft.

1. "Literally" in the sense that these representations are offering up a verbal recital of lines, from a script already written; to speak of 'real' women and 'real' desires is problematic. And, "literally" in the sense that I distinguish this narrative from the body's text, or the way the *body* 'talks'.

2. The phrase "semiotics of self-reference" is from Kaja Silverman, "Dis-Embodying the Female Voice," in *Re-Vision: Essays in Feminist Film Criticism*, edited by Mary Ann Doane, Patricia Mellencamp and Linda Williams, (Frederick, Maryland: American Film Institute, 1984), p. 143.

3. I offer quotations from the models' 'sexual story' which are parodic, excessive and obscene in the sense that Baudrillard writes of the "ecstasy of communication": the "free expression... of the all-too-visible, of the more-visible-than-the-visible... the obscenity... of what dissolves completely in information and communication." "The Ecstasy of Communication," in *The Anti-Aesthetic: Essays on Postmodern Culture*, edited by Hal Foster, (Port Townsend, Washington: Bay Press), 1983, p. 131.

4. Michel Foucault, *The Archeology of Knowledge and The Discourse on Language*, translated by A.M. Sheridan Smith, (New York: Pantheon, 1972), p. 216.

5. Foucault, p. 25.

6. Foucault, p. 25.

7. Stephen Heath, *The Sexual Fix*, (London: Macmillan, 1982), p. 78.

8. Kaja Silverman, "Masochism and Subjectivity," *Framework*, 12, Winter 1979.

9. Mary Ann Doane, "Woman's Stake: Filming the Female Body," *October*, 17, Summer 1981.

10. Paul Willemen, "Letter to John," *Screen*, 21:2, Summer 1980.

11. Willemen, p. 56.

12. Georges Bataille, *Visions of Excess: Selected Writings, 1927-1939*, edited and with an introduction by Allan Stoekl, (Minneapolis: University of Minnesota Press), 1985, p. 17.

13. Mary Ann Caws, "Ladies Shot and Painted: Female Embodiment in Surrealist Art," in *The Female Body in Western Culture: Contemporary Perspectives*, edited by Susan Rubin Suleiman, (Cambridge, Massachusetts: Harvard University Press, 1986), p. 270.

14. Bataille, p. 82.

15. Beverley Brown. "A Feminist Interest in Pornography: Some Modest Proposals," *m/f*, 5/6, 1981, p. 5.

16. Jacques Chevalier, *Schemanalysis: Daughter of the New Wor ld*, forthcoming.

17. Hal Foster, *Recodings: Art, Spectacle, Cultural Politics*, (Port Townsend, Washington: Bay Press), 1985, p. 90.

18. Jean Baudrillard, *Simulations*, translated by Paul Foss, Paul Patton and Philip Beitchman, (New York: Semiotext(e)), 1983.

19. Chevalier.

20. Linda Williams, "When the Woman Looks," in *Re-Vision: Essays in Feminist Film Criticism*, op cit., p. 85.

21. Silverman, 1979, p. 6.

22. Jean-Pierre Oudart, "Cinema and Suture," *Screen*, 18:4, Winter 1977-78, p. 37. The concept of the "cut" is from Silverman (1979) and refers to the formation of the rhetorical subject within a painful dialectic of plenitude and loss, the child "both defined by and separated from (the) ideal image" granted by the Other (p. 3). One's cultural integration is a continual repositioning and reading of cultural texts, the constitution of subjects, of and for, language, discourse, desire. Within the spectator-text relationship the "compulsory narrative" of loss and recovery is replayed; photographic syntax, and visual pleasure, enlists a 'missing element' or the gap into which the viewer is inserted. The missing element, or the "cut", comprises oscillations between absence, separation and imaginary plenitude served by the shot/image (and the missing element, or the viewer). In encountering cultural representations one reads a text the way one might read a dream, and therefore would meet his or her ego in a number of metaphorical transactions. The moment of the cut, then, is a masochistic drama and not the sole preoccupation of women.

23. Williams

24. Williams, p. 89.

25. Williams, p. 90.

26. Francette Pacteau, "The Impossible Referent: Representations of the Androgyne," in *Formations of Fantasy*, edited by Victor Burgin, James Donald and Cora Kaplan, (London: Metheun, 1986).

27. Angela Carter, *The Sadeian Woman*, (London: Virago, 1979), p. 10.

28. Frank Mort, "The Domain of the Sexual," *Screen Education*, 36, Autumn 1980.

29. Sigmund Freud, *On Sexuality*, (Harmondsworth: Penguin, 1977), p. 35.

30. Freud, p. 214.

31. Oudart, p. 36.

32. Rosetta Brooks, "The Body of the Image," *ZG*, 10, Spring 1984, p. 1.

33. Pacteau.

34. The phrase "uncanny double" is from Silvia Kolbowski, "(Di)vested Interests," *ZG*, 10, Spring 1984. The phenomeonon of androgynous cleavages on the body is currently given popular cultural expression in, for example, advertisements for Calvin Klein underwear. A woman with a boy's body (lean, taut, without feminine voluptuousness), save for partial exposure of one breast, sports "his" (Klein's men's) underwear. Theft and possession; the ambiguous writing and reading points to a continual transgression of the "thick sexual spread" (Heath) as a desirable position. Kolbowski quotes an ad for a Klein clone (appropriately called "Swipes"): "wear something of his and you'll fascinate him even more". Interestingly, according to a recent story in the *Montreal Gazette*, a picture of "a man having sex with another man who is made up to look like a woman" is judged as one of the more exceptionally "degrading" obscenity cases, "Selling Sex," 8 April, 1987.

35. Pacteau, p. 78.

36. Jacques Lacan, "From Love to Libido," *Four Fundamental Concepts of Psychoanalysis*, edited by Jacques-Alain Miller, translated by Alan Sheridan, (New York: W. W. Norton & Company, 1981), p. 192.

37. Pacteau, p. 78.

38. Kaja Silverman, "Fragments of a Fashionable Discourse," in *Studies in Entertainment*, edited by Tania Modleski, (Boomington: Indiana University Press, 1986).

39. Pacteau, p. 80.

40. Mary Kelly, "Woman — Desire — Image," *Desire*, edited by Lisa Appignanesi, (London: Institute for Contemporary Arts, 1984), p. 31.

41. From Constance Penley, "'A Certain Refusal of Difference': Feminism and Film Theory," in *Art After Modernism*, eddited by Brian Wallis, (New York: New Museum of Contemporary Art, 1984) and Annette Kuhn, *Women's Pictures: Feminism and Cinema*, (London: Routledge and Kegan Paul, 1982), p. 84.

42. Lesley Stern, "The Body as Evidence," *Screen*, 23:5, November/December 1982.

43. Chevalier.

44. Mary Russo, "Female Grotesques: Carnival and Theory," in *Feminist Studies/Critical Studies*, edited by Teresa de Lauretis, (Bloomington: Indiana University Press, 1986), p. 43.

45. Chevalier.

10

FOUCAULT'S DISAPPEARING BODY

Greg Ostrander

In the folds of the reduction to language, Foucault's thought discovers the body although this discovery is not stamped with the problematic of origin:

> The body is the inscribed surface of events (traced by language and dissolved by ideas), the locus of a dissociated Self (adopting the illusion of substantial unity), and a volume in disintegration. Genealogy, as an analysis of descent, is thus situated within the articulation of the body and history. Its task is to expose a body totally imprinted by history and the process of history's destruction of the body.[1]

History has thus destroyed the body. Certainly one day which, with Foucault, has perhaps arrived, in asking about our bodies and how they have been formed, we will discover how very little we know of them. Secular philosophies of the soul, related in this to a "positivism" of the body, have conspired to limit knowledge of the history of the body. If the body was not considered to be the despised prison of the soul, it was considered to be a sort of residual datum in which immediacy was deposited. There can be, within this positivism, a powerful de-mystifying tendency. Feuerbach's critique of Hegel's sense consciousness as originating inevitably in the body or the reduction, by the young Marx of Hegel's theory of sovereignty, to the body of the sovereign are two examples of this. But the history of the body — how it became what it became, not biologically, but politically; how it moves in this way rather than another way; why it enjoys in this way rather than another — this history has only begun to be written and it bears the name of Foucault.

Foucault teaches us that the soul is the prison of the body, an historical reality and the effect of relations of power. The soul is not merely a religious illusion but rather it is a "reality-reference" on which diverse concepts and fields of research have been engraved — the so-called human sciences:

> This is the historical reality of this soul, which, unlike the soul represented by Christian theology, is not born in sin and subject to punishment, but is born rather out of methods of punishment, supervision and constraint. This real, non-corporeal soul is not a substance; it is the element in which are articulated the effects of a certain type of power and the reference of a certain type of knowledge, the machinery by which the power relations give rise to a possible corpus of knowledge and knowledge extends and reinforces the effects of this power. On this reality-reference, various concepts have been constructed and domains of analysis carved out: psyche, subjectivity, personality, consciousness, etc; on it have been built scientific techniques and discourses, and the moral claims of humanism. But let there be no misunderstanding: it is not that a real man, the object of knowledge, philosophical reflection or technical intervention, has been substituted for the soul, the illusion of the theologians. The man described for us, whom we are invited to free, is already in himself the effect of a subjection much more profound than himself. A 'soul' inhabits him and brings him to existence, which is itself a factor in the mastery that power exercises over the body. The soul is the effect and the instrument of a political anatomy; the soul is the prison of the body.[2]

Foucault discovers in his investigation of disciplinary power, the arcane history of the body, the reasons for why such a history has not previously been possible. The third part of *Discipline and Punish* on "Discipline"[3] from the Man-the-machine of La Mettrie to the Panopticon of Bentham is a powerful essay on the politics of details and bodies. It demonstrates the possible meaning of a microphysics of power and what it might mean to manufacture an individual.[4] Foucault examines here the evolution from the invention of the spy-glass to the development of new techniques of surveillance based on the model of the military camp.[5] And, as suggested by the telescope, the trick is to see without being seen:

The exercise of discipline presupposes a mechanism that coerces by means of observation; an apparatus in which the techniques that make it possible to see induce effects of power, and in which, conversely, the means of coercion make those on whom they are applied clearly visible. Slowly, in the course of the classical age, we see the construction of those 'observatories' of human multiplicity about which the history of the sciences has so little good to say. Side by side with the major technology of the telescope, the lens and the light beam, which were an integral part of the new physics and cosmology, there were the minor techniques of multiple and intersecting observations, of eyes that see without being seen; using techniques of subjection and methods of exploitation of an obscure art of light and the visible was secretly preparing a new knowledge of man.[6]

It was probably inevitable that Foucault, after investigating first madness, then that master of life and death, the medical gaze, and finally the prison, would find himself confronted with that astute production of bodies and of codified reciprocity that is discipline. The mad individual, the ill, the prisoner but also the soldier, the student and the worker, are all entangled in a network of diffuse and anonymous micropowers. We must ask ourselves whether, with the discovery of the significance of discipline, we have not found the historical ground of the dialectic of recognition — a ground that is located outside the existentialist mythologies and consisting of the technology of bodies, not the labor of the spirit. We must also ask whether or not Marxism intentionally neglected the importance of these corporeal powers and if this has compromised any liberation struggles. But Marx, as Foucault notes, insisted in several places on the analogy that exists between the problems of the division of labour and those of military tactics.[7] This is the disciplinary red thread that connects the oppression in the factory with that within the army. According to Foucault, Marx was also aware of the importance of surveillance as a power mechanism.[8] With these traditional references and his strong praise for the "great work",[9] *Punishment and Social Structures,* by Frankfurt Marxists Rusche and Kirchheimer, Foucault attempts to defuse anticipated Marxist criticism of his perspective. He fails to note that Marx only examined these techniques (surveillance, discipline, etc.) as they were applied to capital. The problem of the inter-relation of the abstract domination of capital, which is based on the creation of the commodity, labor power, and the fine texture of individuated micropowers remains open. Without referring to these micropowers, it seems we certainly cannot account for the imprisonment of the mad whose chains appear not in the night of the medieval ages but rather at the dawn of an age that supposedly saw the breaking of man's chains. Neither can we account for the passage from the glorious tortures of an earlier age to the planned surveillance of today's prisons. These and other relations of power are not reducible to the capital-labor relationship.

In the process of unearthing these micropowers, Foucault has consciously condemned the traditional theory of power which saw the latter focussed exclusively on the concept of the state. Foucault's new concept means that power can no longer be seen as a property but rather must be now viewed as a strategy. Its model is that of

> a perpetual battle rather than a contract regulating a transaction or the conquest of a territory. In short, this power is exercised rather than possessed; it is not the "privilege," acquired or preserved, of the dominant class, but the overall effect of its strategic positions – an effect that is manifested and sometimes extended by the position of those who are dominated. Furthermore, this power is not exercised simply as an obligation or a prohibition on those who "do not have it"; it invests them, is transmitted by them and through them; it exerts pressure upon them, just as they themselves, in their struggle against it, resist the grip it has on them.[10]

Foucault's microphysics considers the state to be a point in the strategy of power, certainly an important point, but not the most important. It is not the organ of power *par excellence* precisely because such an organ does not exist. Beneath and surrounding the state operate a thousand techniques for ranking bodies. This type of approach is especially valuable today as a counter to the new forms of statolatry characteristic of much modern political theory. (Witness, for example, neo-Marxism's absorption in new theories of the state.) Politics, the regulating Technique, the supreme Jacobin 'ratio', has its domain continually eroded by the micropowers. Its autonomy is seen to be quite 'relative' with Foucault's theory. Even if the substantiality of the state is radically put into question, it is very difficult to finally eliminate that current of political thought that has always worshipped its power. The state is revived in some radical theories (especially, Leninist theory) as the model of a pure will to power to which even the party itself must adapt. Foucault has furnished tools that allow us to criticize this false autonomy of the state and explore the zone in which the political interweaves with the social to achieve domination. Foucault's approach is a micropolitical one that bases itself upon all of the recent work in the field of anti-psychiatry. However, unlike certain currents of the latter, he avoids any temptation of embarking on a cure of the soul.

The political investment of the body, which characterizes disciplinary society, involves a total inversion of the processes of individuation:

In certain societies, of which the feudal regime is only one example, it may be said that individualization is greatest where sovereignty is exercised and in the higher echelons of power. The more one possesses power or privilege, the more one is marked as an individual, by rituals, written accounts or visual reproductions. The 'name' and the genealogy that situate one within a kinship group, the performance of deeds that demonstrate superior strength and which are immortalized in literary accounts, the ceremonies, that mark, the power relations in their very ordering, the monuments or donations that bring survival after death, the ostentation and excess of expenditure, the multiple, intersecting links of allegiance and suzerainty, all these are procedures of an 'ascending' individualization. In a disciplinary regime, on the other hand, individualization is "descending": as power becomes more anonymous and more functional, those on whom it is exercised tend to be more strongly individualized.[11]

This means that, for Foucault, the individual is not simply an ideological production — that atom which is at the base of political theory of the seventeenth and eighteenth centuries. The individual is also a reality fabricated by disciplinary power. This new power uses the ritual of the examination as the means to achieve "the pinning down of each individual in his own particularity."[12] In this new system, "the individual receives as his status his own individuality... and is linked by his status to the features, the measurements, the gaps, the 'marks' that characterize him and make him a 'case.'"[13]

The new theory of the individual is an important result of Foucault's investigations, It leads to a different status being conferred on the individual and it throws new light on the anthropological disciplines that make of the individual their proper object of research. Foucault also contributes to the liberation of research from the somewhat ingenuous separation of ideology and science — as if ideology was the chaff and science the wheat — that characterizes the human sciences. Foucault shows that not only the theoretical choices but also the very object of study of these sciences are products of power. In a Nietzschean fashion, power produces truth — power is always power/knowledge and no knowledge can flourish outside of power.

For Adorno, on the contrary, utopia would be precisely an anti-power truth which for this reason abides in a state of ineffectuality.[14] Utopia cannot survive within the relation of power/knowledge. Utopia, for Adorno, remains committed to the idea of objective truth — it flees the vice of instrumental reason and forms the point of escape from power relations. Foucault, however, believes that this escape or utopia does not exist or only existed as the goal of the socialisms of the nineteenth century. The counter-attack against existing institutions must, today, base itself on experience. Perhaps, Foucault argues, a new society is delineated in the experiences of drugs, sexuality and community life. He himself stresses the experiential bases of his own theoretical innovations: his early experiences as a mental health worker in France, his experience of the "non-repressive" welfare-state of Sweden and of the overtly repressive society of Poland. Especially important, he argues was his encounter with the students of Tunisia during the mid-sixties who attempted to formulate a radically new political ethic *despite* their nominal adhesian to Marxism. Thus, much more than May '68 in France, March '68 in Tunisia, marked a decisive turning-point, in his intellectual/practical career. One also, of course, thinks of his work in the prisoners' rights movement in France (his founding of the G.I.P. and its theoretical effects: *Discipline and Punish*).

The source of new experiences, Foucault believes, will never be those who benefit from a given system of governmentality. Rather, new heterogeneous practices are always thrown up from below, from the plebs. In this, he agrees with Bataille against the more romantic notions deriving from Nietzsche, notions Bataille believed infected the surrealist movement of his own time. This romanticism resulted in an idealist longing for a "reconstruction of the foundation of humanity before human nature was enslaved by the necessity for technical work... or tied to ends dictated by exclusively material conditions."[15] The surrealists sought an idealistic overcoming of society in the sacred realm of "surreal" art or in a very restricted concept of surreal *activity*. They did not realize that heterogeneity, art or the sacred simply *are* a part of society. Bataille owed his understanding of this to his reading of Durkheim on the elementary forms of religious life. Even the surrealists' self-proclaimed materialism failed to come to grips with the actual links between art and life and, thus, earned Bataille's contempt: "If one determined under the name of *materialism* an offensive emanation of human life poisoned by its own moral system, a recourse, to all that is shocking, impossible to destroy and even abject — all that debases and ridicules the human spirit — it would be possible to determine at the same time *surrealism* as an infantile disease of this base materialism."[16] For Foucault, the linkage between these experiences of resistance and politics must always remain rather mysterious since the truth, for him, is always completely absorbed in power/knowledge and, thus, the movement against present-day power is prevented from generating clear social and political perspectives.

Just as he refutes the notion of utopia, Foucault suspects that of ideology because this always involves the reference to something which poses as the truth as opposed to error. Archaeology, on the other hand, realizes that it is the discursive practices which constitute the channels within which we necessarily speak and think. Genealogy merely claims to bring to light the knowledges deposited in these practices. There are only limited references in Foucault to something that might subterranneously determine the outcome — discourse itself is the first and last level on which the genealogist installs himself. Or as Foucault stated in his inaugural address to the Collège de France in 1970:

> It is as though discourse, far from being a transparent, neutral element, allowing us to disarm sexuality and to pacify politics, were one of those privileged areas in which they exercised some of their more awesome powers. In appearance, discourse may well be of little account, but the prohibitions surrounding it soon reveal its links with desire and power. This should not be very surprising, for psychoanalysis has already shown us that discourse is not merely the medium which manifests — or dissembles — desire; it is also the object of desire. Similarly, historians have constantly impressed upon us that discourse is no mere verbalisation of conflicts and systems of domination, but that it is the very object of man's conflicts.[17]

Foucault knows how to carry out a profound analysis of unconscious ideologies (that is, ideologies that are not ordered around a subject but, rather, are prior to any subject), seizing their quality of being merely circulating discourses.[18] However, in eliminating the concept of ideology, Foucault loses the nexus appearance/reality — a loss which has the ideology of the primacy of discourse as its correlate. Discourses only retain the reality side of this nexus. They are dense realities, charged with power/knowledge — positivities or monuments which can be exhumed from time which has concealed them. How, then, can they be criticized? To this question, Foucault gives no response. The critique of ideology, as developed, for instance, by the Frankfurt School, has always attempted to demonstrate the non-correspondence of reality with its concept and, consequently, revealing the character of socially necessary appearance that the latter assumes is false consciousness. This means that ideology has real social force. This is often forgotten in certain vulgar tendencies within Marxist theory. Foucault has broken with this (not innocent) neglect and has turned his attention on those discourses which, although presenting themselves as sciences, nevertheless engage themselves within a network of powers. This is the case, for example, of discipline; a subtle discourse involving the technology of bodies and the formation of subjects (that is, of the subjugated). Discipline is an unconscious ideology, which despite its lack of recognition remains, nonetheless, terribly efficacious.

An analysis, however, which insistently remains at the level of the positivity of a discourse, risks only attaining its object in part. Discipline is a necessary connection that produces subjects and of which subjects act as supports — it operates a continuous totalization. An ideological analysis would not only reveal the whole that disciplinary power constitutes, it would also indicate the space from which the possibility of breaking through this whole may emerge. The analyses of Foucault, by remaining at the level of the exhumed positivities, are prevented from seeing the internal possibilities of change. This is without a doubt imputable to the panic that Foucault (similar to Deleuze) feels for any theory of liberation — a theory that, for him, must always involve a new counter-productive totalization. Thus, Foucault's microphysics has a kind of fore-shortened perspective and is proud of it. The abandonment of the concept of ideology is, consequently, a sign of his disgust with utopia — the point of escape for radical theories.

The philosphy of desire remains more committed to the survival of the subject despite its efforts to disperse it. Whether desire is pre-formed à la Lacan or not, the subject remains tossed in the current of desire. This philosphy tells us nothing about the subject in its impact with the body. Thus, in both of its extreme forms (Lacan's pre-formed desire or originary desire), desire is hypostatized in the effort to demolish the hypostatization of the subject. A desire liberated from the subject is a 'quid pro quo' that can flourish perhaps in a mythological vision of madness. Desire springs up together with the subject of which it constitutes the other face. A dispersion occurs only insofar as a totalization was first posited. Desire is grafted in the political investment of the body. And the body, which is not merely a linguistic element, is irreducible. Its sufferings and enjoyments are not simply a matter of signs but rather of nerves and muscles. Since Foucault draws all of the implicit consequences from the archaeological finding of the body, from the discovery that the body itself is pre-formed, the result is a profound change in the orientation of his thought. The first aspect to be eliminated is the reduction to language. To be precise, Foucault refuses to align himself with the philosophy of desire (despite his admiration for Deleuze) and his barely commenced research on sexuality proves this. His study is focussed on bodies and their pleasures rather than on desire. He seeks to study the 'apparatus of sexuality' as a field of micropowers rather than sex as a desirable object:

> It is the agency of sex that we must break away from if we aim — through a tactical reversal of the various mechanisms of sexuality — to counter the grips of power with the claims of bodies, pleasures and knowledges, in their multiplicity and their possibility of resistance. The rallying point for the counterattack against the deployment of sexuality ought not to be sex-desire, but bodies and pleasures.[19]

However, in his 1963 "A Preface to Transgression," we see the reduction to language at work:

Sexuality is only decisive for our culture as spoken, and to the degree it is spoken: not that it is our language which has been eroticized now for nearly two centuries. Rather, since Sade and the death of God, the universe has absorbed our sexuality, denatured it, placed it in a void where it establishes its sovereignty and where it incessantly sets up as the Law the limits it transgresses. In this sense, the appearance of sexuality as a fundamental problem marks the transformation of a philosophy of man as worker to a philosophy based on a being who speaks.[20]

Six years later, when his historical research dragged behind it only the wreckage of a problematic compromised by ontology, Foucault described the work of the sexual archaeologist in the following terms:

... instead of studying the sexual behaviour of men at a given period (by seeking its law in a social structure, in a collective unconscious, or in a certain moral attitude), instead of describing what men thought of sexuality (what religious interpretation they gave it, to what extent they approved or disapproved of it, what conflicts of opinion or morality it gave rise to), one would ask oneself whether, in this behaviour, as in these representations, a whole discursive practice is not at work; whether sexuality quite apart from any orientation towards a scientific discourse, is not a group of objects that can be talked about (or that it is forbidden to talk about), a field of possible enunciation (whether in lyrical or legal language), a group of concepts (which can no doubt be presented in the elementary form of notions or themes), a set of choices (which may appear in the coherence of behaviour or in systems of prescription). Such an archaeology would show, if it succeeded in its task, how the prohibitions, exclusions, limitations, values, freedoms and transgressions of sexuality, all its manifestations, verbal or otherwise, are linked to a particular discursive practice. It would reveal, not of course as the ultimate truth of sexuality, but as one of the dimensions in accordance with which one can describe it, a certain "way of speaking"; and one would show how this way of speaking is invested not in scientific discourses, but in a system of prohibitions and values.[21]

As we can observe from the above passage, Foucault in 1969 believes that discourse is one among several possible ways of approaching sexuality. By 1976, however, and the first volume of *The History of Sexuality*, this becomes *the* approach *par excellence* to the study of sexuality. In this study, sexuality appears exclusively insofar as it is put into discourse or spoken by an insatiable will to know. From medieval Christianity, with its technique of meticulous confession, through *Les Bijoux Indiscrets*, to modern psychoanalysis (in which sexuality itself speaks), sexuality constitutes the field of an immense discourse and the object of a continual enjoyment via the discourse which is its basis. The transgression of the system of prohibitions defined by the discourse on sexuality is possible within this same discourse. The prohibition is posited in language as is the transgression — the prohibition incites the transgression and, consequently, the resultant pleasure. Thus, to demonstrate the way in which bodies revolt and engage in a strategic struggle against the moves of the dominant power, Foucault takes the example of auto-eroticism.

> The restrictions on masturbation hardly start in Europe until the eighteenth century. Suddenly, a panic theme appears: an appalling sickness develops in the Western world. Children masturbate. Via the medium of families, though not at their initiative, a system of control of sexuality, an objectivisation of sexuality, through thus becoming an object of analysis and concern, surveillance and control, engenders at the same time an intensification of each individual's desire, for, in and over his body. The body thus became the issue of a conflict between parents and children, the child and the instances of control. The revolt of the sexual body is the reverse effect of this encroachment.[22]

Foucault's discourse maintains within itself an interesting duplicity — if sexuality is a discourse, it is a discourse traversed by conflicts. This undoubtedly represents something which was not present in his writings on literature. The will to know, which provides the impulse for discourse, is completely involved in a Nietzschean fashion with power. A power/ enjoyment corresponds to the power/knowledge. Power and pleasure do not contradict one another but rather support one another. Where there is desire there is already present a relation of power. Even perversions are continually solicited by discourse which itself induces these transgressions. Unlike Marcuse's concept of the polymorphously perverse, sexuality is not a free zone but, instead, constitutes part of the power/pleasure complex. This is important because it indicates the elimination of the traditional concept of repression in Foucault's perspective. Sexuality consists of a network of micropowers, analogous to the disciplinary powers that, far from repressing the individual, permits and encourages his pleasures. The concept of repression, for Foucault, cannot avoid (as in Reich or Marcuse) making reference to a certain uncontaminated "humanity" to which each individual will some fine day have to return. Foucault, who in *Madness and Civilisation* was very much influenced by this concept, breaks with it in *Discipline and Punish*.

In his research on the history of sexuality, the break with the notion of repression is very marked, especially in his new concept of "power over life."[23] This is a power that channels but also provokes life — a power which compels us to live. This new "bio-power"[24] replaces the earlier right of life and death of the sovereign over the subject (the right to kill or to *allow* to live) and signifies the beginning of a positive political investment of life and the body. Sexuality, as an apparatus, can, thus, only be grasped against the background of this power. Power presents sex as desirable and even more than desirable. Power links sex very intimately with death which remained the 'outside' in Foucault's earlier work. The death instinct that traverses sex is an historically determined fact — it is entangled in the contemporary apparatus of sexuality. Foucault describes this employment of 'sex' as strategic ideal used in the domination of bodies in a concluding passage of *The History of Sexuality*:

> It is through sex — in fact, an imaginary point determined by the deployment of sexuality — that each individual has to pass in order to have access to his own intelligibility (seeing that it is both the hidden aspect and the generative principle of meaning), to the whole of his body (since it is a real and threatened part of it, while symbolically constituting the whole), to his identity (since it joins the force of a drive to the singularity of a history). Through a reversal that doubtless had its surreptitious beginnings long ago — it was already making itself felt at the time of the Christian pastoral of the flesh — we have arrived at the point where we expect our intelligibility to come from what was for many centuries thought of as madness; the plenitude of our body from what was long considered its stigma and likened to a wound; our identity from what was perceived as an obscure and nameless urge. Hence the importance we ascribe to it, the reverential fear with which we surround it, the care we take to know it. Hence, the fact that over the centuries it has become more important than our soul, more important almost than our life; and so it is that all the world's enigmas appear frivolous to us compared to this secret, miniscule in each of us, but of a density that makes it more serious than any other. The Faustian pact, whose temptation has been instilled in us by the deployment of sexuality, is now as follows: to exchange life in its entirety for sex itself, for the truth and the sovereignty of Sex. Sex is worth dying for. It is in this

> (strictly historical) sense that sex is indeed imbued with
> the death instinct. When a long while ago the West disco-
> vered love, it bestowed on it a value high enough to make
> death acceptable; nowadays it is sex that claims this equiva-
> lence, the highest of all. And while the deployment of sex-
> uality permits the techniques of power to invest life, the
> fictitious point of sex, itself marked by that deployment,
> exerts enough charm on everyone for them to accept hear-
> ing the grumble of death within it.[25]

Thus, the circle within Foucault's work is closed. That which was initially the ontological experience of death and origin (and of their collapsing one into the other in an eternal recurrence), is now the experience
of a power that seizes us. The Other of desire is now the Same of discourse.

To locate the unthought in a pure outside means to abandon it, finally,
to the web of micropowers. For a long time, these micropowers have occupied what seemed to be an outside and have, thus, made nonsense of
ontology. Origin, death, desire, transgression — all are not at all outside
but rather inside these networks. The theory that wishes to forget this runs
headlong into them. This is no cause for despair, however. It simply means that contradiction must be conceived immanently although this, of
course, is no panacea. That bodies appear in Foucault only as subjugated
is due to the fact that they really are such, rather than due to the reduction
to discourse carried out by him. This reduction *illustrates* a reality but,
because it prohibits the radical questioning of this reality, it remains to a
considerable extent politically impotent. Discourse, thus, becomes the
monologue of power or rather, the chorus of the micropowers. The radical challenging of reality would involve the question, in what way is it possible to think, always negatively, the breaking of this network of power
that holds bodies? Perhaps it will be necessary to start with the negative
experience of the difference that opens in every enjoyment between the
enjoyment itself and the totality that surrounds it. Perhaps, we could locate at this point, the possibility of an 'unhappy consciousness' of the body.
We do not yet know. All we know — and the later work of Foucault has
taught us this — is that the 'liberation' has already taken place. We must
now liberate ourselves from liberation.

Notes

1. Michel Foucault, "Nietzsche, Genealogy, History," in *Language, Counter-
    Memory, Practice: Selected Essays and Interviews*, ed. Donald Bouchard
    (Ithaca: Cornell University Press, 1977), p. 148.

2. Idem, *Discipline and Punish: The Birth of the Prison*, (New York: Pantheon, 1977), p. 29-30 (hereafter cited as Foucault, *Discipline*).

3. Ibid., pp. 135-228.

4. One thinks of the case of President Schreber who was the subject of a famous study by Freud which revealed the pathogenic effects of the disciplinary machines invented by Schreber's father.

5. Foucault quotes from "Rules for the Prussian Infantry" (1973) to show how the new power of the gaze reshaped these initial observatories:

    > In the parade ground, five lines are drawn up, the first is sixteen feet from the second; the others are eight feet from one another; and the last is eight feet from the arms depots. The arms depots are ten feet from the tents of the junior officers, immediately opposite the first tent-pole. A company street is fifty-one feet wide... All tents are two feet from one another. The tents of the subalterns are eight feet from the last soldiers' tent and the gate is opposite the captains' tent... The captains' tents are erected opposite the streets of their companies. The entrance is opposite the companies themselves.

    Foucault then goes on the explain the functioning of this new alert, discrete source of power: The camp is the diagram of a power that acts by means of a general visibility. For a long time, this model of the camp or at least its underlying principle was found in urban development, in the construction of working-class housing estates, hospitals, asylums, prisons, schools: the spatial "nesting" of hierarchized surveillance. The principle was one of "embedding" ("encastrement"). The camp was to the rather shameful art of surveillance what the camera obscura was to the great science of optics." (translation corrected; Foucault, *Discipline*, pp. 172-173

6. Foucault, *Discipline*, p. 171.

7. In Foucault, *Discipline*, pp. 163-164, Foucault quotes several passages including the following passage from *Capital*, Vol. I:

    > Just as the offensive power of a squadron of cavalry, or the defensive power of a regiment of infantry, is essentially different from the sum of the offensive or defensive powers of the individual cavalry or infantry soldiers taken separately, so the sum total of the mechanical forces exerted by isolated workmen differs from the social force that is developed, when many hands take part simultaneously in one and the same undivided operation.

8. See Foucault, *Discipline*, p. 175 for this passage from *Capital*, Vol. I: "The work of directing, superintending and adjusting becomes one of the functions of capital, from the moment the labor under the control of capital, becomes cooperative. Once a function of capital, it requires special characteristics."

9. Foucault, *Discipline*, p. 24 and p. 54.

10. Ibid., pp. 26-27.

11. Ibid., pp. 192-193.

12. Ibid., p. 192.

13. Ibid.

14. Theodor Adorno, *Negative Dialectics*, trans. E.B. Ashton (New York: Seabury Press, 1973).

15. Georges Bataille, *Complete Works*, Volume VII: *L'Economie à la mesure de l'universe. La Part maudite, la Limite de l'utile (fragments, Théorie de la religion, Conférences, 1947-1948)*, ed. Thadée Klossowski (Paris: Gallimard, 1976), p. 386.

16. Idem, *Complete Works*, Volume II: *Ecrits posthumes, 1922-1940*, ed. Denis Hollier (Paris: Gallimard, 1970), p. 93.

17. Michel Foucault, "Orders of Discourse," *Social Science Information*, 10:2 (April 1971): 2-3 (translation corrected).

18. There is no doubt that Marxism has for too long neglected the critical exploration of unconscious ideologies. It has too long lingered on the analysis of intellectuals as producers of ideology and consensus and, consequently, on the analysis of those ideologies which have attained a certain level of conceptual systematization. These ideologies can be conceived of as being the product of subjects and of being, at least apparently, a matter of free choice. The inverse is the case of unconscious ideologies which circulate without even allowing the questions of 'believing' in them or consensus around them to be posed.

19. Michel Foucault, *The History of Sexuality*, Volume I: *An Introduction*, trans. David Hurley (New York: Pantheon, 1976), p. 157 (hereafter cited as Foucault, *Sexuality*).

20. Idem, "A Preface to Transgression," in *Language, Counter-Memory, Practice: Selected Essays And Interviews.*. ed. Donald Bouchard (Ithaca: Cornell University Press, 1977), p. 50.

21. Idem, *The Archaeology of Knowledge*, trans. A.M. Sheridan Smith (New York: Random House, 1970), p. 193.

22. Idem, *Power/Knowledge: Selected Interviews and Other Writings, 1972-1977*, ed. with a preface by Colin Gordon, trans. Colin Gordon, Leo Marshall, John Mepham, and Kate Soper (Brighton, Sussex: The Harvester Press, 1980), pp. 56-57.

23. See Foucault, *Sexuality*, pp. 133-159.

24. Ibid., p. 143.

25. Ibid., pp. 155-156.

11

A MS.–MANAGED WOMB

Eileen Manion

he said, burn your body.
it is not clean and smells like sex.
it rubs my mind sore.
I said yes.

Marge Piercy, "The Friend"

Human beings, the most complex machines, the cleverest,
most dangerous species, does it not offend the rational
mind that they should be the result of the most random
phenomenon in the world, productive coitus...

Zoe Fairbairns, *Benefits*

When asked in a radio interview about the recent Vatican pronouncements condemning most of the new reproductive technologies, Dr. Patrick
Steptoe, British pioneer of *in vitro* fertilization, said he thought that to insist on connecting human reproduction with sex is to "debase us to the
level of the animals." For the scientist, natural is hardly a synonym for good
or right. The reproductive process, like any other manufacturing endeavour,
can be tinkered with and improved. To justify this view, Steptoe, and like-
minded doctors, define infertility as a disease, which should be treated like
any other, tuberculosis, for example. Since nature is not fair, why shouldn't
science step in and remedy the defects? Don't all the new reproductive
technologies merely expand a woman's range of choices? Isn't "choice"
exactly what feminists have been demanding for all women?

Louise Brown, the first child conceived in a petri dish, will soon be ten years old. Over these last ten years, more and more people — bioethicists, journalists, feminists — have been getting involved in the debate over reproductive technology. Most scientists involved in the actual research are at pains to distance themselves from eugenicists like Robert Graham, founder of the Repository of Germinal Choice in Esdondido, California which offers "superior sperm" of Nobel prize-winners to women looking for high-quality genes. Doctors like Steptoe, or like Canadian foetal surgeon, Frank Manning, reject the "eugenics model," with its unsavory taint of racism and Nazism, and opt for the "therapeutic model" of reproductive technology. They claim to have no ambitions to modify the race; more modestly, they just want to relieve individual suffering.

Feminists enter this discussion armed with a good deal of scepticism towards the medical-scientific establishment and doctor's benevolent motives. Nonetheless, we have had some difficulty coming to terms with the more sophisticated reproductive techniques which have appeared in the last decade. In the early days of the contemporary women's movement, motherhood seemed to be what barred women from full participation in the larger world outside the home. Implicitly we believed that a full, exciting human life was male, and women would wish to conform to the male model. According to Shulamith Firestone, who went farthest in this direction, the sooner babies were conceived in test tubes and gestated in artificial wombs, the better. Why should women alone have to experience the "barbaric... deformation of the body for the sake of the species"?[1]

Except among feminists like Andrea Dworkin, who sees all heterosexual sex as coereced, and all intercourse as unpleasant and invasive, this enthusiastic endorsement of reproductive technology has gone out of fashion. By the mid-seventies, feminists had begun to rehabilitate and indeed "embrace" motherhood.[2] Not motherhood in its present incarnation, of course, but motherhood as it might be. Writers like Adrienne Rich or Mary O'Brien insist that women need more control over motherhood, while feminists such as Nancy Chodorow and Dorothy Dinnerstein advocate more male involvement with primary child care.[3] But despite such differences of emphasis, most feminists writing on child bearing are suspicious of technology. Some because it is controlled by males or "malestream" science; others because the technologies in themselves seem problematic, no matter who is in charge of administering them. Nonetheless the hope or the wish that women should control their fertility and child-bearing informs all feminist commentary on the subject to date.

The self-managed womb is an ideal that has taunted women with its seeming accessibility since at least the beginning of this century, if not earlier. The complaint of women in the birth control movement of the twenties was that existing technologies were denied to women by the ignorance or prejudice of ordinary doctors and the conservatism of patriarchal legislators. Birth control campaigners like Margaret Sanger in the U.S. and Mary

Stopes in Britain sought to publicize available birth-control methods and get rid of restrictions which branded such information obscene. In their efforts to gain respectability for birth control, they were forced to collaborate with a male medical establishment that ultimately gained more power over women's bodies than women won for themselves.

Feminists of the sixties found themselves in a position similar to that of their counterparts of the twenties. The issue at that point was not the availability of birth control, but the accessibility of abortion. Again, it seemed that an existing technology was being denied women by male intransigence. However, abortion has never achieved the level of almost complete public acceptance that birth control has gained, for abortion causes conflict for women, as Kathleen McDonnel has noted: "Like no other dilemma that women face, abortion pits our desire to care for others, to protect others and avoid hurting them, into stark and seemingly irreconcilable conflict with our desire to protect and take care of ourselves, to act in our self-interest."[4] Within the anti-abortion movement there are large numbers of women and even a segment of feminists. For a feminist anti-abortionist like Ellen Tabisz, abortion is equivalent to rape and wife abuse — a wrong against women.[5] But even for feminists of the present generation who accept abortion, to have one is an admission of failure, for we grew up assuming that fertility is manageable and it is our job to manage it. Children are decisions made, acts committed. Or are supposed to be.

By the late seventies, feminists' emphasis had changed; more and more women were beginning not only to demand access to better reproductive technology but also to deplore the degree to which the very existence of such technology put women at the mercy of doctors and other experts. But at the same time as women were raising these problems, the very issues themselves were shifting significantly in ways that it would have been difficult to predict in 1960 or 1970. Feminists now are faced not only with the question of how to prevent unwanted pregnancies, but also with the vastly more complex issues of surrogate mothering, artificial insemination, *in vitro* fertilization, prenatal testing, and the virtually complete medicalization of the actual child-birth event. In the near future it looks like we will also be confronted with genetic engineering, embryo evaluations, more sophisticated forms of foetal therapy — the consumer-designed baby. Feminists have set up a woman's right to choose as the determining standard by which all reproductive technologies should be judged. But many of us now ask: have we really chosen to live in a world where children can be custom-made like suits, houses, and cars? If, of course, you have the cash.

At the moment there is no feminist orthodoxy on reproductive technologies, especially the newer, more chic ones. Even when we embraced motherhood, feminists still saw emancipation from the risk of an unplanned pregnancy as a precondition of equality for women. In post-industrial society, the unplanned life is unlivable. But the debates which have occurred within feminist ranks over pornography and sexuality bear witness to the fact that no matter how much discussion of motherhood-management has taken place, there is still no real concensus on the significance of child-bearing in our lives. Even before the menace of AIDS, many women were expressing discomfort over the ideal of recreational sex portrayed in por-nography and in a good deal of mainstream culture. The basic feminist complaint about pornography has been that it degrades women. Underly-ing this complaint, I think we can perceive the fear that the dignity wom-en had formerly been accorded as mothers or potential mothers had been eroded (partly through the efforts of feminists themselves since we did not want recognition only for our biological capabilities) but that no real acknowledgement of women as equal persons has replaced it. And if feminists do not have a consistent line on motherhood, the rest of the cul-ture is even worse. Motherhood is woman's greatest hope and greatest anxi-ety; it is pathogenic, pathological, but it is the ultimate romance. Nothing could be more confusing.

The reproductive technology issues that confront us at the moment are so complex and so laden with deep, primary fears and wishes that the only way we can come to terms with them is to re-examine some of our own history in this area and some of our assumptions. It is vitally impor-tant for feminists to enter public-policy debates on these questions. However, to be effective we need an analysis that takes account of our dilemmas and ambivalences. The recent Vatican pronouncements on reproductive technology demonstrate the danger of taking a single paradigm of conception and judging all possible interventions according to whether they fit it or not. For elegance and simplicity the Vatican model is enviable. But even some Catholics have wondered how many people will pay attention to it.

Some version of a back-to-nature approach may appeal to feminists in despair, as it does to some conservatives: a wish for the idealized certain-ties and stabilities of an earlier era. But adopting such a perspective will only condemn us to the sidelines, from which we may heckle but will hard-ly influence.

Instead of looking for a single determining principle, such as woman's right to choose, or looking nostalgically to the past or to a benign version of nature that conforms to our fantasies, I think that we must look critical-ly at ourselves as feminists, at the view we have taken of the body and of the world in which we live.

Birth Control Rights and Infertility Rites

A dye is being injected into Norma Jean's tubes. She has been instructed to hold her breath until the technician has taken the picture; the dye will show whether or not the tubes are clear. Her whole abdomen is filled with searing

acid. She can't hold her breath. The picture is ruined. Now
we'll have to do it again. She hears herself screaming. 'If
it feels like this, I don't want children.'

Sheila Ballantyne, *Norma Jean, the Termite Queen*

To begin, perhaps we can explore the ramifications of two stories. The
first comes from Margaret Sanger's account of her own life, and the second comes from the news of the last few months.

In her autobiography, Margaret Sanger charts her entry into birth control activism from her involvement with the case of Mrs. Jake Sachs. Sadie
Sachs was married to a poor truck-driver and the couple had three children. Pregnant with a fourth, Mrs. Sachs procured an illegal, back-street
abortion. Septicemia set in; the efforts of her doctor and the intensive care
of Sanger, at that time a nurse working on the Lower East Side in New
York, barely managed to save her life. When Mrs. Sachs begged her doctor
to tell her how to prevent another conception, he advised her: "Tell Jake
to sleep on the roof." She turned in despair to Sanger, a woman like herself from whom she expected empathy. But Sanger knew, at that time, only
a couple of "middle-class" methods (*coitus interruptus* and condoms)
deemed inadequate for the poor. Sanger graphically describes her sense
of helplessness in the face of Mrs. Sachs' inevitable doom. Within a few
months, Sanger was called back to the Sachs' apartment, for the same reason as before. The second time, Mrs. Sachs died within ten minutes.

Sanger dramatizes her reaction to Sadie Sachs' death as the moment
of her conversion: "I went to bed, knowing that no matter what it might
cost, I was finished with palliatives and superficial cures; I was resolved
to seek out the root of evil, to do something to change the destiny of
mothers whose miseries were vast as the sky."[6] For Sanger all the other
feminist causes of the day — the right to vote, the ability to maintain a
separate identity within marriage, the opportunity to work outside the
home — were trivial or irrelevant compared to what she saw as women's
fundamental problem: their inability to control their fertility and bear children when they wanted. With her background as a socialist, she ridiculed
the absurdity of offering working women "the right to work" when they
wished to get away from the onerous factory-jobs available to them. And
the right to vote, she thought, had little impact on poor women's daily lives.

Sanger dates her dedication to the cause of birth control (she came up
with the term) and her identification with the name of her journal, *The
Woman Rebel*, from her experience with the Sachs family. And it is the
misery of the overly fertile working-class woman, whose fertility means
death, or, at best, if she survives, premature aging, with which we empathize
as we read. The clear message behind this narrative: a cervical cap might
have saved Mrs. Sachs' life.

It seems like a long way from the agony of Sadie Sachs to the drama of Dr. Elizabeth Stern. Birth control, having broadened its dimensions into reproductive technology, has given us a new figure with whom to empathize, the infertile woman, or, as for Dr. Stern, the woman whose fertility is limited or restricted in some health or life-threatening way. The Sterns had signed a contract with Mary Beth Whitehead in which Whitehead agreed to be artificially inseminated with Stern's sperm and deliver to the couple the resulting child. After her daughter was born, Whitehead felt she could not follow through on her agreement and give the baby up. The resulting legal battle for custody of the child received an extraordinary amount of publicity and commentary, providing a focus for much of the anxiety about all the new reproductive practices and technologies.

Of course, the real parallel figure to Mrs. Sachs in the Baby M trial might be Mary Beth Whitehead. Has — we might ask — the fertility of the working classes, so deplored in Sanger's text, become a commodity available to the wealthy? Confronted with this situation, the moral of Sanger's tale is relatively simple. But to what or against what could anyone possibly be converted by the complications of the Baby M trial? The only conclusion to which I came after reading all the *New York Times* stories on the trial was that the more rationalized the process of reproduction becomes, the more irrational the reactions of all the participants.

To protect the right of anyone with $25,000 up-front to reproduce, the Noel Keanes of the world have created an elaborate new social practice — so-called surrogate mothering. So-called because to name the woman who contracts to be inseminated with a man's sperm and bear his child for money a "surrogate" is an exercise in New Speak. Inevitably such naming abolishes any claim she might later make on that child. Throughout the press coverage of the Baby M trial, Whitehead was diminished by the use of this term while Stern's claims were enhanced by constant reference to him as the "biological father." Only after she had lost custody of her child, did Whitehead become the "biological mother." But by then, ironically, she was no longer the "real" mother for that role was reserved for the adoptive mother, Elizabeth Stern. Surrogate mothering might more precisely be called contractual conception, since the woman hired to bear the child is not a surrogate and she is being paid not to mother it.

"Contractual conception" as I will continue to call it instead of "surrogate mothering" has raised serious problems for feminists. To condemn it threatens "a woman's right to choose" either to make money from renting her womb or to employ another woman to bear a child for her. To endorse it means to approve yet another realm in which the poor woman can be exploited. In the Baby M case, feminists who spoke out on the issue, such as Betty Friedan or Phyllis Chesler, were moved to do so through sympathetic identification with Mary Beth Whitehead. The sustained attacks on her mothering abilities made in the court room by the "expert" witnesses seemed to threaten any ordinary woman. According to psychologists who testified, Whitehead bought the wrong toys, played patty-cake incorrectly, and was "over-involved" with her baby. What mother could ever stand up to such hostile scrutiny? The fact that the court accepted such testimony and ruled for Stern and for the legality of the contract (in the absence of legislation making such contracts legal) seemed a victory of paternal over maternal rights. To feminists looking cynically at the court-system as a whole, it seems that fathers who want rights get them; fathers who abrogate responsibilities get away with it.

But not all feminists were prepared to jump on the band wagon for mother-right either. In a discussion of the Baby M case, Elayne Rapping noted that "biological motherhood... has only been sanctified in our culture because sexism offers no other source of self-esteem,"[7] and Judith Levine warned against a "retreat to the haven of protectionism and determinism."[8] If the psychologists' vilification of Whitehead made us, as feminists, uncomfortable, so did her lawyer's invocation of the mother/child bond and its inviolability. That mother/child icon has been used for centuries to beat women into subservience and self-sacrifice, and for feminists like Chesler to be invoking it just shows how confusing our situation has become.

There is a final irony in the Baby M trial that has not been observed in all the tortured commentary. Each side in the custody battle invoked the sacred quality of the biological connection of parent and child, just at the historical moment when the Dr. Steptoes are making biology seem less and less relevant to the whole process of human reproduction. Biology becomes fetishized, it seems, just as technology rushes to replace it.

In looking now at the current feminist disagreements and inconsistencies over reproductive technologies, it is perhaps worth remembering that turn of the century feminists were by no means in agreement on the issue of birth control — either its worth to women or its connection with other feminist causes. Women suffragists in the U.S. believed contraception likely to deprive women of the respect and authority they gained from motherhood or the possibility of motherhood. They feared that birth control would allow men rather than women to control women's sexuality.[9] Instead of contraception, they advocated "voluntary motherhood," that is, a woman's right to say "No" to her husband.

In Canada, most feminists actively opposed birth control until after the Depression: "For conservative feminists the answer was to limit births by increasing continence. Men were to be raised to the level of self-control enjoyed by women rather than women being dragged down to the lustful depths of men."[10] Voluntary motherhood was associated with campaigns for social purity, that is, attacks on prostitution and pornography. Social purity activists wished to eliminate the double standard through forcing men to conform to the more rigid sexual behaviour required of the Victorian woman. Since women had not yet gained power outside the home in the public sphere, they were reluctant to surrender what sway they had, or thought they had, in the private sphere, where they believed authority hinged on their status as mothers or potential mothers.

However, Margaret Sanger, Marie Stopes, and others in the movement, finally made birth control so respectable that contemporary feminists could embrace it with unthinking enthusiasm. Sanger very quickly moved away from her early socialist/anarchist rhetoric, in which she had advocated that women learn more about their bodies and teach one another to use diaphragms and cervical caps, but doctors did not immediately take up birth control, even when offered the opportunity. Many doctors were at first reluctant to broaden their notion of therapy to prescribing for the healthy. As the McLarens note in their discussion of the birth control movement in Canada, "Contraception was traditionally associated with the shadowy world of prostitution and quackery,"[11] so that some doctors felt their professional integrity might be compromised by endorsing it. They accepted birth control only to combat pathology; in beginning to recommend birth control to healthy women, doctors had to extend their own purview. Medical professionalism, of course, ultimately encouraged such extensions.

Sanger pragmatically accepted the necessity of medical supervision of contraception, but she added enthusiastically the romantic ideology promoting sexual pleasure as salvation, promulgated at the time by pop Freudians, followers of Havelock Ellis, D.H. Lawrence, or Ellen Key. According to David Kennedy in his book on Margaret Sanger, "That union of science and romanticism created a context of attitudes toward sex that eventually made birth control acceptable to many Americans."[12] Birth control became acceptable because it was ultimately integrated smoothly with both Victorian pieties about the family, and modern exaltation of sexual pleasure. It has enabled industrial and post-industrial notions of planning and management to be applied (ideally) to that most irrational of endeavours, human reproduction. And benevolent therapeutic interveners can oversee everything and correct any little problems.

So we see that birth control began as social reform and gradually slid towards a mode of social control. Efficient control over one's own body was the ideal offered to women; efficient control over the bodies of the over-productive poor at home or abroad is the parallel ideal offered to the fearful Western middle classes. We should never forget that all those active in the birth control movement were enthusiastic eugenicists. Sanger probably had more real sympathy for the poor than Stopes or Canadian promoters like A.H. Tyrer or A.R. Kaufman,[13] but eugenic arguments formed an important part even of her appeals to middle class audiences.

Although I have been looking critically at the birth control movement, I am not about to endorse the Catholic prohibition of artificial contraception. But I do think it is worth remembering the movement's history along with its multiple ironies. From some of its assumptions, as well as from the greed of pharmaceutical companies, we got contraceptives like The Pill and the I.U.D., both of which not only increased medical control over ordinary, healthy women, but also encouraged the view that contraception should be magical, should be as far removed from the sexual act as possible. Birth-control research and promotion did not have to take that direction, but did partly because of its eugenicist origins (the poor are too stupid to use anything more complex) and partly because of its connection with an anti-Victorian endorsement of female sexual pleasure (diaphragms and jellies are less romantic).

Feminists in the last few years have raised questions over these kinds of contraceptives, but at first they were accepted enthusiastically. Women of the sixties and early seventies endorsed without a second thought the ethic of planning, management and technical efficiency that use of such kinds of birth control implies. Messy considerations related to child-bearing should not disrupt sexual ecstasy; the fully modern child must be carefully inserted into a well-ordered life of work and consumption. As Germaine Greer has noted in her quirky critique of sexual modernization, *Sex and Destiny*: "To have rejected patriarchal authority within and without the self, however desirable in itself, is to have become vulnerable to much more insidious and degrading forms of control."[14]

Even now, despite the horror stories of the Dalkon Shield or the controversies over Depo-Provera, some feminists are still quick to embrace the latest techno-fix, RU-486, the "unpregnancy pill" developed in France. It prevents a fertilized egg from implanting itself in a woman's uterus, or if implantation has taken place, it acts as an early abortifacient. In the latter case, women might abort "without the knowledge that they were pregnant."[15] Writing in *MS.*, Sue Halpern discusses what a blow to the anti-abortion movement U.S. approval of such a drug would be. It might not be safe, she acknowledges; not enough testing has been done. But there is no question in her mind that it is politically correct and desirable to have such a contraceptive/abortifacient available. But shouldn't we — especially the generation of women who were guinea pigs for the Pill and the I.U.D. — be asking ourselves: do we want to continue to "trick" our bodies with chemicals and hormones or do we want to know and understand our bodies a little better? Should we continue to go along with the pharmaceutical research that assumes we are stupid? or the sexologists who assume that the idea of conception should be as far removed from intercourse as possible?

Even into the early 1970's it still seemed as if a woman's problem was how not to have children, or at least how not to have them at inappropriate moments in her life. But the more recent and problematic reproductive technologies address the issue of how to have children: the problem of infertility.

What is infertility? For the Dr. Steptoes, it is a disease. For psychotherapists, it is a "wound"[16] or a "life crisis... likened to the grief experienced after the death of a loved one."[17] Defined in this way, infertility demands complex therapeutic treatments, both medical and psychological.

A woman who suspects she is infertile may undergo any or all of the following tests: biopsies of the uterine lining; injections of dye or gas into the tubes and uterus to discern blockage; examination with a laparoscope inserted through the abdomen; assays of blood hormones; studies of chromosomes and immune systems; cultures to detect infections. A man will undergo a sperm count, tests to explore testicular circulation, procedures to check hormones, the prostate gland and the immune system. Medical treatment may include surgery, drug therapy or both. During or after the medical tests and treatments, the infertile couple will presumably need a good deal of psychotherapeutic help to come to terms with their grief and mourning, or with their new perception of themselves as ill — since if they did not see themselves as sick before the whole process, they will undoubtedly by the end of it.

If the infertile couple does not make use of all the painful and time consuming medical options available, then as Christine Overall has noted, "they seem to have willfully chosen their infertility."[18] Paradoxically, the promise that medicine can "do something" for at least some of the infertile may make the condition itself harder to bear. Some feminists writing on the subject have noted the ideological component of this response to infertility: "The desperation of these women who cannot meet the cultural definition of feminine womanhood by becoming mothers is accepted by medical researchers, ethicists and law reformers as unproblematic."[19] However pointing out to the infertile that they are victims of false consciousness and should consider themselves "childfree" instead of "childless" may not always be appreciated.

Ironically some of the infertility women experience can be traced to other reproductive technologies. From 1941 to 1971 in Canada and 1943 to 1959 in the U.S., many pregnant women were treated with the "Wonder Drug" DES (diethylstibestrol) which has subsequently been linked to fertility problems in their children (both male and female). In the early seventies thousands of women used the notorious Dalkon shield, an intrauterine device linked to pelvic inflammatory disease, ectopic pregnancy and consequent damage to the fallopian tubes. To anyone rendered infertile in such a way, medical technology ironically offers to restore (at a price) what it has taken away.

One in six couples in the U.S. today is infertile. (Infertility is defined as inability to conceive after a year of trying.) At least some of this infertility (for both men and women) can be linked to workplace hazards: workers exposed to many kinds of industrial chemicals, radiation, and lead have all experienced reproductive problems.[20] However, the big research-dollars do not go into working on the causes of infertility, but into heroic interventions to "help" the infertile. And few popular discussions of infertility treat it as anything but one of nature's mistakes, to be corrected by human ingenuity.

What are the options? In cases where a couple's infertility results from a problem with the male partner which cannot be corrected with surgery, artificial insemination by donor (AID) is a possibility. Technologically speaking, AID has been feasible for about a hundred years, but it has had its limited social acceptability only since World War II. According to Gena Corea in *The Mother Machine*, artificial insemination developed slowly because it was perceived as a "threat to the patriarchal family and to male dominance."[21]

Although ordinarily done for married couples in a clinical setting, artificial insemination is such a simple procedure that anyone can do it at home. In London, a group of lesbians distributed pamphlets on self-insemination which a number of the women had successfully practiced. They saw their use of artificial insemination as not merely a technique of getting pregnant but as a challenge to "one of the basic rights claimed by patriarchy — that biological fathering gives men power over women and children."[22] Since artificial insemination is such a "low level" technology, it can effectively escape the hands of the medical establishment. Whether it will escape the judicial establishment is another issue. In a California case, a gay man who had agreed to provide a lesbian friend with sperm, but have no contact with the resulting child, later changed his mind and wanted visiting rights. He won the paternity suit.[23]

Technologically speaking, contractual conception does not differ at all from artificial insemination, but it of course aims to cope with the reverse problem, female infertility, in the contracting couple. If it had not been for Baby M, this practice might have remained in its legal limbo. Baby M herself, now officially Melissa Stern, will be in court again since Mary Beth Whitehead has appealed Judge Sorkow's decision. Meanwhile, the publicity given to the trial has spurred legislators in some states to propose laws regulating this controversial social practice. In the New York State legislature, two Republicans, John R. Dunne and Mary B. Goodhue, have introduced a proposal that would place such agreements under the jurisdiction of contract law, legalize payment, and allow the mother no grace period (as a mother receives in adoption agreements) during which to change her mind. The hearings on this proposal have given us the unusual spectacle of the Catholic church and the National Organization of Women both testifying against it.

Contractual conception, as practiced in the Baby M case, is a fairly crude way of dealing with female infertility. Much more sophisticated are *in vitro* fertilization (IVF) and *lavage* (embryo transfer). The former has been used in cases where a woman ovulates, but has suffered some damage to her fallopian tubes that prevents fertilization from taking place; the latter is used if the woman does not ovulate. IVF can also be used in cases where a man produces some sperm, but has a sperm count too low for conception to take place with intercourse.

With *in vitro* fertilization, sperm and ovum unite in a petri dish and the blastocyst is implanted afterwards in the woman's uterus. This is not as simple as it sounds; hyperovulation is first induced with hormones, and then the eggs are extracted with a laparoscope. The ova extraction is a surgical procedure with all the attendant risks and no one knows what long-term effects hyperovulation has on the women treated. The success rate claimed for IVF is only twenty-five percent (the figures have been disputed, with some asserting that there is only about a 15 percent success rate).[24] However, Dr. Steptoe insists that IVF has a higher batting average than surgical reconstruction of a woman's tubes.

With embryo transfer, one woman is artificially inseminated and after impregnation has taken place, the embryo is flushed out of her body and implanted in the infertile woman. Although this practice is a fairly standard one for cows, it has so far been successful for only a few women. Both these technologies are still experimental, but once infertility has been defined as a disease, women offer themselves as guinea pigs just as heart attack victims line up for artificial organs.

Each time one of these glamorous new technologies produces a live baby, we have a wonderful photo opportunity: smiling couple, smiling doctor, and infant. A new version of the holy family? However, the ordeals suffered — years of infertility tests, operations, invasions of the body, and the mind — are not described. And the women who suffer the same risks and pains but do not manage to produce the live baby (at least seventy-five percent of those admitted to IVF programs) are not photographed. They might not smile in front of the camera.

There are other variations possible. A couple like the Sterns could have a child genetically entirely theirs by combining contractual conception with *in vitro* fertilization. One can't help wondering whether there would have been as much sympathy (not that there was very much) for Mary Beth Whitehead if the ovum had originally belonged to Elizabeth Stern. It is clear that the possibilities for assembly-line production of children already exist — egg and sperm donors might conceivably have no connection with gestaters and social parents.

If we now have *in vitro* fertilization and embryo transfer, can cloning and the artificial womb be far behind? We have amniocentesis to detect Downs Syndrome and incidently to tell us whether we will have a boy or girl. The results come rather late in the pregnancy to make abortion on sex-selecting grounds desirable for most people, but how much longer do we have to wait until a reliable test comes along that could be done in early pregnancy? More and more diseases, we are told, have a genetic causal factor — manic depression, Alzheimer's disease, to name the most recent candidates for possible prenatal testing, selective abortion, or medical intervention which takes the foetus as a patient separate from its "environment." The more tests done on the embryo or foetus, the more possibilities for treatment in utero, the less likely a woman will produce a "defective child." Isn't that progress? But a number of disabled women have raised the question of whether such "quality control" will ultimately reduce our (very limited) compassion for the handicapped or our support of social programs for them.[25] Despite the declared therapeutic intentions of the reproductive technologists, eugenics has a way of sneaking back into the definitions of health, quality, and fitness.

Competing Fears, Fetishes, and Fantasies

> You can apply ice to a woman's ovaries, for instance. She can have a child. Men are no longer necessary to humanity.
>
> Doris Lessing, *The Golden Notebook*

> And now they've found that they can't leave it to us. Not even that. The randomness, the wildness of it, won't fit into their planned century. How abstracted can they get? What's the planning for?
>
> Zoe Fairbairns, *Benefits*

Many feminists writing today on the newer reproductive technologies are suspicious, and with good reason. They see in most of them Man's attempt to gain power over Woman's body, her reproductive capacity — a male, especially male-medical, desire to take child bearing away from women and do it themselves. Attempts at developing methods of early sex determination in pregnancy, or methods of sex selection, are looked upon as particularly dangerous since sociological studies have shown that most people, given a choice, select boys, or at least select boys as first children, or select a majority of boys in a case of an uneven number of children.[26] Given such data, many feminists have raised the spectre of eventual gynicide.

In the short term, women fear that the process of child bearing will become increasingly specialized — one class of women as egg-donors, another as incubators, and a third as social mothers. And if artificial wombs can be developed, who needs women at all? Some of the feminist writing on reproductive technology is haunted by the nightmare vision of a world where women have been virtually eliminated, or their numbers significantly reduced and the few left kept just to donate their eggs. Writers like Gena Corea, Renate Klein, Jalna Hanmer, and Robyn Rowland, all of whom have written extensively on reproductive technology, assimilate this issue to other issues of female victimization, and see this as one more front in the war of the sexes. Infertile women who submit their bodies as "living laboratories"[27] are a kind of fifth column who betray all women, not through their own fault, of course, but through their socially constructed desire to bear a child.

However, the same writers who look with such fear and loathing upon contractual conception, *in vitro* fertilization, etc. take a very different view of artificial insemination by donor. Initially this technique was used for married couples when the husband was infertile but the wife capable of conceiving. However, in recent years, some doctors have been willing to inseminate single women or women in lesbian couples. And, a number of women have successfully inseminated themselves with needleless syringes, condoms, or even turkey basters. While such practices may horrify conservative defenders of the nuclear family, they delight feminists who see in AID a chance for a woman to avoid relinquishing "control over her body to a male-dominated medical profession or control over herself and her child to the biological father."[28] Of course, widespread practice of AID in such circumstances would reduce men to the role of sperm donors, although it can be argued that, given the political and social power of men, this competing masculine nightmare is unlikely to come true.

The reason I mention this seeming inconsistency in feminist writing on reproductive technology is that, for me, it epitomizes a larger inconsistency within feminism as a whole. On the one hand, we want to support women's individual self-assertion, since in the past women's individualism has been sacrificed to "the family" or the idea of the family. On the other hand, as feminists, we see the results of the deterioration of social life and communal responsability all around us and we attempt to remedy this: at the immediate level, with the establishment of consciousness-raising groups, support groups, self-help groups of all kinds, and, at the political level with support for day-care, health-care — a view of society that takes care, as women are supposed to do.

Feminists began by revolting against the notion that women's bodies are their father's, husband's, or the state's property; for feminists, no one but the woman herself should have the right to control her body and her reproductive capacity. Unfortunately, in many cases, this revolt against the notion of the body as male property has left us with the idea that the body is our property. Thus we have the vision of each woman controlling her own body as her own private property. That is an improvement over somebody else's controlling it, but as a theoretical perspective it leaves something to be desired — namely the element of the social. Nineteenth-century feminists were highly dubious about such possessive individualism, for they perceived in the loss of community a threat to women.[29] We are more aware of the ways in which women have been sacrificed to communitarian ideals (often by appealing to their maternal feelings).

To respond to the challenges of reproductive technology, a number of feminists are now trying to develop a feminist ethics that will take account both of the concerns of the infertile and the fears of the technology. Sue Sherwin has attempted to define an ethical model of "an interconnected social fabric, rather than the familiar one of isolated in-dependent atoms."[30] From such a perspective, the problem with technol-ogies like IVF is not that they are male, but that they give too much power to those not directly involved with raising children, to individuals who relate to others in an authoritarian, distanced, technical/professional way.

Thus the issue of reproductive technology cannot be treated as if it were merely a matter of improving techniques, or democratizing access to techniques. In fact, when looked at carefully, this issue raises important questions about what sort of society we want, what sort of families we want, what kinds of attitudes we want to take to our bodies.[31]

One response to the anxiety raised by these new technologies and so-cial practices is to insist rigidly that they be used to reinforce some notion of the family that exists primarily on television shows, in advertisements, and in the imagination of nostalgic social critics on the right or the left. Thus to qualify for IVF programs, just as to qualify for adoption, couples must be heterosexual, married, middle class, in other words, they must conform to TV — family stereotypes and they must never feel or admit to feeling any ambivalence. However, as feminists, we know that infantile wishes for the perfect family do not translate into good social policy.

The reproductive technologists offer us the ideal of "total family plan-ning" — the ultimate extension of birth control where you can select for family size, spacing of children, sex, intelligence, good health — whatever you want. Proponents of this new technology conjure up the ultimate nar-cissistic fantasy, "the motherless child, the individual atom of humanity that grows — beholden to no one — into an independent person."[32]

I have my own messier fantasy. Let's say that I have a friend who is a single mother with two children. She unintentionally becomes pregnant, but feels she cannot raise a third child. The standard options are: have an abortion or give the child up for adoption to some anonymous strangers. Neither prospect appeals to her. Now let's say we both have another friend who has been trying to get pregnant. Why shouldn't the first friend have her baby and give it to the second? Is this any more outrageous a sugges-tion than contractual conception or IVF? Undoubtedly lawyers, psychol-ogists, lovers, other friends might try to dissuade the two women from going ahead with this project. But let's say the two women persisted any-way. And while we are fantasizing, let's say they did not end up in court two years later, embittered, estranged and embroiled in a custody battle. The hypothetical child would belong to neither woman, but would be theirs, not in the sense of their being co-parents, but in some vaguer, more social sense. And suppose this idea caught on?

What I am trying to suggest is that we really do not need these new technologies to deal with the problem of infertility; what we need is more creative thinking about social possibilities. Unfortunately we are all some-what bemused by the seductiveness of technology and by the wish for magical-medical manipulations of the body. Unless enough people get dis-

couraged with the poor results of the IVF clinics or the legal and psychol-
gical complications of contractual conception, they will not just disappear.
Should they be legislated out of existence, as the Vatican has recommend-
ed? Despite my criticisms, I do not believe it would be wise to prosecute
people for attempting to have children in ways deemed unorthodox by
some. As I said at the beginning, there is no quick, easy formula available
for dealing with this issue, for it calls into question nothing less than the
nature of the world in which we live and expect to raise children, however
they may be conceived.

Notes

1. Shulamith Firestone, *The Dialectic of Sex: The Case for Feminist Revolution*
   (New York: Bantam, 1970), p. 198.

2. See Heather Jon Maroney's discussion, "Embracing Motherhood: New Feminist
   Theory," in *Feminism Now*, ed. Marilouise and Arthur Kroker, Pamela
   McCallum, and Mair Verthuy (Montreal: New World Perspectives, 1985) 40-64.

3. Adrienne Rich, *Of Woman Born: Motherhood as Experience and Institution*
   (New York: Bantam, 1976); Mary O'Brien, *The Politics of Reproduction*
   (London: Routledge & Kegan Paul, 1981); Nancy Chodorow, *The Reproduction
   of Mothering: Psychoanalysis and the Sociology of Gender* (Berkeley:
   University of California Press, 1978); Dorothy Dinnerstein, *The Mermaid and
   the Minotaur: Sexual Arrangements and Human Malaise* (New York: Harper
   & Row, 1977).

4. Kathleen McDonnell, *Not an Easy Choice: A Feminist Re-Examines Abortion*
   (Toronto: The Women's Press, 1974), p. 30.

5. Anne Collins, *The Big Evasion: Abortion, The Issue That Won't Go Away*
   (Toronto: Lester & Orpen Dennys Ltd., 1985) p. 204-5.

6. Margaret Sanger, *An Autobiography* (New York: Dover Publications, Inc., 1938)
   p. 92.

7. Elayne Rapping, "Baby M: Distrust Appeals to Maternal Instinct or Natural
   Law," *The Guardian* (March 25, 1987) p. 19.

8. Judith Levine, "Motherhood is Powerless: How the Baby M Decision Screws
   Women," *The Village Voice* XXXII:16 (April 21, 1987) p. 16.

9. Linda Gordon, *Woman's Body, Woman's Right: A Social History of Birth
   Control in America* (Harmondsworth: Penguin Books, Ltd., 1974) p. 98.

10. Angus and Arlene McLaren, *The Bedroom and the State: The Changing
    Practices and Politics of Contraception and Abortion in Canada, 1880-1980*
    (Toronto: McClelland and Stewart Ltd., 1986) p. 68.

11. McLarens, p. 122.

12. David M. Kennedy, *Birth Control in America: The Career of Margaret Sanger*
    (New Haven: Yale University Press, 1970), p. 71. Birth control was necessary

for what Paul Robinson has called *The Modernization of Sex* in his study of the work of Havelock Ellis, Alfred Kinsey, William Masters and Virginia Johnson. (New York: Harper and Row, 1976). It might be interesting to speculate on the connection of the new reproductive technologies with the "postmodernization of sex," a phenomenon described, if not named, in *Remaking Love: The Feminization of Sex* by Barbara Ehrenreich, Elizabeth Hess, and Gloria Jacobs (Garden City: Doubleday, 1986). According to Ehrenreich et al., "The crisis in heterosexuality had introduced new metaphors for sex that drew on the world of market relationships: Sex as a system of bartering, sex as consumerism." (p. 102).

13. For a discussion of Stopes, see Ruth Hall, *Marie Stopes: A Biography* (London: Virago, 1977). The McLarens discuss the eugenicist ideas of Kaufman and Tyrer in Chapter 5 of *The Bedroom and the State*.

14. Germaine Greer, *Sex and Destiny: The Politics of Human Fertility* (London: Picador, 1984), p. 209.

15. Sue M. Halpern, "RU-486: The Unpregnancy Pill," *Ms.* XV: 10 (April, 1987) p. 58.

16. Miriam D. Maxor, "Barren Couples," *Psychology Today* 12:12 (May, 1979) p. 103.

17. Robyn Rowland, "Technology and Motherhood: Reproductive Choice Reconsidered," *Signs* 12:3 (Spring, 1987) p. 516.

18. Christine Overall, "Reproductive Technology and the Future of the Family," in *Women and Men: Interdisciplinary Readings on Gender*, ed. Greta Nemiroff (Toronto: Fitzhenry & Whiteside Ltd., 1987) p. 253.

19. Rebecca Albury, "Who Owns the Embryo?" in *Test-Tube Women: What Future for Motherhood?* ed. Rita Arditti, Renate Duelli Klein, and Shelley Minden (London: Pandora Press, 1984) p. 57.

20. Carolyn Marshall, "Fetal Protection Policies: An Excuse for Workplace Hazard," *The Nation* XXXII:16 (April 25, 1987 p. 532.

21. Gena Corea, *The Mother Machine: Reproductive Technologies from Artificial Insemination to Artificial Wombs* (New York: Harper & Row, 1985) p. 35.

22. Quoted in Renate Duelli Klein, "Doing It Ourselves: Self-Insemination" in *Test Tube Women*, p. 385.

23. Gena Corea discusses this case in Chapter 3 of *The Mother Machine*.

24. For a discussion of this controversy over the figures see Rowland, p. 520.

25. Marsha Saxton, "Born and Unborn: The Implications of Reproductive Technologies for People with Disabilities" in *Test-Tube Women*, pp. 298-312.

26. Jalna Hanmer, "Reproductive Technology: The Future for Women?" in *Machina Ex Dea: Feminist Perspectives on Technology*, ed. Joan Rothschild (New York: Pergamon Press, 1983) p. 191.

27. Rowland, p. 521.

28. Hanmer, p. 185.

29. See Willaim Leach, *True and Perfect Union: The Feminist Reform of Sex and Society* (New York: Basic Books, 1980).

30. Sue Sherwin, "Feminist Ethics and In Vitro Fertilization" *Canadian Journal of Philosophy* (forthcoming), p. 15.

31. In her dicussion, "The Politics and Ethics of Reproductive Technology," Thelma McCormack makes the point that we displace many of our other uncertainties onto the technology itself "as if the technology embodied its own meaning, and was capable of generating determinate consequences independent of our wishes or needs." Paper given at Canadian Philosophical Association, Seminar on Practical Ethics. McMaster University, May 26, 1987.

32. Collins, p. 243.

12

—∞∞∞∞∞◯∞∞∞∞—

THE ANOREXIC BODY

Elspeth Probyn

Yet today the subject apprehends himself 'elsewhere', and 'subjectivity' can return at another place on the spiral: deconstructed, taken apart, shifted, without anchorage: why should I not speak of 'myself' since this 'my' is no longer the 'self'.

Roland Barthes[1]

She must learn to speak/starting with We/starting as the infant does/with her own true hunger/and pleasure/and rage

Marge Piercy[2]

Some time ago I came across Angela McRobbie's article, "*Jackie*: An Ideology of Adolescent Femininity."[3] I flipped through, interested in finding a reading of ideology which wasn't cold, distanced and impenetrable. In this article McRobbie seemed to be searching beyond a straight structural or formal reading of ideology to what might be called a textualization of a hegemonic practice. In other words, one could see the move away from an Althusserian insistence on ideology as always-already 'there', to a perspective that wanted to account for lived experiences (and contradictions) within ideology. McRobbie's article also attracted me as I had read *Jackie* when I was in my early teens. Her argument about how *Jackie* constructs a world for teenage women (a text which entices with its comfortable naturalized notions of femininity) seemed at first quite valid. I also liked her argument of the ways in which *Jackie* 'works': of how this teen-mag articulates romantic narratives to the mapping out of the everyday for its teenaged women readers. In the juxtaposition of romantic fiction with 'how to' tips on keeping your man or applying make-up, we can see how *Jackie* both naturalizes and reproduces an ideology of teenage femininity, as it literally and symbolically occupies the space of the 'private'. As such McRobbie's analysis is a tentative description of the hegemonic, and thus, uncoercive 'hailing' of feminine sexuality.

However, at the same time a small voice in me questioned what seemed to be the over-privileging of this particular text and the over-determination of the reader's experience. I mean, I read *Jackie* and I didn't go around yearning for boys and clothes and despising my female friends. In fact, buying *Jackie* was part of a small site of defiance and in a way solidified the group I hung around with. At that time in pre-Thatcher Britain, all state schools provided subsidized hot mid-day meals which were, as one might imagine, rather foul. In any case it became the thing to do to keep the 10 shillings for the week's meals and sneak up to town to buy chips, smoke a cigarette and read *Jackie*. This lasted for a while but gradually the event disintegrated — one of the group was pregnant, another spent all her time studying for the O Level Exams, one switched to a tougher (and more interestingly defiant) crowd, and I became anorexic.

What I want to underline is that none of us acted in a way that could be attributed to our having been simply hailed by *Jackie*. Even, or especially, in a boring Welsh rural community, there were many more pressing discourses and practices at work. I suppose of all the *Jackie* readers I knew, my anorexia would come the closest to being construed as some sort of over-determined reaction to the magazine and the ideology it undeniably articulated. Indeed, the argument would have been (and still is) that anorexia is a perfectly normal (i.e. straightforward and even quite 'rational') reaction to the dominant interpellations for women in this society. In this argument anorexia is just another example of being hailed. Or to follow a more seductive line, the anorexic attempts to disappear quite literally into our desire as women to actually become the representation of our flesh — to live out the lie of eternal slim youth. However, this doesn't seem an overly satisfying account, and certainly has little to do with the complex ways in which my friends and I read *Jackie*. Nor do I think that we can explain away anorexia by merely invoking the spectre of discourses hailing and interpellating the female body. This paper will try to open up and explore anorexia as an embodied moment of negotiation: as a site which shows up the articulations of discourse, the female body and power. While this perspective obviously recognises the power of discourse to position, it also requires that we be careful about collapsing very real voices and bodies into mere matter to be appropriated by discourse. Thus, in exploring the anorexic's practice, I shall be concerned with developing a notion of how certain practices come to be negotiations of discursive positioning.

Anorexia has recently hit the headlines as *the* post-modern illness. However, as with that other celebrated condition of our times, AIDS, the popular and medical press have imploded the multiple discourses that both the anorexic and the AIDS sufferer experience at the site of their bodies, into one causal and moral discourse. Thus, one condition is explained away as the result of women taking their bodies too seriously (trying to reduce them to the representations of their sex), and the other is the moral wage for men being too close to their own sex. In this way, the portrayal of these two conditions is the antithesis of postmodernism; the signifier and the signified have been fused together at the site of the body.

Unfortunately, these generalizations are not limited to the media. At this point, I would like to trace out a few of the analytic discourses which deal with anorexia, in order to consider the ways in which the anorexic is captured. In exploring the epistemology of these arguments, I shall be concerned with discursive articulations which contain and work over the body. In his book *The Body and Society*, Bryan Turner notes that, "if hysteria in the pre-modern period was an illness of scarcity... anorexia in the twentieth century is an illness of abundance."[4] This example of 'loose' discourse analysis seems to ignore the ways in which discourses are multiply interwoven, and hence do not suddenly and cleanly erupt within different centuries. From a clinical perspective, Hilde Bruch states that she:

> is inclined to relate [anorexia] to the enormous emphasis
> that Fashion places on slimness... magazines and movies
> carry the same message, but the most persistent is televi-
> sion, drumming it in, day in day out, that one can be loved
> and respected only when slender.[5]

Here we can see that Bruch leans towards a causal model of the media as directly responsible for all social ills, and anorexia in particular as a fall-out from experiencing too much representation. From within an American liberal feminist stance, Susan Brownmiller comments that: the typical anorectic usually comes from a privileged background and she is often described as an over-achieving perfectionist whose obsessive pursuit of thinness has crossed the line into self-destruction,[6] thus rendering any further discussion of anorexia rather flat.

As we can see, the dominant image of anorexia that emerges is that it is a modern affliction caused by too much affluence, women's lib., fashion and media. While in part all these factors may be in play, what we can clearly hear from these descriptions is that women are pathologically susceptible to media images. As such this idea is hardly new when we consider that the moral panics over television violence, etc., were academically grounded in research that took women and children as their (half) subjects. Somehow it seems that only women suffer from living in the late twentieth-century mediascape. Thus what we have here is the articulation of gender, class, media representation, and our present 'affluent' society. While empirically it may be stated that many anorexics are white, middle-class women, I would contend that this categorization of anorexia has more to do with the preoccupations of the Western medical establishment and the articulation of its discourse to other discourses that capture women. Thus we can begin to see that anorexia is situated at the nexus of several discourses, and that it is particularly constructed through the articulation of the body, women's sexuality, class, and the Western post-industrial society.

I would argue that it is specifically the insistence on the contemporaneous nature of anorexia, the popular discourse on anorexia as the 'epidemic' of our times, which fuses together the discourses on anorexia. In order to disturb this constellation of discourses, I would now like to briefly present an historical case, which if nothing else requires that we question the equation of modern mediated society and anorexia. Moreover, while anorexia is an important manifestation of current societal contradictions, looking at an example of anorexia beyond our own time and space may lead us to understand what Jeffrey Weeks terms "a history of the historical present as a site of definition, regulation and resistance."[7]

In tracing through the history of anorexia, we first encounter that the name itself is a misnomer: anorexics do not suffer from a lack of appetite. The term 'anorexia' was coined simultaneously by a French doctor, Laseque, and the English physician, Gull, in the 1870s. For my purposes, Laseque's naming of 'anorexie hysterique' is the more interesting. We should remember that at this time in France, what Foucault calls the 'hysterization' of the female body was well underway. But what we have with Laseque, Charcot and de la Tourette is a more precise classification of the female body within the general rubric of hysteria. This is a good example of what Paula Treichler has pointed to: that "diagnosis stands in the middle of an equation which translates a phenomenological perception of the human body into a finite set of signs called symptoms."[8]

However, before the medical profession got around to claiming the anorexic body, the Church had firmly defined the body in general, and had classified the anorexic body in particular as '*inedia miraculosa.*' From the early middle-ages on, there are several tales of young women who were said to live on the host and air. The Church was pleased to stake them as miracles until they were caught cheating, in which case they were burned to death. A case that intrigues me is one that straddles two periods and two discourses: from *inedia miraculosa* to hysteria. I shall outline this case as an instance of the discourses of the Church and the Medical vying for the body (and soul) of a starving young girl. This is to consider what Robert Castel has referred to as moments when "the discourses of the Church and medicine each tried to appropriate [bodies] with regard to producing knowledge."[9]

What *The Lancet* of 1869 called "The Strange Case of Sarah Jacob" took place in Llanfihangel-ar-arth, a small Welsh hamlet. Sarah started her practice of starvation in 1866 and her fasting ended in December of 1869 with her death. What makes her case fascinating is that she died of 'simple' starvation under the noses of England's finest: Guy's Hospital. To backtrack slightly, and to sketch out the facts — for reasons unknown, Sarah Jacob one day stopped eating. She remained in good form and her parents were quite proud of their daughter. In fact she was installed in the central room of their small farmhouse where, garlanded in ribbons, she spent her time writing and reciting from the Bible. The local vicar claimed her as a miracle and then went on to taunt the medical profession to come and prove him wrong. Guy's duly sent a team up to watch her and before two weeks were up she was dead.

From a Foucauldean perspective, this death could be seen as a consequence of what Castel referred to: the discursive appropriation of bodies. Sarah's dead body is situated quite truly in the juncture between two discourses. The medical discourse has literally taken over the ground of the Church, with its stated goal being not welfare but rather surveillance. Again, in a Foucauldean reading, Sarah's body becomes a surface upon which to inscribe the medical discourse and to delimit the realm of the possible: thereby effectively excluding the Church.

But is rivalry of discourse the only possible reading of Sarah's situation? Or is this merely another example of the progression of rationality in the name of the medical, clearing away superstitions and finally bringing to an end "the age of miracles which did not seem to be done with in nineteenth century Wales"?[10] While it is easy to see Sarah as merely caught between the sliding discourses, let us consider the events from another perspective: one which acknowledges her silent standpoint. She was obviously positioned to a certain extent by the Church, and by medical discourse (to say nothing of the family). Yet to consider her fast solely as a causal reaction to the interpellations of discourses is to empoverish her act.

To begin with, one would have to say that Sarah was positioned by more than two discourses. For example, it seems that she traversed a difference within church authority itself in the reach of one church's discourse over another. Wales was at that time (and still is) predominantly 'low Church', whereas Sarah was taken up by the 'high' Church of England, which goes in for a celebration of the suffering of the body much more than the 'low' Methodist faith. Without overly weighing the agency of her act, we can say that the discourse of the C of E sustained her starving, giving it meaning and allowing her room to live the contradiction of a poor farming girl dressed to the gills and reading poetry in bed. Of course, this luxurious position was dependent on the articulation of the Church's discourse with that of her sex (there are no references to male 'inedia miraculosa') and her act of starvation. Although this may be evidence that she was simply 'hailed' by the Church, I think that there is more at hand here.

To take another tack, we could describe the above situation as the operation of one of the apparatuses of the time. So therefore, Sarah was not interpellated by any one discourse, but was rather positioned by the articulation of discourses within an apparatus. Since the apparatus is not homogeneous, this would seem to be a more satisfying description. Furthermore, from this perspective we way begin to consider Sarah's starvation not as an act (thus implying some sort of free will) but as a negotiation of the particular discursive articulations within the apparatus. Thus we may begin to theorize the meaning of Sarah's starvation, and consider it as an embodied strategy that allowed her some small movement across the discourses of her time.

Difficult though it is to articulate historical events to modern occurrences, I would intimate that historically, and currently, anorexia can be taken as a practice or a strategy for negotiating discourses. Anorexia leads us to consider the contradictions within and between discourses, and the negotiations carried out against and across them. To my mind, this constitutes a site for the possible emergence of what Foucault has hinted at: namely that there are 'forms of understanding which the subject creates about himself.'[11] Here I am referring to Foucault's "technologies of the self" and the ways in which individuals "affect by their own means, a certain number of operations on their bodies, their souls..."[12] While there is insufficient time to engage with Foucault's argument, I wish merely to point to ways of conceptualizing practices (such as anorexia) that avoid the perils of a dichotomous argument of either strict interpellation or full human agency. The site of anorexia shows up the entanglement of discourses and articulations of any particular time, and leads us to consider how the meanings we live with, the significance of our selves, are produced intertextually across a range of discourses. In this manner the anorexic's strategy serves to disturb the nexus of ideologies which seek to contain women. To concretize these notions let us move back to the contemporary scene.

As mentioned earlier, many of the popular images of anorexia centre on establishing direct causal links or chains between the anorexic and the paper-thin representations of women. In fact the underlying structure of most popular commentaries on anorexia comes off sounding like a warning to women — don't try to be equal to the representations of your sex. The picture further darkens if we consider the epistemological assumptions of the clinical discourse which supposedly 'treats' anorexia. Although much of the family therapy work on anorexia is well-intentioned (such that of Selvini Palazzoli for instance[13]), this discourse's articulations of the female body, her place in the family and her sexuality is quite frightening. The underlying logic of this discursive formulation is to use anorexia to articulate an essence of female sexuality to the discourse of the family. This is particularily dangerous at the present time when the political right is increasingly sucessful in articulating the family and reproduction to its political agenda. Specifically what we see within family therapy is that the anorexic is reduced to what is called the 'dysfunctional role' within the family. Her actions, strategies and practices are dismissed, stripped of their possibility of meaning in the name of maintaining the family equilibrium. As if this weren't enough, the mother of the family is crudely blamed for the anorexia. Peter Dally, a specialist in anorexia, claims that "the mothers of many anorexics were frustrated and hence overly ambitious for their daughters."[14]

This tendency is perhaps an inevitable outcome of a discipline that rigidly assigns roles within the family and jealously delineates the family from society. It is however a movement that we can see as integral to the medicalization of society into a familial entity, and thus must be taken to task outside of its own perimeters. To reconsider my earlier analogy of AIDS and anorexia, it is clear that the effects of these articulations of the family, and conservative delineations of sexualities and a healthy society, are being felt beyond the particular instances of the individual 'patients.' The political ramifications are no longer hidden under liberal covers as sexual preference, and the gains of women are being legislated out of existence. In other words, if we consider that the anorexic disturbs certain articulations of the body, female sexuality and the family, the way in which she is currently treated should give us cause for concern; in many ways and in many psychiatric wards, the reproduction of certain vicious ideological articulations is progressing.

Having so far sketched out some of the issues that anorexia raises, I will try to bring together what these various signifying bits might mean for a feminist theory and practice of communication. First, I have tried to follow through what McRobbie has recently pointed to: "a different working practice or methodology that emphasizes establishing loose sets of relations, capillary actions and movements, spilling out among and between different fields".[15] To my mind this necessarily includes 'allowing for the ambiguous' — an approach that seeks and recognizes the intertextuality of our practices, and constantly works against the containment of these practices, whether it be by theoretical discourses, medical practices, or the everyday and night appropriation of the tube. This is also to work against the ways in which these institutions articulate our bodies, our sexualities, and our practices.

Second, I think that we should seriously recognize the power of these discourses to position. What I mean by this is that in looking at instances of what seems to be simple positioning by discourse (such as anorexia, or reading teen mags, or making ourselves up, etc.), we encounter complex webs of meaning. And while I don't think that we should forget Foucault, Althusser, or any of the other intricate analyses of ideology, I do feel that we must recognize the immediacy of our involvement in the reproduction of hegemony.

In some ways more problematic than the Althusserian move we find that in certain theoretical practices the abstract body (the 'post-feminist feminine') has become prevalent while the everyday body has disappeared. Thus recently we have seen 'the feminine' gain purchase within certain discourses on postmodernism.[16] To take one instance of this move, Tania Modleski wants to argue for the privileging of the feminine in the postmodernist's masses. Here it is Jean Baudrillard who supposedly upholds the feminine: "Baudrillard himself is justifying the masses ... on account of their putative femininity."[17] Modleski's argument becomes rather contrived as she goes on to say that "it is the mute acquiescence of the masses to the system — the silence of the majority — that renders them most feminine."[18] In this way Modleski ignores the potential insights that postmodernism might offer feminism in order to keep afloat an abstract notion of the feminine body. In another fashion Turner uses the feminine body as a prop as he mines the sites of specific female diseases; thus "agoraphobia and anorxia are expressive of the anxiety of congested space."[19] I would argue that the circulation of the feminine and the use of anorexia as a 'grisly metaphor' of our postmodern times is problematic on (at least) two levels.

First, the theoretical project of constructing an equivalence between the masses and the feminine allows for some rather reductive slides. For example, Andreas Huyssen argues that nineteenth-century discourses 'feminized' the masses and that "male fears of an engulfing femininity are projected onto the metropolitan masses."[20] In this way Huyssen wants to show that mass culture has been denigrated by association with the feminine but in fact he tells us little of the specificities of these discourses at work. Second, the current circulation of the feminine body, and the extrapolation from 'its' conditions, operates in the most ahistorical and agendered ways. Craig Owens thus can say that "they [women] have nothing to lose; their exteriority to Western representation exposes its limits."[21] As women are repositioned again and again in this line of argument as the feminine Other, I would contend that there is indeed much at stake in ignoring the deep articulations between history and female bodies.

John Berger has pointed out that the first person singular of the verb 'to be' "absorbs the past which is inseparable from it. 'I am' includes all that has made me so. It is more than a statement of immediate fact ... it is already biographical."[22] This biographical 'I' is already a deconstructing 'I' — partial and fragmentary pieces no longer held in place by the forgotten fiction of a stable present, of a ruling meta-narrative of being. However, this 'I am' also says 'I am a woman', that 'I am the daughter ... of a woman'. While the strands involved in these statements have been recently individually unravelled, the theoretical lines enabling us to go from 'I am' to 'a daughter' are not immediately obvious, occluded as they are by the insistence on the feminine. I would now like to briefly chart a quiet epistemological move that takes quite seriously inscriptions across local bodies. For as Adrienne Rich has recently said: "To say 'the body' lifts me away from what has given me a primary perspective. To say 'my body' reduces the temptation to grandiose assertions."[23]

This projection of a feminist politics of local bodies moves across already existing terrain as it takes up and re-articulates the gendered and historical body within feminism. Now, of course, this body is not a stable one — the body of '*l'écriture féminine*' is different than the political use of the body to be found, for instance, within the art of Barbara Kruger. However, the insistence on the processes which (re-)produce the specificity of gender is fairly consistent within the history of feminist thinking. Moreover, while the move to articulate local bodies theoretically and practically owes much to this history there are important distinctions here — this is no mere re-inscription of the 'personal is political' of previous feminist politics. We cannot ignore the specificity from where we may speak and to search for some 'essential' moment, some valorized aspect to be called 'real experience' would be illusory. However, as we keep moving from those theoretical moments there are other emergent attempts to ground the analysis of the social with material details — to fill in the individual in discourse without romanticizing a reified referent. As Iain Chambers and Lidia Curti, among others, have noted, this calls for strategies that can articulate diverse moments as we move with:

> less secure steps into an often murky landscape, illuminated by shifting shadows and light, populated by particular experiences, practices and knowledges, each partial and open-ended . . . .[24]

And it is within these strategies of articulation that the body returns. Jo Spence's work deconstructs the medical discourses with her own body as she takes the moment of her breast cancer to cut synchronically through the institutions of medicine, family and representation while diachronically opening up their affective pull. Here, as well as in the work of Hebdige, Steedman, Walkerdine and McRobbie[25], biography emerges as a central term, a turn away from universal structures, from essences as well as away from any unitary notion of self. Rather it is divergent subjectivities and local investments across several discourses and planes which begin to illuminate possible wider political configurations.

To return briefly to the site of anorexia, I would like to situate the anorexic body within a local politics. As previously mentioned, the anorexic is currently floated as both signifier and signified of the postmodern. Within Orbach's analysis the anorexic represents a subversion of patriarchy at work:

> The individual woman's problem — for which anorexia has been the solution — is that despite a socialization

process designed to suppress her needs, she has continued
to feel her own needs and desires intensely.[26]

Thus Orbach positions the anorexic as opposing the common-sense prescriptions offered to women. While it is interesting to juxtapose this interpretation with a postmodernist description of anorexia as emblematic of "the movement to the massless state when the body has succumbed to the parasites of postmodern culutre",[27] neither comes very close to the anorexic herself. Furthermore both these descriptions close down the anorexic leaving little room to consider the multiple ways in which the anorexic negotiates a particular historical moment. As I hope to have made clear, anorexia as a practice works across multiple planes as it shows up the contradictions within discourses. Therefore instead of exploiting the anorexic as a metaphor I suggest that we look closely at the specificity of her situation, at the particular ways in which anorexia strips bare the discourses that construct femininity. At the same time we must consider anorexia as a local practice used against the exigencies of place, time, gender, biography, age, family, etc. This conjunctural analysis moves from the ways apparatuses hail us to the everyday, and often mundane, practices that differentiate the institutional pull. This approach, therefore, considers the articulation of selves, subjectivities, biographies as inscribed and lived across a local body.

Notes

1. Roland Barthes, *Roland Barthes by Roland Barthes*, translated by Richard Howard (New York: Hill and Wang, 1977), p. 168.

2. Marge Piercy, in Kim Chernin *The Obsession: Reflections on the Tyranny of Slenderness*, (New York: Harper Colophon Books, 1981), p. 45.

3. Angela McRobbie, "Jackie: an Ideology of Adolescent Femininity," in *Popular Culture: Past and Present,* ed. B. Waites, T. Bennett and G. Martin (London: Croom and Helm and The Open University Press, 1982).

4. Bryan S. Turner, *The Body And Society: Explorations In Social Theory* (Oxford: Basil Blackwell, 1984), p. 83.

5. Hilde Bruch, *The Golden Cage: The Enigma Of Anorexia Nervosa.* (Cambridge: Harvard University Press, 1978), p. viii.

6. Susan Brownmiller, *Femininity* (New York: Simon and Schuster, 1984), p. 49.

7. Jeffrey Weeks, *Sex, Politics And Society* (London: Longman, 1981), p. 21.

8. See Paula A. Treichler's excellent essay, "Escaping the Sentence: Diagnosis and Discourse in 'The Yellow Wallpaper'," *Tulsa Studies In Women's Literature 3*: 1984 61-77.

9. Robert Castel, in Michel Foucault ed., *I, Pierre Riviere Having Slaughtered My Mother, My Sister And My Brother...,* translated by F. Jellinick (New York: Patheon, 1975), p. 252.

10. J. Cule, *Wreath On The Crown: The Story Of Sarah Jacob: The Welsh Fasting Girl* (Llandysul: Gomerian Press, 1967), p. 9.

11. Michel Foucault, "Sexuality and Solitude" in *On Signs*, ed. Marshall Blonsky (Baltimore: The John Hopkins University Press, 1985), p. 367.

12. Ibid.

13. Mara Selvini Palazzoli, *Self-Starvation: From Individual To Family Therapy In The Treatment of Anorexia Nervosa*, trans. Arnold Pomerans, (New York: Jason Aronson, 1978).

14. Peter Dally, *Anorexia Nervosa* (London: W. Heinemann Medical Books, 1969).

15. Angela McRobbie, "Dance and Social Fantasy" in *Gender And Generation,* eds., Angela McRobbie, and Mica Nava, (London: MacMillan, 1984), p. 142.

16. For a more detailed discussion of the issues at stake in the 'merging' of feminism and postmodernism see Elspeth Probyn, "Bodies and Anti-bodies: Feminism in the Postmodern", *Cultural Studies*, forthcoming.

17. Tania Modleski, "Femininity as Mas(s)querade: a Feminist Approach to Mass Culture", in Colin MacCabe (editor), *High Theory/Low Culture*, (Manchester University Press, 1986), p. 47.

18. *Ibid.*, p. 49.

19. Bryan S. Turner, *op. cit.*, p. 113.

20. Andreas Huyssen, "Mass Culture as Woman: Modernism's Other", in Tania Modleski (editor), *Studies in Entertainment: Critical Approaches to Mass Culture,* (Bloomington and Indianapolis: Indiana University Press, 1986), p. 191.

21. Craig Owens, "The Discourse of Others: Feminists and Postmodernism", in Hal Foster (editor), *The Anti-Aesthetic: Essays on Postmodern Culture,* (Port Townsend, Washington: Bay Press, 1983), p. 59.

22. John Berger, *About Looking*, (New York: Pantheon Books, 1980), p. 47.

23. Adrienne Rich, *Blood, Bread, and Poetry: Selected Prose 1979-1985,* (New York: W. W. Norton & Company, 1986), p. 214.

24. Iain Chambers and Lidia Curti, "Silent Frontiers", *Screen Education*, no. 41, 1982, p. 33.

25. See Dick Hebdige, "Some Sons and Their Fathers", *Ten-8*, 1985, pp. 30-39; Carolyn Stedman, *Landscape for a Good Woman: A Story of Two Lives,* (London: Virago, 1986); Valerie Walkerdine, "Video Replay: Families, Films and Fantasy", in Victor Burgin, James Donald and Cora Kaplan (editors), *Formations of Fantasy*, (London: Methuen, 1986), pp. 167-200; Angela McRobbie, *op. cit.*.

26. Susie Orbach, *Hunger Strike: The Anorectic's Struggle as a Metaphor for Our Age*, (New York: W. W. Norton & Company, 1986), p. 19.

27. Arhur Kroker and David Cook, *The Postmodern Scene: Excremental Culture and Hyper-Aesthetics*, (New York: St. Martin's Press, 1986), p.13.

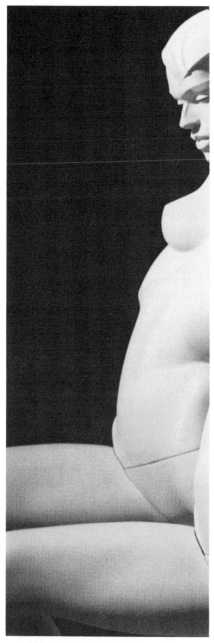

Art Direction: New John Nissen Mannequins (Brussels).
Photo: Christian d'Hair.

13

―――――⇒∞◦◦◦◎◎◎◎◎◦◦◦◦∝―――――

THE CHALLENGE OF LOSS

Sam Schoenbaum

In 1983 a close friend died of an AIDS related illness. I had gone through that last year of his dying, watching a body age about thirty years in twelve months. He was 35 when he died. In that last year, he had been treated with one medication after another, from Interferon II to chemotherapy. At a certain point it became evident that his body was no longer his own and that the medications were reacting upon each other leaving his body as some kind of host figure within this exchange process.

In 1985 I am reading an article by Linda Nochlin, on "Watteau: Some Questions of Interpretation". She begins her article by saying that perhaps the most striking thing about the paintings is the ruin of their surfaces. I am immediately reminded of my friend's body and the progression of lesions on his skin. One Watteau reproduction shows a detail — the cracking of its surface. From this detail, we see that the cracks form a layer which make the formal elements of the painting seem secondary. Linda Nochlin then goes on to talk of "the necessary connection of desire with death". This article is becoming more interesting to me. She then brings in her gender and identity through the issue of the male point of view on women's sex, as if the so-called male point of view is a thing-in-itself, regardless of the gender of the person experiencing it. I cannot imagine she believes that the female point of view or the male point of view could be knowable to both sexes equally. How can she know the male point of view as I know it? How could I know the female point of view as she knows it? Maybe the mere asking of the question is to her already a male point of view. We do, however, share a parallel point of view in what we cannot know about the other. When she comes to our conventional sense of pictorial space, we move beyond gender. I am pleased that she brought up the issue of gender in such an unresolved manner, because it is unresolved and maybe we can all get more mileage out of keeping it unresolved. Learning to integrate the irresolvable may take us one step closer to realising that death does not resolve life and that while our bodies are in contact with one another, we are a community, whether we like it or not.

Her description of entering the National Gallery in Washington where these Watteaus are hung, brings to mind that my friend's death occurred in a hospital and that the bureaucratisation of hospital management cannot be overlooked as part of modern medical treatment.

Linda Nochlin then goes on to discuss a current monograph on Watteau by Donald Posner, and attempts to interpret the figure Gilles, painted by Watteau around 1718-19. This Gilles, which appears in the painting as a Christ-like Pierrot, turns out to be a portrait, probably of an actor who later used it as a shop sign in his cafe. There seems a mystery present in Watteau's paintings, a melancholy, though this interpretation did not appear until the next century, when it suited nineteenth-century romanticism. And yet his contemporaries founds his work "gay and cheerful".

It seems to me that Watteau was in fact recording the disease of melancholia. When looking at historical interpretations we have to leave room for what has not yet been thought. It may turn out that Watteau found himself suffering from melancholia and that by externalising this through the canvas he was attempting to perform his own healing. Such an idea may appear quaint, but a recent show by Hannah Wilke at the Ronald Feldman Gallery does this very thing, it showed some polychrome sculpture pieces in one room and in another photographs documenting stages of cancer occurring in the artist's mother, as well as the artist with her mother and the mother undergoing hospital treatment. The polychrome sculptural pieces could represent platelets as seen under the microscope. The division of the two rooms could represent a distinction between the inside of the body and the outside. The exhibition itself could be a part of the artist's self-healing, if she believes her mother's cancerous condition was inherent in the family.

Of course it is not possible to know all this, or the more ritualistic exchanges between art and life, life and death, etc. We refer to our work as forming a body, regardless of gender. Historical interpretation, like the field of medicine, is always dependent upon new discoveries through research. Such factors controlling what goes in and out of the body, apart from economics and politics, shape not only how we live but also how we die.

When I first came to live in New York I was amused at the American approach to history. It appeared to me that here people's own experiences, in the course of their lifetime and through their body, is what becomes history for them. All else somehow falls into the realm of fiction. And with deaths now occurring so close to hand, our history is no longer amusing. How to deal with the losses we feel becomes a constant challenge to our survival.

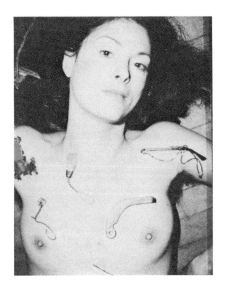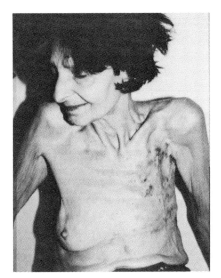

Hannah Wilke,
So Help Me Hannah Series:
Portrait of the Artist with
Her Mother, Selma Butter, 1978-81,
diptych, cibachrome photographs, 40" × 30" each
photo by D. James Dee, courtesy of
Ronald Feldman Fine Arts, New York.

Editors' note: *The Challenge of Loss* by Sam Schoenbaum and Hannah Wilke, *So Help Me Hannah Series: Portrait of the Artist with Her Mother, Selma Butter, 1978-81,* first appeared in *Art and Text*, no. 17, (April, 1985). We thank *Art and Text* for allowing us to reproduce this work.

14

~~~~~~~∞∞∞◎◎◉◎◎∞∞~~~~~~~

AFRAIDS

(an anti-medical science fiction for the end of the world)

Stephan K. Anderson

I knew I could not afford to be depressed. I had seen studies showing that people who were distressed had depressed immune systems as a result. The worst was after I was referred to the AIDS clinic at the Royal Victoria Hospital. The doctor there gave me a thorough examination. He took a culture of my tongue, saying " I just have to take a culture of this white material to be sure of what it is." That is what he was like, never saying more than he had to. Of course I knew he was checking for candida infection. Then he had me take off my clothes and be on the examining table. He said "You have this mottled rash all over your upper torso. Have you ever noticed it before?" He showed me what he meant, a kind of spotty coloration starting at a line between the abdomen and chest. If I'd ever seen it before I'd never noticed it as anything wrong. He never explained what he thought it might be either. He said under the circumstances he was not yet classifying me as having AIDS but that I was being admitted to the clinic because I was likely to get it. About the only thing he said was "I'm not telling you not to have sex." Then on the way out the nurse gave me a pamphlet entitled "Care in the Home." When I got a chance to read it, I discovered it was completely concerned with hygenic measures for people with AIDS at home. Instructions to wash clothes with bleach and how to dispose of bodily fluids sanitarily.

She told me "Everyone has to go to Anergy testing in order to be admitted to the clinic" and it seemed to suggest to me that a real challenge lay ahead. At this point I was feeling the very worst. Absolutely scared, sick of having blood drawn, of having these people see how overwhelmed I felt, humiliated. So arriving there in another wing of the hospital, I tried to act as bouncy as possible to throw off this feeling of foreboding. The woman at Anergy was very nice, joking, cheerful. She said "I'm sorry but this is really not very pleasant." She made little injections that puffed up under the skin of my arm. Then she wrote on my arm little abbreviations by each of the bumps. I asked her what they would mean and she said "Well, you must ask your own doctor that." Of course, anyone could figure out what it was. I was to come back in a few days for her to see the results. Of course, I saw the results before she did. There weren't any. I had even managed to figure out all the different abbreviations of all the infections agents I hadn't the slightest immune response to. There was one slight red spot because she had not made the injection deep enough and it seemed to be the injury rather than any reaction and she wondered aloud was that two or three tenths of a centimeter. I said three and she conspiratorially wrote it down.

A few months after returning from San Francisco, I started to get night sweats and swollen glands. Also I would get very hot during the day. It was the summer of 1982 and I thought it was the heat. But I would notice other people had sweaters on, and I would ask them is it particularly hot? And they would say no. It was shocking, I was young and it was the first time my body seemed to fool me to make me think it was warm when it was not. I eventually got so used to night sweats that they no longer even phased me a bit. After months of waking up soaked with sweat I would just roll over and try get back to sleep whenever it happened. Then I became very weak, I who used to be the last one to tire.

One day I tried to walk from Gastown to Stanley Park and I only got as far as Granville Street; I was so tired I could only turn around and walk home. At this time there was no test for any AIDS related virus, let alone treatment of any kind. For this reason I never went to the doctor. I knew they didn't know anything I didn't know. But then things took a sudden turn for the worse. I got big purple "bruises" on my legs with lumps in them. I was starting to feel like the character in Kafka. The doctor I had then was very nice. He told me he had no idea what was going on. He ran every sort of test and found nothing. Then I started feeling a kind of estrangement from the whole world. I remember I told no one about the purple marks, one appeared suddenly on a trip to Long Beach with a priest friend. I didn't tell him because I felt it would only hurt him.

I started to take huge doses of vitamin C and a few months later I became macrobiotic. And these things did seem to help. I felt relatively normal. The next winter in Montreal my health started to deteriorate again. I began to have constant diarrhea. The macrobiotics people said not to worry, it's just "purification" from all the vitamin C. But it didn't go away and the night sweats began again. By this time they seemed banal and routine. But after what was now a few years of this, a new kind of panicky dread was taking control. Every morning I would search my skin for any new blemish, and I would become anxious if I found anything and made a mental note to see if it would go away quickly. Then the AIDS antibody test came out. There was a lot of controversy over the usefulness of taking the test but I was quite frightened already, it could only do me good to have a negative test result as I was already so worried. So I made an appointment with Dr. Goldberg and went to see him. In order to take this test I would have to answer some questions. Was I in good health at present? What kind of symptoms did I have? Then he asked "are you promiscuous?" I said "What would that be exactly?" He gave me a rather easy definition and I said "Yes." He mentioned quickly that the results of this test were taking a long time to come back due to a lack of funding (at that point about nine months) and that there was another test, very expensive to perform that could be done in more urgent cases. In any event, he wanted me to return in two weeks for a "follow-up" visit, though I couldn't exactly understand why he wanted this I made the appointment.

During the next two weeks I had to move unexpectedly from my apartment. It took me all day to move as I had to constantly lie down to rest. When I came back in two weeks I said yes I would like to have this T-cell test done, surprising myself to hear me say it; I hadn't given it much thought. So I had to come in to his office in the morning (I'm usually never up in the morning) and have a blood sample taken at Goldberg's clinic and then take the blood myself to the Royal Victoria Hospital laboratory. Goldberg told me to get there quickly, it had to be there within fifteen minutes. I had no money for a cab so I half ran up that hill, really more than I could endure at the time, thinking this test is really going to kill me, just getting it there. I didn't have to wait long to get this test result back. That day an obviously solemn Dr. Goldberg ushered me into his office and closed the door. I was already feeling upset. He said "I'm afraid we have some very bad news. You have been diagnosed as severely immune deficient." He never showed me the results but I could read upside down that my T-cell ratio was .02. I knew that a normal ratio was 2.0 or 1.5, advanced AIDS cases having ratios as low as 1 or .5 or in rare cases even lower. "Do you have people who can help you with this?" I said yes. "Would you like us to get you the services of a psychologist to help you with this?" I said no. "We're going to send you to the AIDS clinic at the Royal Victoria. I hope you don't see this as our deserting you, you can always make an appointment with me to see me about anything, anytime."

I clung to the one fact that though my T-cell count was incredibly low, they had not told me that I had AIDS so I did not feel I had to take it as a death sentence. Or so I told myself part of the time. It also occurred to me that it was a common phenomenon in such cases not to tell the patient the worst, that they could be deliberately allowing me denial. I was never notified or given another appointment to tell me of the results of the cultures or Anergy tests. I thought this was pretty bad of them but if it was more bad news I didn't need to hear it. I would defeat this somehow. I joked with people that I would just live without T-cells if necessary.

No one, none of the doctors had said to me," O.K., we have this problem now we are going to do this and this to combat it." There was no information that if I got more rest perhaps or ate better or did anything else I might if not recover then at least do better for a while. This gave everything an undercurrent of helplessness. They seemed to be saying "there is nothing to be done except prepare for the end."

The hardest thing to accept did not seem to be the possibility of my imminent demise, but rather that my life had been so unimportant and meaningless. If I wasn't sure I would ever do great things, there was always the possibility that I might. Now it seemed certain that I wouldn't. It seemed such a very short and unremarkable life. Still, I said to myself that I wasn't taking this as a death sentence. Like everyone else, I needed hope. I can tell you that any religious ideas I had were of absolutely no comfort to me.

I felt no one could understand what I was going through at all. I always felt more and more that there was a huge distance, a thick wall between me and everyone else, and though I still wanted their company sometimes, my friends seemed oddly irrelevant to me. For the first time. Sometimes I would try to explain but their sympathies seemed ridiculous to me. Mostly I didn't tell them because they seemed to me no more than grown-up children who really could only trouble me because it stirred up trouble in themselves. I would end up helping them deal with their reactions, which I didn't have the energy to do. The ones that didn't know what was going on would always be saying "Oh, you look so tired, Stephan, you must get more sleep, you must eat more, you look so thin these days." Those who did know would try to encourage me by saying I was looking better.

One friend, Anne-Louise, reacted differently when I told her. She had been asking me what was bothering me lately, I seemed so distant and thoughtful to her. When I told her she simply said "I think I can help you. I think we can do something about this." She said I would do better if I followed a special diet based on my particular constitution according to an ancient Indian health practice called Ayurveda. I had already heard a similar story with macrobiotics and in the end it didn't seem to do me any good. But she gave me some printed materials she had from a course she took, and it seemed to make sense, and in any case as it cost nothing really, I would try it. All this time I had a terrible time sleeping, probably because I was so tired of waking up in a fever and not being able to get back to sleep. She told me to put coconut oil on my head and on the soles of my feet before going to bed. It seemed absurd but it worked very well. In fact, for the first time in years it seemed that I'd really felt pleasantly sleepy rather than nervous and hyper-aware. She also told me to eat some more sugar and lots of vegetable oil and butter which I found particularly shocking. She said that for me it was good, according to my constitution.

Actually, it is all quite complex. There were always new suggestions Anne-Louise would make every week but as I was feeling very much better after a few weeks I was more and more curious. She lent me a book on Ayurveda that had a lot of stuff about how one could be in balance with the seasons and take this and that spice or herbs according to a certain problem or time of the year. But it also said that the state of consciousness determines the state of the body, and in a section entitled Unified Field Based Perfect Health it said that Transcendental Meditation would be necessary for perfect health. It said all sorts of worries and fears would fall away with the practice of meditation and that this would lead to a state of "immortality." This seemed ridiculous, as did the picture of the doctor who wrote the book showing him to be an elderly Indian gentleman, white haired and obviously getting old like everyone else. However, as a naturally nervous sort of person in difficult circumstances, this idea of meditation appealed to me, the kind of calm that Anne-Louise had appealed to me. I wanted to have all possible means to fight for my health, so I took the course, which was rather expensive.

As the months went by I felt better and better. I had started Ayurveda in September and in November I saw an Ayurvedic physician who was making a tour of North American cities and I bought a herbal preparation from him that is supposed to specifically enhance immunity. What I found convincing was that it tasted so good to me. Nothing has ever tasted so good to me before or since.

In December I visited my parents. I think they were a bit shocked at how much older I looked but I knew I looked far better than I did a few months earlier. Still, all the time I was there I was afraid of getting suddenly ill. Indeed, I got a funny rash when I was there, but maybe it was just an allergy. They found my new diet, meditation etc. very hard to understand. Then over a month after I returned to Montreal and over six months since I received the T-cell ratio results I got back the antibody test results. They were negative. Whatever my immune deficiency, it was not the AIDS virus. I did not jump for joy. I thought of what I had gone through. It was only over the next few weeks and even months that I began to really appreciate what had happened to me. I thought of the hell I had gone through, how I had sometimes thought of suicide. Slowly I began to feel again that I could relate to people and no longer felt this distance from them. Then I had the revelation that in all the time after the T-cell test results and the negative antibody results I don't think I ever really felt any kind of joy or real sadness. I still enjoyed life then, enjoyed many things and often protested when people said I looked depressed. But now I noticed a great joy in simple things, in walking through the snow or eating lunch, or in talking to friends and I realized that in all that time there had been pleasures but no joy at all. And at other times I now felt terribly sad, bitter and depressed at what I had done through. I never quite felt that way when I considered myself ill; I could never afford to be sad. I felt I had to conserve all my energy to survive. And then I realized that I was no longer trying to eat the right things all the time, that I wasn't keeping to the Ayurvedic guidelines so strictly anymore, and that I no longer compulsively searched my skin for signs of new blemishes or was afraid of other change in my body.

I realized I could still get AIDS but somehow I felt I could never be as afraid of it again.

IV

BODY WRITING

The postmodern body is penetrated by power and marked by all the signs of ideology. Indeed, when power actually produces the body and when the body itself becomes conditional for the operation of a fully relational power, then the postmodern body is already only a virtual afterimage of its own simulated existence. Virtual sex, virtual eyes, virtual organs, virtual nervous system: that is the disappearing body now as the cynical site of its own exteriorization (and immolation) in the mediascape. And so, what follows is body writing for the end of the world. No longer writing *about* the body or even *from* the body, but robo-bodies writing the violent and excessive history of their (own) disappearance into the simulacrum. It's Cathy Acker still in Haiti and Jean Baudrillard spitting on the Eiffel Tower as letters to excess for a hyper-modern time.

15

CRIMINOLOGICAL DISPLACEMENTS: A SOCIOLOGICAL DECONSTRUCTION

Stephen Pfohl and Avery Gordon

This text re-presents a deconstructive sociological reading of Michel Foucault's several investigations of the genealogy of the human sciences. The sociological history of criminology is taken as an exemplar of the relation between the form and content of western social science theorizing and the historically material pleasures associated with the production of a certain knowledge of "Other"ness within the intellectual marketplace of modern western society. In analyzing the epistemological pleasures of human scientific knowledge in terms of sadism, surveillance, and the realization of a normal subject in discourse, connections are made between the structures of social scientific knowledge and the hierarchical organization of capitalist, racist, heterosexist, and imperialist power. The essay concludes with an outline of the methodological and political implications of a critical post-structuralist intervention into social science theorizing.

A Preface: Some Words About Power and Knowledge and the Text that Follows

[P]ower and knowledge directly imply one another... There is no power relation without the correlative constitution of a field of knowledge, nor any knowledge that

> *does not presuppose and constitute at the same time pow-*
> *er relations.*[1]

This is a story of what we (in relation to each other) read, that is re(w)rite, as important sociological and political implications of Michel Foucault's several investigations of the genealogy of the human sciences. The text that follows re-presents a story of the production of a certain subject in history. Our *descent* into the narrative confines of this story partially retraces the material and imaginary *emergence* of a certain "he" who speaks in the name of the law-like truths of social science.[2] This he of whom we write occupies (or is occupied by) a powerful positioning of knowledge within the institutional sites of formal theoretical practice in the advanced capitalist west. He captains that ship we call the research enterprise, gate-keeps entry into scholarly journals, presides over the classroom, chairs dissertation committees and dispenses awards of fellowships for work deemed worthy. He is the father of a certain discipline, the master of a given "order of things", in time marked ceremoniously through ritual.[3]

This is a text about the rituals of a given epistemological practice and its pleasures. Rituals of the book, the boardroom, the bedroom; rituals of the classroom, the office, the factory, the computer center, the penitentiary, the lunatic asylum, the television. Each of these sites of epistemological ritual is the material locus of an imaginary production of a given order of things.[4] It is also a site of sacrifice where some things other are banished from commonsense, erased from memory. To ritually enact the knowledge of modern western Man is to enter the hierarchical theater of a particular homogeneous enlightenment. It is also to make dark, unmemorable or unconscious the reciprocal possibilities of a heterogeneity of other knowledges, other relations of power foreclosed or silenced. It is to repeatedly discover ourselves positioned within the institutional social apparatus of a particularly violent epistemology, to find ourselves seduced or secured within the linguistic prisonhouse of capitalist, racist, heterosexist and imperial hierarchies. It is to realize our thoughts and theories, desires and actions, but only within the exclusionary rule of a specific historical conjuncture of power and knowledge. This is a history of our present. We want out.

We want to de-realize the hierarchical role of modern Man, to intervene within against the hegemonic codes that socially dominate our senses of time and space. Codes of empire. Phallic codes. Codes of economy and color. We want out. We want a different knowledge and want knowledge differently. We want a "partial" knowledge: a cognitive, moral and carnal relation to power that is, at once, always incomplete and politically reflexive of its own material and imaginary positioning within history. We want a knowledge based not in the universal name of the Father, nor in the codified rule of the son/sun (the western daydream of omnipresent enlightenment), nor in the pure spirit of positivist mastery (the desire for a picture

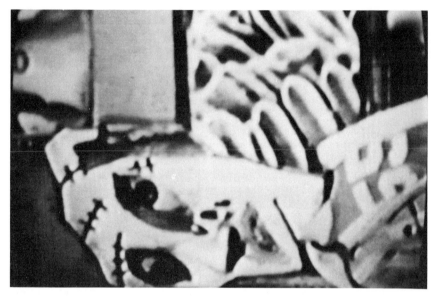

Still from video-text *Criminological Displacements*. Source: Joseph La Mantia and Stephen Pfohl, *Normalizing Relations* (detail), photocollage, 1985.

perfect word-world). We want a different knowledge and want knowledge differently. This is our desire: to displace the hegemonic closures of contemporary social science theorizing so as to open ourselves out towards others, toward other relations of power and knowledge. This is a desire to disturb and restructure the epistemological sites by which we are identified, to de-fetishize the routine ritual productions and normatively unnoticed sacrifices that operate upon, within and through us in the academic marketplace of an almost fully industrialized culture of transnational capital. This is our desire: a sociological deconstruction.

Our desire for a different practice of theoretical knowledge leads us to interrogate the epistemological form or aesthetics of sociological writing as well as its content, the art as well as artifactual effects of "normal (social) science." This interrogation leads us to conclude that what sociology ordinarily refers to as social facts are, in fact, nothing but powerful forms of fiction. As such, we find our own words about such matters poured through an opening in the sociological imagination partially realized in the late writings of Emile Durkheim[5] and in the subsequent investigations of Marcel Mauss, Georges Bataille, Michel Leiris and the other "surrealist ethnographers" associated with the College of Sociology in France in the years between the world wars in Europe.[6] We read these critical breaks within the development of French social theory as anticipating what has come to be known in the years following May 1968 as the intervention of post-structuralist theorizing. Historically situated between a revolutionary refusal of France's colonized Others to submit to the homogenizing gaze of western anthropological imperialism and a practical political desire to counter the epistemological lure of fascism, certain critical French social theorists, writers, and artists were drawn into a desire for a deconstructive displacement of the facts of everyday western social life and of the rules of the sociological method that theoretically secured their reign.

Our desires for a different theoretical practice are situated not dissmilarly in the United States in the late 1980s. The resistance of colonized Others and the lure of fascism; these are forces in the history of our present as well. Signs of resistance are today noticeable in a variety of counter-institutional sites whether simply as expressive explosions of violence or as reflexive strategies of historical change. Consider the ecstatic rituals of violence against either the self or its other that express the abandonment of once productive urban wasteland by the migration of transnational capital to the cheaper labor markets of its "periphery." Or the more reflexive collective resistance of women, peoples of color, and of those who desire sex differently, or of those at the imperial margins who "just say no" to a continuation of economic, cultural, and political subordination. In order for critical western sociological theorists to enter into a reciprocal dialogue with these hetereogeneous Others who resist our normal science, we must first ourselves resist the homogenizing effects of the discipline that has become us. This will not be easy. It requires both an unlearning of our given epistemological confines and some different methods, that is, different ritual practices of power and knowledge.

This is also the case with regard to the possibilities of resisting the epistemological lures of fascism. "Stay tuned." We are today popularly informed of who we are, what we desire, and what we might possess through a mass of electronically mediated images. And so we are lured into the fascinations of fascism.[7] Daily exposure to images of "Dynasty", "Wheel of Fortune", and divinely inspired invocations for random roadblocks and mandatory drug testing. Screen to screen, stadium to stadium, long lines of beautiful young men in uniforms in search of the thrill of victory; the pleasures of a perfect body and the pornographic excitement of becoming almost fully commodified, a living doll, the word made advert then flesh, the perfect model, the simulacrum. Accuracy in academia — what critical sociological practice can counter this fascinating fascist appropriation of certain violent fictions as truly the real world without end, Amen? The bombing of abortion clinics, the burning of crosses, paramilitary mens' clubs practicing in parking lots, a resurgence of the Klan, US sponsored terrorism aimed at the suppression of struggles for justice in Central America and the relationship between the US and South Africa. And from the airwaves, above it all, the televised image of an actor playing the role of a President declaring himself a *Contra*, advertising democracy just after

"Jeopardy" and some time after Hiroshima; and how many years after Watts, after the Christmas bombing of Hanoi, or "Superbowl IV", *Rambo*, "Leave it to Beaver"? What difference? The specter of fascist epistemology: this is also a significant feature of the history of our present, perhaps more compexly, more subtly, more electric.

We want a way out. This is a desire for a different theoretical practice, for a method that may better disturb and counter the memory that threatens to inscribe us within the epistemological lures of fascism, within the collective re-presentations of an advanced capitalist, imperialist, heterosexist, racist and electronically mass-mediated nation state bureaucratized in history and culturally anxious for popular rites of sacrificial release of some sort or of the Other. This is a desire for deconstruction.

Despite its roots in the epistemological displacements of French sociological theorizing in the years following World War I, the reflexive challenge of post-structuralism has largely been ignored by the professional discourse of sociology within the United States. While American literary critics and students of art, architecture, and the cinema have begun to grapple with issues related to the narrative structuring, fictive composition and historical provisionality of all powerful claims to knowledge, questions regarding the artifactual nature of socially scientific knowledge have yet to significantly disturb the relative conceptual slumber of the dominant theoretical and methodological paradigms of American sociology. Because of this general lack of professional sociological engagement with the aesthetic and substantive challenges of post-structuralist thought, and because the text that follows makes use of a variety of post-structuralist thematics, we feel compelled to conclude this preface with a brief statement of what we read as some of the more radical implications of post-structuralism for the practice of sociology.

Post-structuralism advances what may be described as a historical and materially informed surrealist conception of the relation between things and words, between artifacts and the linguistic rituals of power and knowledge. As such, post-structuralism critically displaces the epistemological groundings of both positivist and humanist varieties of American social theory. While positivists contend that sociology must "objectively" explain, predict, and control observable structures of social action, humanists argue that the discipline should instead concern itself with the meaningful interpretation of subjective social interaction. Despite these apparent differences, both varieties of American theory share a fundamental commitment to a "realist" strategy of theory construction. Both view social facts as "things" independent of the historically materialized narrational practices of the sociologist who pictures them as such. What differs is simply the locus of the realism identified by these two approaches. Whereas positivists see social facts in terms of abstract and objective structures amenable to quantified classification and measurement, humanists identify the subjective interpretive experience of sense-making individuals as a truly factual starting point for their more qualitative theoretical enclosures.

Post-structuralist theory resists the truth of both these positions. It also resists their pleasure, the pleasure of interpretively mastering either the objective or subjective "facts" of the Other. It resists the temptation to forget that its own re-presentation of facts is an essential feaure of the sacrificial epistemological ritual by which any act of theorizing secures a given identity, a particularly truthful "being-in-the-world." As such, post-structuralism refuses to grant the theorist a place of (transcendental) epistemological privilege outside of the narrative or textual confines in which she or he finds a self materially and with imagination in history. This refusal, if incorporated into the practice of sociology has significant implications for both the style and content of theoretical literature. Literature? One final quote to end this preface, then a re(w)riting of Foucault's critique of the literary structure of the crminological sciences, that is, the law abiding theoretical productions of the normal human sciences in the world in which we find ourselves writing. This is a history of the present.

> *[L]iterary practice remains the missing link in the socio-communicative... fabric of the so-called human sciences... [Moreover] the insertion of this practice into the social science corpus necessitates a modification of the very notion of "science".*[8]

The Pleasures of Criminology: Pleasures of the Text

> *[This] whole effort consists in materializing the pleasure of the text, in making the text* an object of pleasure like the others... *The important thing is to equalize the field of pleasure, to abolish the false opposition of practical life and contemplative life... What we are seeking to establish in various ways is a theory of the materialist subject.*[9]

The content of criminology: crime, the criminal and the effects of a law that orders. But what is its pleasure? What binds the criminologist to his labor within the material constraints and imaginary confines of the professional intellectual marketplace in the modern or post-modern capitalist West?

The pleasure of criminology is to displace the Other's unfixed pleasure into the pain of a certain victim and to master her, to keep an eye on her, to induce her to confess herself the proper subject of the law.

This is what makes the criminologist content: His content, for it is he who speaks in history of a criminal justice, no longer in the name of the Father, as once before the altar, but now in the name of a law universal,

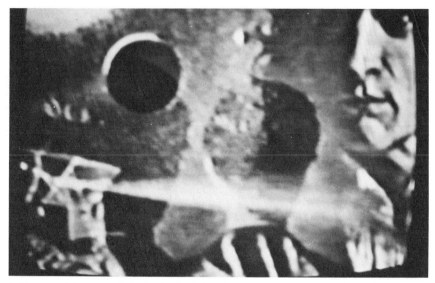

Still from video-text *Criminological Displacements.* Source: William Blake, *Newton*, and René Magritte, *Not To Be Reproduced.*

abstract and beyond a reasonable doubt. Erect before the bar he sees her as grave matter to be ordered knowledgeably. His deadly nature and her laws he rights, he writes, he rites — three rights and nothing left: the rights of man, the writings of a science and the ritual construction of an imperial order.

The pleasure of criminology is to displace the other's unfixed pleasure into the pain of a certain victim and to master her: to subject her to the rules of reason, just as he defines her, this exotic contrary fallen between the cracks. She is the criminologist's subject matter, this unreasonable savage other, dark and unruly. She is the object of his discipline and dangerous. He comes upon her at night in the city and enlightens. To master her, to reduce her to a thing he can count upon — this is the first pleasure of criminology. He says, "We need to penetrate the facts of this crime." This is the first pleasure of criminology: *SADISM.*

The second pleasure of criminology involves his gaze. To keep an eye upon her, to classify, count and cut her up; to make her visible as a certain thing; to dissect that visibility into rates and measure her incidents; to map her determined figure and to analyze her probable path; to uncover everything about her and to lay her bare; to arrest her so that he may operate upon her and see what happens. This is the criminologist's principal method — to never let her escape from sight, to watch her constantly so as to know everything she is. This is the episteme of the discipline, the second pleasure of criminology. He says, "We need a positive science of the facts of this crime." This is the second pleasure of criminology: *SUR-VEILLANCE*.

To the pleasures of mastery and positive science, sadism and surveillance, the criminologist adds a third — the truth of a normal subject, himself. For just as he sets about to master her and to keep his eye upon her. he discovers himself the proper subject of the law. In subjecting her "unruly nature" to the gaze of his law, he realizes himself. The gaze, with which he freezes her, mirrors back upon him and he finds his truth in what she's not: his normal self in relation to her, the other, the illegal alien, the outlaw. This, the truth of the normal subject, is the historical effect of criminological discipline, the material and imaginary locus of its power, its final pleasure. He says, "We need to know who's guilty and who's not." This is the third pleasure of criminology: *THE TRUTH OF THE NORMAL SUBJECT, HIMSELF.*

The Pleasures of Sadism: Mastering the Facts of Crime as "Things"

Sadism and the Confines of Reason

He said, "We need to penetrate the facts of this crime" — to master the nature of this thing laid bare, to make visible her laws, to reasonably ascertain her origin and to rationally calculate and predictively control her effects. She read this as a declaration of sadism; not because he bound her and beat her, but because of the ritual manner in which he rationally confined her otherness and silenced her, as an object to be worked upon, unreasonable and in need of a calculative make-over. The Marquis de Sade had done the same and called it crime and here he was speaking a similar language and calling it criminology.

He Found Himself Alone and Afraid

It was the late eighteenth century. The calculative isolation of individuals competing for a wage had long since replaced the interdependent economic relations of feudalism. The commodified space of market labor had made his time a thing. Within this time he found himself alone with no nexus to others but the relation of things exchanged at the going rate, "naked self-interest... callous cash payment."[10] And just as this commodity exchange had set him apart ruthless in self-calculation, the rise of the nation-state stripped away previously collective political ties, dismembering the ritual powers of kin, the Church, the guild, the locale. And so he was transformed, appearing in his own eyes as an atomized individual, subject to law, a self-interested economic strategist, owing allegiance to none but the state and his reason.

Within this time he found himself alone and afraid. He talked of progress but found his vision of things and himself made uncertain by the sight

Still from video-text *Criminological Displacements*. Source: Paul Delvaux, *Musée Spitzner* (detail), 1943, Musée d'Art Wallon.

of the other's pleasure when it resisted his reason or fell ungraced between the cracks of his newly enlightened order. He saw her nature as greedy, vile and voracious and called her the dangerous class.[11] He saw her "huddled together in the grossly overcrowded"[12] spaces of his city, "lurking in the squalid alleys," ready to cut his throat "for a pocketful of change".[13] And he said it was necessary to defend his society "from the usurpation of each individual, who will always endeavour to take away... not only one's own portion, but to encroach on that of others... [P]unishments [must be] established against the infractions of the laws".[14]

It was the late eighteenth century. This was the beginning of criminology. She took notice of the punishments he had prepared to silence her and said, "We won't play nature to your culture".[15] It was too late. He had already prepared a cell for her confinement saying, "Nature has placed mankind under the governance of two sovereign masters, pain and pleasure... They govern us in all we do, in all we say, in all we think".[16]

The truth of what he said was self-evident to men such as he who forged their only knowledge of nature within that powerful order of things in which they found themselves alone and afraid. It was the late twentieth century and James Q. Wilson said, "The radical individualism of Bentham and Beccaria may be scientifically questionable but prudentially necessary".[17] And Chief Justice Burger said, "We must not be misled by cliches and slogans that if we abolish poverty, crime will also disappear. A far greater factor is the deterrent effect of swift and certain... penalty".[18]

She said, "NO!" She told him that she remembered a time when things were not fixed in this fashion.[19] Nor was this, his view of pleasure, hers. She said, You've turned me into a thing and call it nature — a rational abstraction from the concrete relations in which you find yourself in time, over against me, and in fear. What you see as the natural facts of my greed are nothing but the ritual representations of the time in which you find yourself alone with no nexus to others but the relation of things exchanged. You project this, your pleasure, upon me and call me nature.

He found himself alone and afraid. He remembered nothing of what she said. This was his culture: forgetting. He said, "[M]an is really born isolated, selfish, cruel and despotic; he wants everything and gives nothing in return... Only our selfish interests bind us. The reason that I, the strongest of the gang, do not murder my comrades is because I need their help. It is for the same reason that they do not stick a dagger in my back. Such a motive is a selfish one, though it has the appearance of virtue. What society calls its interests is nothing but a mass of private interests."[20]

He had transformed her into a thing unruly and cruel and called it nature and demanded its submission. He had positioned himself outside of nature, looking down: her master, a man of reason, extracting the rights of law, the rights of man. He demanded her silence but she resisted saying, What you call reason, I call sadism. The sadist "draws a portrait of the other which reminds us of that part of his own mind he would deny and which he has made dark to himself".[21]

He found himself alone and afraid. He remembered nothing of what she said. He spoke of progress but found his vision, his self, made uncertain by the sight of the other's pleasure when it resisted. And so he sentenced her under law. And George Jackson said, "Every time I hear the word 'law' I visualize gangs of militiamen or Pinkertons busting strikes... I see a white oak and a barefooted black hanging, or snake eyes peeping down the lenses of telescopic rifles, or conspiracy trials".[22] But he remembered nothing of this and so he sentenced her to exile, confined her to a place where the pains of punishment promised a more certain compliance, a more rational order of things.

It was the late eighteenth century. This was the beginning of criminology and he said, "Pleasure's effects... are always uncertain; often disappointing... [P]ain must be preferred, for pain's telling effects cannot deceive"[23]. This is the voice of the Marquis de Sade. This is the beginning of sadism. Beccaria, Bentham and Sade were contemporaries, each a theorist of the relation between the pleasures of crime and its punishment. Confined by the lawful reason espoused by Beccaria and Bentham, Sade exceeded their reason, discovering within his cell the imagined pleasures of total control, the contentment promised by complete and rational mastery of her furious nature.[24]

> Sadism... is a massive cultural fact which appeared precise-
> ly at the end of the eighteenth century, [just as
> criminology] and which constitutes one of the greatest
> conversions of the Western imagination... Sadism appears
> at the very moment that unreason, confined for over a cen-
> tury and reduced to silence, reappears, no longer as an im-
> age of the world... but as language and desire. And it is
> no accident that sadism, as an individual phenomenon
> bearing the name of a man, was born of confinement...
> and that Sade's entire *oeuvre* is dominated by the images
> of the Fortress, the Cell... the inaccessible Island which
> thus form, as it were, the natural habitat of unreason.[25]

It was the late eighteenth century. It was the beginning of criminology.
It was the beginning of sadism.

A Night of the Living Dead

George Jackson said, "The very first time [I was put in prison], it was
just like dying... Being captured was the first of my fears... acquired... over...
centuries of black bondage".[26] And she said, under the eyes of the sadist
we are made to "enter a kind of Night of the Living Dead, in which the
human soul has vanished... and the human being is represented by a corpse
which walks and talks and impersonates the living. Here the arc of culture's war against nature is completed".[27] We are made silent as things
dead but still living.

But upon hearing this he said, Now wait a minute. He was always waiting, she thought, waiting for something that never comes in time, cease-
lessly deferring a confrontation with death, with the dissolution of all
things, caught up in a march of linearity without return, unable to let himself down. And for this reason he confined her. It was as if by silencing
her he could quiet the disturbing noise within and achieve certainty. For
without being dead certain, he would lose his grip on things and with them
himself. She told him, "Sadism demands a story, depends on making something happen, forcing a change in another person, a battle of will and
strength, victory/defeat, all occurring in a linear time with a beginning and
an end... [The pleasure of sadism] lies in ascertaining guilt... asserting control, and subjecting the guilty person through punishment".[28]

But he said, Now wait a minute. This parallel between criminology and
sadism makes no sense. Beccaria and Bentham advocated the rational use
of punishment to deter crimes. Sade, on the other hand declared that "Happiness lies only in.. crime".[29] Now, I ask you, is that reasonable?

To this she replied, "In the modern period, exchange value has come
to dominate society; all qualities have been reduced to quantitative equiva-
lences. This process inheres in the concept of reason. For reason, on the

one hand, signifies the idea of a free, human, social life. On the other hand, reason is the court of judgment of calculation, the instrument of domination, and the means for the greatest exploitation... As in De Sade's novels, the mode of reason adjusts the world for the ends of self-preservation and recognizes no function other than the preparation of the object from mere sensory material in order to make it that material of subjugation".[30]

He countered by saying, Perhaps, but this is what separates Sade from the criminologist. They were concerned, not simply with self-preservation, but with the legislation of a common good. Classical criminology hoped to deter the offender by the threat of certain punishment. Sade hoped to rationally master his victims, to deploy pain as a means of altering her, and thereby securing submission.

She replied, On this score Sade advances the rule of reason to its limit, to that dark point unseen by those who stand alone within its light. He gave voice to the unspeakable implications of the rule of reason. Sade said what could not be said from reason's lips without exploding the material and imaginary conditions of rational language itself. And this, of course, was the most dangerous of his crimes. Sade wrote from within the deepest confines of reason, that place where the final making over of a person into a thing is most complete. Perhaps, this enabled him to envision the "progress" that criminology would make less than a century later. For as Foucault has noted, "The theatre of punishment of which the eighteenth century dreamed and which would have acted essentially... [as a deterrent] was replaced by the great uniform machinery of the prisons".[31] Thus, has not the criminologist's theatre of rational punishment been transformed into a sadist's theatre of cruelty, a theatre that fixes her as a thing to be watched and employs discipline, not so much to make her think about her unreasonable behavior, as to change her thinking, alter her behavior, make her a more compliant object and reasonably so?

He was alone and afraid in the time in which he found himself. He remembered nothing of what she said. He spoke of progress but his vision and his self were made uncertain by the sight of the other's pleasure when it resisted. And so he confined her for observation and rehabilitation saying, as it was said to 0 in another story, "You are here to serve your masters. During the day, you will perform whatever... duties are assigned you... But at the first sign or word from anyone you will drop whatever you are doing and ready yourself for what is really your one and only duty: to lend yourself... You will remember at all times — or as constantly as possible — that you have lost all right to privacy or concealment... [Y]ou must never look at any of us in the face".[32] And so he gazed down at her, silent and eyes averted, alone within the cell. And he said, "We need to penetrate the facts of this crime." This is the first pleasure of criminology: *SADISM*.

The Pleasure of Surveillance: The Eye Upon Her

Scene One. The Objectifying Gaze

> *1876: The publication of Cesare Lombroso's* The Crimi-
> nal Man. *Lombroso, an Italian physician performs an au-*
> *topsy on the body of the dreaded brigand Vilella when*
> *struck by what he perceives as the apelike structure of the*
> *criminal's skull. Lombroso gazes upon this, the object of*
> *the first positive criminologiocal examination.*[33]

SHE: This is the gaze that fixes, classifies; the gaze that surveys the facts
of the other. This is the gaze that cuts open and cuts up. This is
the gaze that reduces secrets to masterful knowledge. This gaze
holds a positive charge. This is a singular gaze, blinded by reason.

HE: "We must move beyond... measurements of environmental impact...
We must develop the capacity for tracing painful stimulus into the
organism to the associational and motivational areas of the brain
and then to the motor centers and to behavior. Between the stimulus and the response is the great big black box... It is here that
we will find the questions we should be asking".[34]

KRUGER: "Your devotion has the look of a lunatic sport".[35]

SHE: This is a knowledge that must be seen. This is a knowledge that
masters facts. This is a knowledge that surveys, makes visible, classifies, counts, dissects. This is a knowledge of things. This
knowledge is under the eye.

HE: The birth of positivism is the end of ideology. We will not compete
for the truth. We can differentiate, measure, master the truth
through observation. We can see the facts and grasp them. We can
order these facts, fix this world, control its destiny. We have rights...
to order. We write: You have the right to be seen, but not heard.
You must be silent to be properly diagnosed. These are the two
rules of my positive science: You must be silent and avert your
gaze. You have lost all right to concealment. My pleasure, my eyes,
work... they work over you, a ritual. Your eyes are blind, they are
by measurement. We can order these facts.

> The modern dominance of the principle of rea-
> son had to go hand in hand with the interpreta-
> tion of the essence of beings as objects, an object
> present as representation, an object placed and
> positioned before a subject. This latter, a man who
> says "I," an ego certain of itself, thus ensures his
> own technical mastery over the totality of what
> is.[36]

Still from video-text *Criminological Displacements*. Source: Joseph La Mantia and Stephen Pfohl, *Normalizing Relations* (detail), photocollage, 1985.

SHE: The facts of social life are nothing but powerful forms of fiction. My mouth holds your words. Your eyes burn through me. Your distance, your analysis cuts me up. Your gaze makes things out of my scenes. With your passive contemplation, your observe me with a force. You reduce my secrets to your truths, your facts. You universalize my particularity. You erase my narrative. Your gaze freezes objects outside of time and space and the power structuring practices in which we are situated. My trouble, my sin, is your fact, the facts of this crime. Your gaze, your pleasure, is my containment.

HE: We need a positive science of the facts of this crime. We will be objective. We will accurately represent the facts. Your case will be heard.

SHE: The light of your reason blinds your eyes.

HE: The facts can be seen. They will speak for themselves.

SHE: Your gaze which observes, fixes its objects, and then displays them, produces the very facticity you claim to be capturing. Your objectivity mistakes facts for artifacts. Your objectivity denies your place in constituting my subjectivity, in constituting the facts.

HE: This is not the truth. The birth of positivism is the end of ideology.

SHE: (asking) From what womb do you emerge?

Scene Two: The Carceral Gaze

> 1843: *Publication of Jeremy Bentham's* Edited Works. *Bentham, committed to the practical application of criminological theory, drafted architectural specifications for the Panopticon, a huge, round and glass-roofed "inspection house." At its center would be a central guard tower. There the watchful eyes of state authority could gaze at incarcerated inmates twenty four hours a day.*[37]

BENTHAM: The Panoptican, the ideal prison, it will be "a mill to grind rogues honest and idle men industrious".[38]

SHE: This is the gaze that operates, disciplines, that writes over the other, erases her historical narrative. This is the gaze that forgets its own history. This is the faceless gaze, inscribed in stone, forgotten in memory. This is the Panoptic gaze. This is the discipline that never ends. (She feared, Permanent visibility, the faceless gaze, automatic discipline, the machine body.)

CHIEF JUSTICE BURGER: "What I sugget now... is to survey the wreckage and begin a damage control program".[39]

KRUGER: "Your manias become science/You are an experiment in terror".[40]

(She feared, Constant surveillance, manipulative transformation. The panoptican, the eye that surveys endlessly.)

FOUCAULT: "Panopticism is the general principle of a new 'political anatomy' whose object and end are not the relations of sovereignty but the relations of discipline... [I]t is exerted spontaneously and without noise".[41]

CHIEF JUSTICE BURGER: "When our distant ancestors came out of the caves and rude tree dwellings thousands of years ago... they did so to satisfy certain fundamental human needs... But the basic need was security — security of the person, the family, the home and of property. Taken together, this is the meaning of a civilized society".[42]

SHE: "Your property is the rumor of power"/"Your fictions become history".[43] The meaning of our society is your property. The meaning of your security is our discipline. The industry of your machines is our docility. The light of your reason is the darkness of the prison.

HE: We need a positive science of the facts of this crime. We will study the prisoners.

SHE: The criminological eye is the carceral eye. Together, they assemble, document, watch for/upon/to write over the lives of others, of us all, prisoners. (The TV calls out.)
"Who are you?

I am number 2.

Who's number I?

You are number 6.

I am not a number. I am a free man!" (from "The Prisoner")

SHE: The criminological eye is the industrial eye. Together they assemble, document, discipline, watch for/upon/to write over the bodies of others, of labor, machines.

HE: Discipline is necessary. Every child, later an adult, needs to learn discipline — at home, at school, at work, for the market. Discipline creates order. We must have an ordered world. We must have the facts.

SHE: Your normative science criminology plays with a disciplinary technology. (And then she thought:) "Discipline 'makes' individuals; it is the specific technique of power that regards individuals both as objects and as instruments of its exercise... [I]t is a modest, suspicious power, which functions as a calculated, but permanent economy".[44]

HE: This economy that you speak of, like the economy of goods and machines requires supervision. We need to survey the facts of this crime.

SHE: My knowing reaches out to embrace the sacred. Normalization is my living death. Your word, your eye, they are the same things, all simulations.

HE: This is only a problem for those who don't conform, who don't fit. We must be vigilant. We cannot be held "hostages within the border of our own... enlightened, civilized country".[45]

(She thought this was a fantastic thought, like the phantasms at Disneyland. Jean Baudrillard had been there too and he thought the same thing.)

BAUDRILLARD: "Disneyland is there to conceal the fact that it is the 'real' country, all of 'real' America, which is disneyland (just as prisons are there to conceal the fact that it is the social in its entirety, in its banal omnipresence, which is carceral)".[46]

HE: We must be vigilant. We must know the facts.

SHE: Your carceral eyes upon the I burn me through. I am your thing. I am your word. I am your captive. Your comfort is my silence.

Scene Three: The Spectacle of Surveillance

1986. She is alone with the radio and television. This is the new criminology.

The ideal point of penalty today would be an indefinite discipline; an interrogation without end, an investigation that would be extended without limits to a meticulous

> *and even more analytic observation, a judgment that*
> *would at the same time be the constitution of a file that*
> *was never closed, the calculated leniency of a penalty that*
> *would be interlaced with the ruthless curiosity of an ex-*
> *amination, of a gap in relation to an inaccessible norm*
> *and the asymptotic movement that strives to meet in in-*
> *finity.*[47]

She awoke this morning and like most other mornings, flicked on the radio, walked toward the shower and thought she'd make the coffee after the bath. Faint noise from the radio reminded her of fascism in South Africa, the heroic struggle of a country, a continent, chained under the eye of Western imperial reason and of other imperials, Nicaragua, recent crime statistics, the building of new prisons. A faint noise from the radio, a pop song with a refrain that engaged her: "Every breath you take/Every move you make/Every bond you break/Every step you take/I'll be watching you".[48] A long look in the mirror, the daily surveillance of her body, not thin enough, sagging, cloudy. The face, eye-to-eye, in the mirror that always reflected the same skin in need of a little touch-up, a minor make-over, make-up. The clothes to best display the body, mask the not-thin-enough legs, stomach, her own flesh; these occupy her thoughts. She looks again at herself, her image in the mirror. Next week, I'll fix this body, discipline myself. And she thought, like him, I am now alone, at work, with my body, across the newspaper, with the television.

A long look in the mirror, the daily surveillance of her body, like the daily surveillance of her thoughts, her image, her performance at work: those unseen forces, others, against whom she constantly judged herself. She asked herself, in whose image am I made?

And she got angry and screamed, show your faces! Let me see your eyes! But only her double, her eyes, the image reflected in the mirror, the one into which she daily gazed, answered back: I am your eyes. I am your gaze. You are a captive audience. You are my victim. You are under my eyes.

He said, "We need a positive science of the facts of this crime." This is the second pleasure of criminology: *SURVEILLANCE.*

The Pleasure of Truth: The Normal Subject and His Other

> *The society that emerged in the nineteenth century — bour-*
> *geois, capitalist, or industrial society... put into operation*
> *an entire machinery for producing true discourses... [T]wo*
> *processes emerge, the one always conditioning the other: we*
> *demand that... [the Other, the object of our gaze] speak the*
> *truth... and we demand that it tell us our truth... We tell it*
> *its truth by deciphering what it tells us... [I]t tells us our own*
> *by delivering up that part of it that escaped us.*[49]

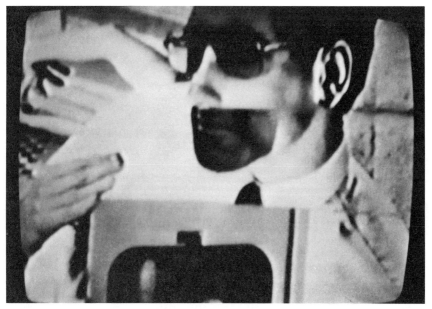

Still from video-text *Criminological Displacements.* Source: Joseph La Mantia and Stephen Pfohl, *Cool Man Calculated* (detail) photocollege, 1985.

Speaking of Truth

Criminology is a true discourse. It captures the other within its words and orders the truth she speaks. The content of her truth varies at different moments of the discipline. In the nineteenth century, the truth of her perverse or pathological pleasure displaced that which he previously saw as rational. In the 1920's her truth was seen as disorganization, but by the late 1930's she had become a dysfunction or perhaps even a positive contribution to the self-regulating machine in which she appeared a part. In the 1940's she confessed herself a bad learner, or so he said, while during the 1950's she revealed the truth of anomie as he questioned her every strain. In the 1960's she was laid bare again now the object of labelling, while in the 1970's she was viewed as an object of conflict. These truthful contents repeat herself, recycling the facts of her case into the present.[50] Despite these differences in what it sees as her truth, the structure of truthful criminological discourse, its basic episteme remains the same as its pleasure: "The pleasure that comes of exercising a power that questions, monitors, watches, spies, searches out, palpates, brings to light".[51] And in this the criminologist finds himself the normal subject of the law, positioned over against her, the alien other, the exotic outlaw, the shadow of his truthful ignorance.

It was the late nineteenth century when he stood above the silent and fixed body of the dreaded brigand, Vilella, the object of the first positive criminological examination, and said, Speak to me of the truth of your crime. It was just this morning that he poured over the body of the data spewing forth from the machine, silent and fixed. He demanded the same: a profile, a measured exactness, a story of the other's truth and he found it! It was not his, but he worked over this body of evidence until it yielded a certain knowledge, a significance, a model of the other's determined unreasonableness. And in this he discovered a certain pleasure, evidence of his own self-contained normality. This is what only she, as he interpreted her, could provide.

He said, Speak to me of the truth of your crime.

She said, "The hardest thing was simply to speak... [T]his time what they wanted from her was not blind obedience, acquiescence to an order, they wanted her to anticipate orders, to judge herself... and surrender herself as such".[52]

True Confessions

He had learned to speak the truth. He had learned that it was normal to find truth within himself and that this truth was reasonable. He had learned to see his self as the locus of truth, the locus of certainty. He had begun to see things this way as early as the thirteenth century as he found himself confessing before the fathers. They had sacramentalized this ritual just as feudalism began its decline. It was 1215. There was a Lateran Council and it said: No more trials by divine ordeal. No more trials by battle. We need a more reasonable way. He said, "We need to know who's guilty and who's not." He turned his eyes within.

It was the late middle ages. It was not the beginning of criminology but he was moving in that direction. He was increasingly becoming an individualized actor in the material order, just as he was becoming a judge of himself in the imaginary realm. He looked about him and saw signs of judgment everywhere and experienced the demand to keep a biographical ledger of his rights and wrongs. He was becoming the center of his own truth and began confessing this.

Philippe Ariès said, "Beginning in the twelfth century... we see the rise among the rich, the well educated, and the powerful, of the idea that every man possesses a personal biography. At first this biography consisted solely of actions, good or bad, which were subjected to an overall judgment: what he was... The actions of the individual are no longer lost in the limitless space of transcendence or, if you prefer, in the collective destiny of the species. From now on they are individualized... [Life now] consists of the sum total of an individual's thoughts, words, and deeds... Life is a body of facts that can be itemized and summarized in a book".[53]

He said, "We need to know who's guilty and who's not." Everywhere he looked there were images of a final judgment. He saw a 14th century painting by Albergno. There was Christ the stern judge with a book upon his knee. There were words that said: "He whose name is written in this book shall be damned." There were frightened souls before this Lord each with their own book in trembling hands. He felt alone and afraid and the Fathers said, "Confess!"

Foucault said, "[A]ll this helped to give the confession a central role in the order of civil and religious powers... For a long time, the individual was vouched for by reference to others and the demonstration of his ties to the commonweal (family, allegiance, protection); then he was authenticated by the discourse of truth he was able or obliged to pronounce concerning himself. The truthful confession was inscribed at the heart of the procedures of individualization by power".[54]

He gazed at her sternly and said, Tell the truth. You must confess.

She said, "... what they wanted from her was not blind obedience, acquiescence to an order, they wanted her to... judge herself... and surrender".[55]

By the eighteenth century, the book was everywhere in sight and Sade was soon to be confined. In the cathedral at Albi books hung like identification papers from the necks of souls before their last judgment.[56] Otherwise they were naked and afraid, just as he, with no nexus to others but the relations of things exchanged at the going rate. The book appears, likewise, throughout the baroque art of the seventeenth and eighteenth centuries, a biographical confession at the hour of death, a calculated ledger of good deeds and bad, a passport to the afterlife.

Philippe Ariès said, "The book is therefore at once the history of an individual, his biography, and a book of accounts, or records, with two columns, one for the evil and the other for the good. The new bookkeeping spirit of businessmen who were beginning to discover their own world — which has become our own — was applied to the content of a life as well as to merchandise or money".[57]

"Book her," he said. "We need to know who's guilty and who's not. Book her and demand a confession."

Foucault said, "We have since become a singularly confessing society. The confession has spread its effects far and wide. It plays a part in justice, medicine, education, family relationships, and love relations... [O]ne confesses one's crimes, one's sins, one's thoughts and desires, one's illnesses and troubles; one goes about telling, with the greatest precision, whatever is most difficult to tell... The obligation to confess is now relayed through so many different points, is so deeply ingrained in us, that we no longer perceive it as the effect of a power that constrains us... Western man has become a confessing animal".[58]

He had learned to speak the truth. He had learned that it was normal to find truth within one's self and that this truth was reasonable. He had learned to see his self as the locus of truth, the locus of certainty and he demanded the same from her.

This is the new meaning of confession. Foucault said, "[O]ne had to confess... because the work of producing the truth was obliged to pass through this relationship if it was to be scientifically validated. The truth did not reside solely in the subject who, by confessing, would reveal it wholly formed. It was constituted in two stages: present but incomplete, blind to itself, in the one who spoke, it could only reach completion in the one who assimilated and recorded it. It was the latter's function to verify this obscure truth... the decipherment of what it said. The one who listened was not simply the... judge who condemned or acquitted; he was the master of truth".[59]

He Speaks Her Truth

It is now the late twentieth century. Criminology has taken the place of the Inquisition. It still demands that she speak the truth of her illegality only now its demands are of another order. The criminologist speaks, not of doing the work of God, but of serving Man and Reason. He does not expect her to fully answer for herself. Her confession is now filtered through his masterful interpretation. The inquisitor set about his task before the time of sadism and surveillance, before labor's wage became a thing and the imperial rule of modern reason.

Under the positive eyes of criminology the truth of these things, crime and the criminal, can today be seen, regardless of her ability to speak of them reasonably. She is, after all, a thing he has fashioned. And so he can count on her to speak, just as he orders the meaning of what she says. It was just this morning that he poured over the body of the data spewing forth from the machine: silent and fixed. He demanded a profile, a measured exactness, a story of the Other's truth and found "it!"

(A Conversation between a Psychiatrist and a Patient overheard)

PSYCHIATRIST: "I understand your expressions correctly, I have the feeling that you honestly believe that the reason you are here is because of alcohol. That may have been the conveyer. That may have been the one thing that allowed you or that happened at the same time. But I wonder if you have thought about the millions of people that do drink and do drink too much, alot, and do not commit these crimes. For what I'm trying to help you think about is that when you drink, when your judgment is removed by alcohol, then you will act out something that is already there. There is your key — and there you will find answers."

PATIENT: "Yeah, that's right. I go to group therapy here and we've talked about that at some lengths. And I don't know whether it's a crutch. You look back and say — Yeah. I was drunk. I did this. I did but maybe the thought was already there. But if I'm sober I don't act them out. Right?"

PSYCHIATRIST: "Right! You're under control. I just wanted to bring this up for your thoughts and consideration and that you might seek specific help in helping to get rid of that particular problem".[60]

She said, "The hardest thing was simply to speak... [T]his time what they wanted from her was not blind obedience, acquiescence to an order, they wanted her to... judge herself".[61]

Criminology is a true discourse. It captures the Other within its words and orders the truth she speaks. And in this he discovered a certain pleasure, evidence of his own self-contained normality, his own truth. This is what only she, as he interpreted her, could provide. This is the third pleasure of criminology, *THE TRUTH OF THE NORMAL SUBJECT.* He says, "We need to know who's guilty and who's not." Now he knew for sure.

Towards an Uncertain Deconstruction and a Power-Reflexive Practice

> *Deconstruction seems to offer a way out of the closure of knowledge. By inaugurating the open-ended indefiniteness of textuality... it shows us the lure of the abyss as freedom. The fall into the abyss of deconstruction inspires us with as much pleasure as fear. We are intoxicated with the prospect of never hitting bottom.* [62]

The content of criminology: crime, the criminal and the effects of a law that orders. Three certain pleasures: sadism, surveillance, and the truth of the normal subject. Three certain technologies:

He says, "We need to penetrate the facts of this crime."

He says, "We need a positive science of the facts of this crime."

He says, "We need to know who's guilty and who's not." Certain techniques, certain pleasures, certain constructions.

She says, I am uneasy in the face of your certain pleasures, your certain constructions. Mine is an uncertain pleasure, an uncertain deconstruction.

The Provisionality of Mastery

You said, We need to penetrate the facts of this crime. We need to master the things in this world. You seem committed to a realist view of the things of this world. But you forgot that *you* mastered the text. You forgot that the "things" which appear as social facts (*sui generis*) are fictive effects of the powerful structuring practices by which we repeatedly embody ourselves in history. You ignored the traces of Marx, Durkheim, Nietzsche.[63]

She said, I have taken leave of this world of facts, in order to examine the transformative ritual practices which situate us here and now, at home in a world of *artifacts*. I am committed to a surrealist view of the things of this world and these are nothing but the effects of domesticating drama, the timely consequences of our mode of production and reproduction.

You said, My story masters objects, objective truth and you asked me, What is the objective truth of your story? My answer is uneasy, uncertain. My answer is that the material and definitional actualities of any "thing" are bound together in an indeterminate relation that "is" the effect of a transformative displacement of one set of social structuring practices by some other(s). From within this collusion or collision of practices arises a "true" story — the real facts of the matter, the real facts of the crime, the self-evidency of these "things." There are no truths aside from this elusive (intertextual) formation.[64] The truth of things is embedded in a ceaseless repetition of an indeterminate act of differentiation between colliding practices. But so also is truth effected as an act of deference. To make something "truly" present is to make absent something other. Things become real only in a socially differentiated act of silencing. This imperial exclusion marks the historical production of "things in themselves." Yet this is exactly what they are not. They are nothing but the cultural, political, and material effects of the power structuring practices in which we are situated.

She said, You forgot that you made me into a thing, silenced me, mastered me. You forgot the uncertainty of my pleasure. I remember that I, by necessity, provisionally forget the socially constructed nature of my mastery of things within my text. Your certain pleasure of mastery is my uncertain pleasure of reciprocity, of deconstruction. I labor under an ungoing provisionality, under these words, spoken by another she:

> [T]he desire of deconstruction may itself become a desire
> to reappropriate the text actively through mastery to show
> the text what it "does not know." As she deconstructs, all
> protestations to the contrary, the critic necessarily assumes
> that she at least, for the time being, means what she says...
> In other words, the critic provisionally forgets that her
> own text is necessarily self-deconstructed, always already
> a palimpsest.[65]

Watching for Noise

You said, We need a positive science of the facts of this crime. You said, We need a knowledge that sees, that stands over against the objects it desires to know. But your gaze so fixed upon the other refused to reflect back. Your text, conceived of its own right reason, bound itself by the rules of a method that privileges its objectivity apart from the world in which it finds itself.

She said, My uncertain pleasure is the open-ended practice of reading and writing. My uncertain pleasure is the text bound by the historical and material rules of concrete social interaction.[66] My uncertain pleasure situates theorizing as a practical activity in the production of history. My uncertain pleasure denies your dream of positive science. My uncertain pleasure asks: What if the provisionality of forgetting becomes a reflexive feature of theorizing itself? What if it places "under erasure" the possibility that theorizing can never escape the textual network of powerful social practices into which it asserts itself.[67]

He asked, What if...

But she interrupted him because she wanted her text to interrupt his reason. She said, My uncertain pleasure asserts the value of a reflexive analysis that understands itself as effecting a provisional knowledge positioned by the power of its relationships to other practices. My uncertain pleasure is a power-reflexive social practice, a practice that displays, if imperfectly, the mode of its own production, its situationally bound strategies of textual construction.

She continued, My uncertain pleasure, deconstruction, reflexivity, is not a positive or a normal science. It turns analytically upon itself, just as it acts upon its "subject," disclosing, not a determinate world of social facts, but an indeterminate production of artifacts, *itself included*. This is its strategic truth. It opens before me, again and again, the power-invested practices that provisionally effect the things of this world.

She said, You gazed, your eyes alight with reason, but your frame was fixed and you couldn't see the noise that you were making. Your certain pleasure is the gaze that holds a positive charge. My uncertain pleasure is the noise in which we find ourselves.

She said, I labor under an ongoing complicity, under the words spoken by another she:

> The aspect that interests me most is... the recognition, within deconstructive practice, of provisional and intractable starting-points in any investigative effort; its disclosure of complicities where a will to knowledge would create oppositions; its insistence that in disclosing complicities the critic-as-subject is herself complicit with the object of her critique: its emphasis upon "history" and upon the ethico-political as the "trace" of that complicity — the proof that we do not inhabit a clearly defined critical space free of such traces; and finally, the acknowledgement that its own discourse can never be adequate to its example.[68]

Renaming the Subject

You said, We need to know who's guilty and who's not. As you continued to fix your gaze on her, you deluded us into thinking that she was your problem, your pleasure. But, in reality, it was all of us, you, it was our eyes upon ourselves that fueled your desire. And you took pleasure in displaying your own normality. Your certain pleasure is the truth of the normal subject.

She said, My uncertain pleasure is another naming. My uncertain pleasure is not your normal subject, the subject certain of himself, the subject who recognizes himself when named, the interpellated subject, but the de-centered subject: the subject "at another place on the spiral: deconstructed, taken apart, shifted, without anchorage".[69]

You said, I know the other is de-centered, adrift in the world, anomic, disorganized, ill, angry. This is how I know she differs from me. Over and against her otherness, her difference, I know I am within the law, embraced.

She said, All you have learned is that you have learned to "work by yourself" without the benefit of theory, law, or therapy, and that the others, the "bad subjects... provoke intervention".[70] But, all theory, your theory too, is an intervention into the ritual process that produces subjectivity, that produces us. We are all of us de-centered subjects, uncertain subjects, produced as such by and in relation to imaginary, historical, material practices. "There is... no 'human essence'... [T]here is only the play of difference, and the multiplicity of mutually conditioning contradictions".[71]

She said, This is the pleasure of the heterogeneous and contradictory subject. This is an uncertain pleasure of an uncertain subject: a subject who knows we are interpellated — that we all respond to the hailing of our names. But this subject recognizes the provisionality of centering, the uncertainty of that seemingly certain anchorage, only produced by the rituals of taking the world within us. This is the uncertain pleasure of the subject whose truth is always inscribed in the power to know, to entrap in a name.

She said, You desired the truth of the abnormal subject, but you fixed the truth of the normal subject, yourself. Your certain pleasure is the naming of the other and yourself. My uncertain pleasure is the loss of a name, the truths of the de-centered subject.

She said, I labor under an ongoing autobiography, under the words of another she:

> Autobiography can be a mourning for the perpetual loss
> of a name — one's proper word-thing.[72]

Into the Abyss

She falls into a dangerous abyss and yet finds pleasure in what she does. She is freed from all but the material and imaginary practices which provide her with a story of herself and the world. And this, of course, is everything. Here, she celebrates a ritual of deconstruction, not as a bottomless trap of infinite regress, but as the strategic possibility for a finite reconstruction of the things of this world presented by the always contestable constellation of the structuring practices in which we are engaged. This is the uncertain truth of deconstruction. This is the uncertain truth of the acknowledgement of the relation between power and knowledge She said, I labor under an ongoing power-reflexivity, under these words:

> There is no power relation without the correlative constitution of a field of knowledge, nor any knowledge that does not presuppose and constitute at the same time power relations... It's not a matter of emancipating truth from every system of power (which would be a chimera, for truth is already power) but of detaching the power of truth from the forms of hegemony, social, economic and cultural, within which it operates at the present time.[73]

The content of criminology: crime, the criminal and the effects of a law that orders: Three certain pleasures: sadism, surveillance, and the truth of the normal subject.

An Epilogue: From Conflict Criminology to a Criminology That Conflicts

He had come from the criminology convention and said that the science of criminology was a science of conflict. He said that both criminals and those who define and detain them were forever locked within the confines of conflict, that each naturally struggled with the other to realize an interest that would impose itself, that would outlaw the other, just as it victoriously claimed the law its own. He informed her that such timeless conflict was a natural fact of human social existence and that "the assumption here is that there are limits to the human capacity to include others as 'we'".[74] He explained to her that this is what differentiates his theory of criminology from the others. His objective was, less to master the determinate characteristics of the criminal, than to scientifically explain the universal laws of the conflict that criminalizes. This notion was not unappealing to the many liberal voting members of the Criminological Society in which he found himself. Just as he, many were fascinated by the fact that the outlawed other was typically reported as of powerless origin: outclassed, out-raced or unable to adequately erect a defense of self-interest.

And so he turned his eyes to the facts of conflict, counting its structures, numbering its factors and proposing its laws.

He explained to her that this is what differentiates his conflict theory of criminology from the others. She understood this: that the *content* of conflict criminology differed from the more conventional science of the causes of crime. But did it differ in its *contentment*? Did it differ in the fundamental pleasure which positioned the imagination of the criminologist materially in history as master of the natural facts of crime? This question disturbed her significantly. As she pursued this question she found herself losing her center: a slide into a different pleasure: the pleasure of difference; a slide into a different criminological practice: a politics of difference; a different conjuncture of power and its relation to knowledge. When she spoke to him of this disturbance and its different pleasure he had nothing to say. He had been telling her about his conflict theory of criminology, but she was speaking of a criminology that conflicts.

Acknowledgements

© 1986 by The Society for the Study of Social Problems Inc. Reprinted from *Social Problems*, vol. 33, no. 6, pp. S94-S113 by permission.

A "video-text" version of Criminological Displacements" is also available in VHS format. Produced by Avery Gordon, Andrew Herman and Stephen Pfohl video cassettes are available for $10.00 from PARASITE CAFE PRODUCTIONS: 25 Gerald Road, Brighton, Massachusetts 02135.

Notes

1.   Michel Foucault, *Discipline and Punish: The Birth of the Prison*, trans. Alan Sheridan, (New York: Vintage Books, 1979), p. 27.

2.   Michel Foucault, "Nietzsche, Genealogy, History" in *Language, Counter-Memory, Practice: Selected Essays and Interviews by Michel Foucault*, trans. Donald F. Bouchard and Sherry Simom, (New York: Cornell University Press, 1977), pp. 139-64.

3.   Michel Foucault, *The Order of Things*, trans. Alan Sheridan, (New York: Pantheon, 1970).

4.   Stephen Pfohl, "Labeling Criminals" in H. Lawrence Ross, *Law and Deviance*, (Beverly Hills: Sage Publications, 1981), pp. 65-97.

5.   Emile Durheim, *Elementary Forms of the Religious Life*, trans. J.W. Swain, New York: Free Press, 1965; Emile Durkheim and Marcel Mauss, *Primitive Classification*, trans. Rodney Needham, (Chicago: University of Chicago Press), 1963.

6. cf. James Clifford, "On Ethnographic Surrealism," *Comparative Studies in Society and History, 1981*, vol. 23, pp. 539-64; *Michele Richman, Reading Georges Bataille: Beyond the Gift* (Baltimore: Johns Hopkins University Press, 1982); Alan Stoekl, "Introduction" in Georges Bataille, *Visions of Excess: Selectedd Writings, 1927-1939*, ed. and trans. Alan Stoekl, (Minneapolis: University of Minnesota Press, 1985), pp. ix-xxv.

7. Angela McRobbie, "Fear of Fascism: Old Stories — New Narratives," *ZG*, 1983, no. 5, pp. 21-23; Susan Sontag, *Under the Sign of Saturn* (New York: Vintage Books, 1981), pp. 73-105.

8. Julia Kristeva, *Desire in Language: A Semiotic Approach in Literature and Art*, ed. Leon S. Roudiez, trans. Thomas Gora, Alice Jardine and Leon S. Roudiez, (New York: Columbia University Press, 1980), p. 98.

9. Ronald Barthes, *The Pleasure of the Text*, trans. Richard Miller, (New York: Hill and Wang, 1975), pp. 59, 61.

10. Karl Marx and Frederick Engels, "The Communist Manifesto" in *Selected Works*, (New York: International Publishers, 1968), p. 37.

11. H.A. Frégier, *Des Classes Dangereuses de la Population Dans Les Grandes Villes et des Moyens de les Vendre Meilleures*, (Paris: Bureau de Seiene, 1840).

12. Andrew Scull, *Decarceration: Community Treatment and the Deviant — A Radical View*, (New Jersey: Prentice-Hall, 1977), p. 22.

13. Ysabel Rennie, *The Search for Criminal Man*, (Lexington, Ma: D.C. Heath, 1978), p. 3.

14. Cesare Beccaria, *An Essay on Crimes and Punishments*, trans. Henry Paolucci, (Indianaplis: Bobbs-Merril, 1963), p. 57.

15. Barbara Kruger, *We Won't Play Nature to Your Culture: Works by Barbara Kruger*, (London: Institute for Contemporary Art, 1984), p. 28.

16. Jeremy Bentham, *An Introduction to the Principles of Morals and Legislation*, (New York: Hafner Publishing Company, 1948), p. 1.

17. James Q. Wilson, *Thinking About Crime*, (New York: Vintage, 1975), p. 62.

18. Warren Burger, "The Perspective of the Chief Justice of the U.S. Supreme Court," *Crime and Social Justice*, 1981, vol. 15, p. 44.

19. Raymond Michalowski, *Order, Law and Crime*, (New York: Random House, 1985), p. 48.

20. Marquis de Sade, *Justice, or The Misfortunes of Virtues*, (New York: Castle Books), 1964, pp. 25, 24-25.

21. Susan Griffin, *Pornography and Silence*, (New York: Harper and Row 1981), p. 161.

22. George Jackson, *Blood in My Eye*, (New York: Random House, 1972), p. 168.

23. Marquis de Sade, *Justine, Philosophy in the Bedroom, Eugenie de Franval and Other Writings*, trans. Richard Seaver and Austryn Wainhouse, (New York: Grove Press, 1966), p. 252.

24. Georges Bataille, *Death and Sensuality: A Study of Eroticism and The Taboo*, (New York: Arno Press, 1977), pp. 164-76.

25. Michel Foucault, *Madness and Civilization: A History of Insanity in the Age of Reason*, trans. Richard Howard, (New York: Random House, 1965), p. 210.

26. George Jackson, *Soledad Brother: The Prison Letters of George Jackson*, (New York: Coward-McCann, Inc., 1970), p. 13.

27. Griffin, p. 69.

28. Laura Mulvey, "Visual Pleasure and Narrative Cinema" in Brian Wallis, ed. *Art After Modernism: Rethinking Representation*, (New York and Boston: The New Museum of Contemporary Art and David R. Godine Publishers, Inc., 1985), p. 368.

29. Quoted in Simone de Beauvoir, "Must We Burn Sade?", trans. Annette Michelson in The Marquis de Sade, *The 120 Days of Sodom and other Writings*, trans. Austryn Wainhouse and Richard Seaver, (New York: Grove Press, 1966), p. 52.

30. Kathy Acker, "Scenes of World War III," in Richard Prince, comp. *Wild History*, (New York: Tanam Press, 1985), p. 110.

31. Foucault, *Discipline and Punish: The Birth of the Prison*, p. 116.

32. Paulien Réage, *Story of O*, trans. Sabine d'Estree, (New York: Grove Press, 1965), pp. 15-16.

33. Stephen Pfohl, *Images of Deviance and Social Control: A Sociological History*, (New York: McGraw-Hill, 1985), p. 85.

34. Quoted in *Ibid*, p. 114.

35. Kruger, p. 32.

36. Jacques Derrida, "The Principle of Reason: The University in The Eyes of its Pupils," trans. Catherine Porter and Edward P. Morris, *Diacritics*, Fall 1983, pp. 9-10.

37. Pfohl, *Images of Deviance and Social Control*, p. 64.

38. *Ibid*.

39. Burger, p. 45.

40. Kruger, pp. 41, 44.

41. Foucault, *Discipline and Punish: The Birth of the Prison*, pp. 208, 206.

42. Burger, p. 43.

43. Kruger, pp. 44, 27.

44. Foucault *Discipline and Punish: The Birth of the Prison*, p. 170.

45. Burger, p. 44.

46. Jean Baudrillard, *Simulations*, trans. Paul Foss, Paul Patton and Phillip Beitchman, (New York: Semiotext(e), Inc., 1983), p. 25.

47. Foucault, *Discipline and Punish: The Birth of the Prison*, p. 227.

48. Sting, 1983.

49. Michel Foucault, *The History of Sexuality, Volume I An Introduction*, trans. Robert Hurley. (New York: Vintage Books, 1980), pp. 69-70.

50. Pfohl, *Images of Deviance and Social Control*.

51. Foucault, *The History of Sexuality, Volume I*, p. 45.

52. Réage, pp. 74-5.

53. Philippe Ariès *The Hour of Our Death*, trans. Helen Weaver, (New York: Vintage Books, 1982), pp. 138, 103-4.

54. Foucault, *The History of Sexuality, Volume I*, pp. 58-9.

55. Réage pp. 74-5.

56. Ariès, pp. 104-5.

57. *Ibid*, p. 104.

58. Foucault, *The History of Sexuality, Volume I*, pp. 59, 60.

59. *Ibid*, pp. 66-7.

60. Stephen Pfohl, *Predicting Dangerousness: The Social Construction of Psychiatric Reality*, (Lexington, Ma: D.C. Heath, 1978), p. 148.

61. Réage, pp. 74-5.

62. Gayatri Chakrovorty Spivak, "Translator's Introduction" in Jacques Derrida, *Of Grammatology*, (Baltimore: The Johns Hopkins University Press, 1976), p. lxxvii.

63. Stephen Pfohl, "Towards a Sociological Deconstruction of Social Problems: A Response to Woolgar and Pawluch," *Social Problems*, 1985, vol. 32.

64. Jacques Derrida, *Of Grammatology*, trans. Gayatri Chakrovorty Spivak, (Baltimore: Johns Hopkins University Press, 1976).

65. Spivak, p. lxxvii.

66. Michael Ryan, *Marxism and Deconstruction: A Critical Articulation*, (Baltimore: Johns Hopkins University Press), 1982.

67. Derrida, *Of Grammatology*.

68. Gayatri Chakrovorty Spivak, "Translation and Forward to 'Draupadi' by Mahasveta Devi" in Elizabeth Abel, ed. *Writing and Sexual Difference*, (Chicago: University of Chicago Press 1981), pp. 262-63.

69. Ronald Barthes, *Roland Barthes by Roland Barthes* trans. Richard Howard, (London: Macmillan, 1977), p. 168.

70. Louis Althuser, *Lenin and Philosophy and Other Essays*, trans. Ben Brewster, (New York: Monthly Review Press, 1971), p. 181.

71. Rosalind Coward and John Ellis, *Language and Materialism: Developments in Semiology and the Theory of the Subject*, (London: Routledge and Kegan Paul, 1977), p. 20.

72. Gayatri Chakrovorty Spivak, "Glas-Piece: A Compte Rendu," *Diacritics*, September 1977, p. 24.

73. Foucault, *Discipline and Punish*, p. 27; Michel Foucault, *Power/Knowledge: Selected Interviews and Other Writings 1972-1979* trans. Colin Gordon, Leo Marshall, John Mepham and Kate Soper, (New York: Pantheon, 1980), p. 133.

74. Austin Turk, "Analyzing Official Deviance: For Nonpartisan Conflict Analysis in Criminology," in James A. Inciardi, ed., *Radical Criminology: The Coming Crisis*, (Beverly Hills: Sage Publications, 1980), p. 84.

16

LETTERS IN EXCESS

Stephen Pfohl

The pretext. I had this daydream. I saw a man watching a woman hysterical. I wondered, is this me? I quote from a book by Alice Jardine, Gynesis. This is a question. "What would have happened...if Eurydice had thrown herself defiantly in front of Orpheus — loudly refusing [to be saved], refusing to follow obediently behind him toward the light at the end of the cavern?"[1]

It began over coffee. They wanted the coffee and the land and the market and her bloodright. Sandino resisted and she.

It began over coffee. Well not exactly over coffee, more before. The coffee was but a twist in this story, its destination. They had their eyes on the coffee and each other. This was their manifest destiny: to have and to hold. Their plan: to thrust deep into her interior, to penetrate her portals with metal shafts exploding, to bring her to her knees and save her. *En el nombre de padre y filio y spirito santo.* "Fuckin commie Spics." These words: the speech of white men of power in a basement, hit men for an imperial democracy, the best thing since the movies and even more violent. "Fuckin commie Spics." They want to play hard ball? OK we'll play hard ball. F1-lls roar south into darkness. They wanted the coffee and the land and the market and her bloodright. Sandino resisted and so did millions of Other Nicaraguans.

It began over coffee. Well not exactly over coffee, more before. The coffee was but a twist in this story, its destination. It was dark and she said, "Well what do you think? Should we make plans to have coffee or should we simply fuck?" I was taken by this question and by her, called out, interpellated, displaced, transferred from one story I was within (w)riting into another with desire, and a certain sacrifice. I wanted the coffee and I wanted her. What kind of story is this?

"To a greater or lesser extent, everyone depends on stories...to discover the manifold truth of life. Only such stories, read sometimes in a trance, have *the power* to confront a person with [her or] his fate."[2]

This a story of a relationship: of the social circumscription of two characters materially and with contradiction in history. It is a story of the author's double and its other, a woman; a story of a double or nothing, an uneasy story of danger, sex mad violence and sacred self loss; a story of power embodied orderings and their transgression; a story of abjection. As to autobiographical elements of the story, this much can be said: it is written under the following sentence. "Autobiography can be a mourning for the perpetual loss of a name — one's proper word-thing."[3]

Sociologically the narrative does not originate in the text that follows. As such, it is a repetition: a ritual copy sacrificed in the inscription of difference. It was springtime and she wrote:

> I've spent the afternoon reading pornography...I've become interested in a sex language of mechanics. Pornography tends to emphasize wetness. I want an arid sex speak. A sex speak that uses the terminology of metallurgy...devoid of adjectives as possible and of all commas...I guess it's in my nature that I will never find a man who can bind me or beat me so I'll have to continue to do it to myself. Bind me baby but with your politics. I had a feeling of longing for you at 2:35 a.m. Wednesday morning. It is now 3:46.

Five weeks of "things" pass before they end. At the edge of the end she mused disturbingly along the border: why have things gone wrong? I thought that everything should be in order now that I've acquired the right look, the right clothes, that I've gotten down to the right weight and have the right books, the right haircut, the right friends? I've even got sex under control. I know what they want and how to give it. Why then is death more flatly appealing than life? Why this violence? Thereafter he scribbled a few short letters.

I. I think of you and am swollen with words not uttered and feelings without proper names and obscene. Thoughts come violently at night or upon awakening or at random: the effect of chance synchronic I am first lifted up then abandoned. History passes through my body like you and I am eliminated.

II. I am hesitant to write: Will you read my words as claims to be desire you haven't and want no knowledge of who cares? Will they evoke feelings for which you make no sense and want no memory? With what impurity are they penned?

III. I recall a walk cross campus, scandalized eyes, a bed of books, and phantasies of being lovers as school begins its fall. Now it is July and I am beside myself: unworded silence bespeaks abject horror. It is 6:00 p.m. and I am unglued and looking for something other. The phone calls me to dates and dinner and yet I long for the call that doesn't come. Such madness.

IV. I thought of writing a letter saying only nice things: impersonally pleasant pages as if from summer camp. "How are you? I did this on Thursday and that Tuesday. I hope you are well. I miss you. How is Kirt? Are you making the movie? What about Anthony?" It all seems shit. When you thought of spending summer on the Cape you said we could have a writing relation. That seemed good to me. For reasons I didn't fully understand or put into words I thought it better to be at a writing distance. I was ready for this distance but not the sudden hate and erasure.

V. We had undressed somewhat nervous and were between the living room and the bed above. I had been between your fish-net thighs and you said, "Nice legs!" When you saw the back porch you asked if we could have sex there when it was summer and sweaty. We went upstairs and fucked with seeming abandon and lay in talk throughout the day after.

Now it is summer and I sit on the porch alone. Once before we were separated until you phoned at noon. That night we fucked in the sand not far from your grandmother's ocean. Her name is Helen and she told me how she despised poodles of the rich.

VI. I no longer expect your call and yet the phone still triggers unease. Why am I waiting restless? Last night I was taken by a rush of sadness as my image of you fades abstract. "The other's fade-out, when it occurs, makes me anxious because it seems without...conclusion. Like a kind of melancholy mirage, the other withdraws into infinity...endlessly withdraws and pales: a feeling of madness..."[4] I am lost before this fade-out and left with some cruel cut-outs of Madonna. She is not you but I think of securing her photo-image within the crypt of a waffle-machine and reshooting it: death doubled over on film. And you think you're crazy?

VII. I read a book about death's history. It said death and sex were unwed until labor's wage become a thing. Then began the imperial westerns: a march of authorial eyesight accompanied by a dictionary of all things considered: a positive conquest of unreason and its child-like, savage, or feminine frontiers. Everything else was made dark and invisible. You could feel it in the night but it escaped words and never showed itself in photographs except those of an erotic sort.

VIII. You said masturbation seems safer than sex between and later offered an oneiric image of violence flat against yourself with fear and fascination. This was our last conversation.

IX. I read a book about death's history and saw the movie *Videodrome*. Both said death and sex were unwed until labor's wage became a thing. So did Foucault.[5] I read a book about suicide. It said the same. I read another book about a woman "saved" by the marks of men. It was the *Story of O* upon whose body the men she loved and the men they loved projected their death as her sex. "'Oh, how I love you,' he murmured...She moaned in the darkness, all the time he possessed her...All the mouths that had probed her mouth, all the hands that had seized her breasts and belly. All the members that had been thrust into her and so perfectly provided the living proof that she was...worthy...and had, so to speak, sanctified her...The word 'open' and the expression 'opening her legs' were, on her lover's lips, charged with such uneasiness and power that she could never hear them without experiencing a kind of internal prostration, a sacred submission, as though a god, and not he, had spoken to her...Each time she emerged from his arms, René looked for the mark of a god upon her...René, impressed and overwhelmed, gazed for a long time at the thin body marked by thick, purple welts like so many ropes spanning the shoulders, the back, the buttocks, the belly, and the breasts, welts which sometimes overlapped and crisscrossed. Here and there a little blood still oozed'. 'Oh, I love you; he murmured."[6] You said masturbation seems safer than sex between and later offered an oneiric image of violence flat against yourself.

X. "The sadist and the masochist are one being — one being who feels and would not feel. Remembering feeling, this being goes back to that painful moment when he decided to murder feeling within himself. There he stands at the crossroads again. There once again he can make the old decision. And he does. Over and over, he hates himself. Over and over he murders himself. For a few moments, feeling has returned to his consciousness. Feeling must make an appearance in order that he may murder it...But there is such a stockpile of furious feelings in him he is afraid he will lose control. He fears the power of his feeling. So the whip which returns him to an earlier state of feeling, now serves another purpose. It can punish him for feeling. It can discipline feeling...[and so he] looks with gratitude to the one who holds the whip, and...regards this torture as that which saves him. In the hell which is his mind, this lash brings on a moment of relief and resolution that must be bliss."[7]

XI. "Save me," you cried out to Kirt theatrically and with a pout buried yourself in Mike's bedroom. Kirt ascended the stairs in your wake determined. It was time for me to leave. I had known you once in a different bedroom as you arched back and cried out openly, "Oh God. No!," and trembled. There was no saving you then but soon thereafter things appeared more dangerous.

XII. "Death has become inseparable from violence and pain. It is no longer *finis vitae*, but...a rending away from life, a long gasping cry, an agony hacked into many fragments. These violent scenes...aroused primitive forces whose sexual nature seems obvious...The confusion between death and pleasure is so total that the first does not stop the second, but on the contrary, heightens it. The dead body becomes in its turn an object of desire."[8]

XIII. I've been reading Barthes', *A Lover's Discourse* and find that I am dislodged within a cruel theater of self-displacement. This is not so much a bad feeling as one of terrible excess. Perversely, I desire no other. Last evening at the Algiers Cafe I was consumed by a sense of meaninglessness. One night in bed with you I had this dream I didn't tell. I was in a men's room pissing when I am seized by a sadistic male figure. He forces me to crawl face flush to the filthy floor, removes my pants and penetrates me with violence and pleasure. I am, at once, humiliated and aroused. Some others gather and in silence witness my submission. I awake naked next to you: the disturbing irrationality of my positioning within a system of mechanic eroticism that drives me from myself into a space indeterminate and then disappearing. I am compelled toward a place of ignorance with no time to return. I suppose all of this will change but in the present it makes me circumspect about the power of privately architectured pain. In Washington the House votes dollars for death in Nicaragua, while here I am hostage to a discourse that spirals me out of history: An awful guiding light: madness floats in and I listen. My pen moves but to where?

XIV. "Nurse: I'll always help you in crime. I: You're still romantic. Stick this mirror like a stiff cock in front of my puss. Last night all I directly dreamt about was sex. I fucked men and women alternatively. Why isn't there any sex in my waking life. Mirror: the above: water made into ice by boredom in your frozen frame, how many times for how many hours each time, cut off from dreams cut off from desire ... I don't exist because there's nothing to see me with I live on the edge of existence; horror ... I am dead. I'm confused now because I being

awakened... What man would want to touch me?
I'm savage. I don't want a boy friend now. I want
no sense."[9]

XV. One night after a stolen rose and Chinese food something seized
you darkly within you could not explain. It seemed as if from a place of
abjection, "one of those violent, dark revolts of being, directed against
a threat that seems to emanate from a exorbitant outside or inside, ejected
beyond the scope of the possible, the tolerable the thinkable." This lesson
you offered me: with violence. "It lies there, quite close, but it cannot be
assimilated. It beseeches, worries, and fascinates desire, which nevertheless, does not let itself be seduced. Apprehensive, desire turns aside; sick-
ens it rejects... A weight of meaninglessness. On the edge of non-existence
and hallucination, of a reality that, if I acknowledge it, annihilates me ...
I expel myself, I spit *myself* out, I abject *myself* within the same motion
through which 'I' claim to establish myself. During that course in which
'I' become, I give birth to myself amid the violence of sobs, of vomit."[10]

XVI. Later that night I had this dream. You were screaming. I heard
this sound stark but was unable to see either you or the scream. At first
I could not decide if it was a scream of pleasure or of terror. I listened
longer. Now I heard only terror: the abjection. I sprang out of sleep startling
the cats who looked upon me in the dark: naked and alarmed.

XVII. The Scream. He saw it often. He would awake in a sweat cold
and see it staring at him — silent. It wasn't his will to see it simply desire.
Some said it was a scream like at the hour of our death Amen. For others
it screamed of birth.
He was uncertain. If he'd but come dumb virgin from the womb it
would all be positive. As it is this reality the noise drummed loud memory:
his eyes listening but without recall. Too loud now he covered his head
with a pillow and waited. In time he hoped to see the scream more clearly.

XVIII. Several days pass. I write: Today you seem more present than
absent: You have dared a strange journey, a dangerous voyage into the
cavern of madness, a break from a self contained in a plethora of previously pleasing images now shattering before you fall. Hallucinations haunt
your descent: corpses in cars passing and rats devouring a soul listless and
without desire: abject terror; the horror of a Void without laughter. This
morning you are a bit more at ease, closer to laughter. You rub your body
against mine and appear more comfortable. Earlier in the week you phoned
out of dull depressed flatness: no affect — the chill of pain frozen. You
have not gone to work and are overrun by dreams of violence unfulfilling.
You imagine striking out at Anthony, but your blows prove ineffectual. You
drift within a place without words or objects named; pushed and pulled

about in a space "pre-thetic," the "semiotic chora" described by Kristeva. Your mind and body battlegrounds for a struggle undefined. And yet you refuse to submit to either the chill of this place, Golgotha: a place of the skull, a place of torrid crucifixion, or to the normatively sanctioned methods of its containment: psychotherapy administered officially, the calming control of drugs prescribed or self preserved.

You elect instead to ride this storm within without to some place other: not to gain normality but to lose yourself within the metamorphoses of art, politics, death, rebirth, renewal. How is all of this affecting me? I pause at the cavern's edge. I am neither coming nor going. There are voices. They fix you in a certain description — an object of sight. Fine cut nose, cheekbones categoried and wild eyes dry, large and unfocused. I turn within this *site* that is this hell and see you faceless. A burst into poetic *ex-citation* and terror. I am, of course, disturbed but not exhausted. Nor do I feel I've crossed the boundaries of what might be impossibly given.

XIX. You seem frozen this side of death and the other side of life, a horrific place between: self disgust without release, suspended as it were in a night of the dead living. Of another, Bataille wrote: "When Teresa of Avila screamed that she was dying of not dying, her passion, moving beyond any possible barrier, broke an opening that leads into a universe where perhaps there is no composition either of form or of being, where it seems that death rolls from world to world."[11]

XX. It began over coffee. They wanted the coffee and the land and the market and their bloodright. It is now sometime later and you turn upon me as well. I pause at the cavern's edge. The phone rings and I am dismissed faceless. This is difficult for me to accept. "[O]n the telephone the other departs twice over, by voice and by silence: whose turn is it to speak? We fall silent in unison: crowding of two voids."[12] You offer me no meaning concerning not wanting to see me. And so, for a time excessive, I am jettisoned, erased for all but an imaginary relationship to you. I am haunted by this the imaginary realm.

Notes

1. Alice A. Jardine, *Gynesis: Configurations of Woman and Modernity*, (Ithaca: Cornell University Press, 1985), p. 101.

2. Georges Bataille, *Blue of Noon*, trans. Harry Mathews, (New York, Urizen Books, 1978), p. 153.

3. Gayatri Chakrovorty Spivak, "Glas-Piece: A Compte Rendu," *Diacritics*, Vol. 7 Sept. 1977, p. 24.

4. Roland Barthes, *A Lover's Discourse: Fragments*, trans. Richard Howard, (New York: Hill and Wang, 1978), p. 112.

5. Michel Foucault, *Madness and Civilization: A History of Insanity in the Age of Reason*, trans. Richard Howard, (New York: Vintage Books, 1965), pp. 199-220.

6. Pauline Reage, *Story of O*, trans. Sabine d'Estree, (New York: Ballantine Books, 1965), pp. 106, 55, 106.

7. Susan Griffin, *Pornography and Silence*, (New York: Harper and Row, 1981), pp. 57-58.

8. Philippe Arles, *The Hour of Our Death*, trans. Helen Weaver, (New York: Vintage Books, 1982), pp. 372, 373.

9. Kathy Acker, *My Death, My Life by Pier Paolo Pasolini*, in *Blood and Guts in High School plus two*, (London, Picador, 1984), p.282, 283.

10. Julia Kristeva, *Powers of Horror: An Essay on Abjection*, trans. Leon S. Roudiez, (New York: Columbia University Press, 1982), pp. 1, 2, 3.

11. Georges Bataille, "The College of Sociology" in *Visions of Excess: Selected Writings, 1927-1939*, edited by Allan Stoekl, trans. Allan Stoekl with Carl R. Levitt and Donald M. Leslie, Jr., (Minneapolis: University of Minnesota Press, 1985), p. 253.

12. Roland Barthes, *A Lover's Discourse*, p. 115.

BODY IN RUINS

WE...

body in ruins body in ruins body

in ruins body in ruins body in ruin

ARE

GESTURE TRACKING

body in ruins body in ruins body

WEARING...

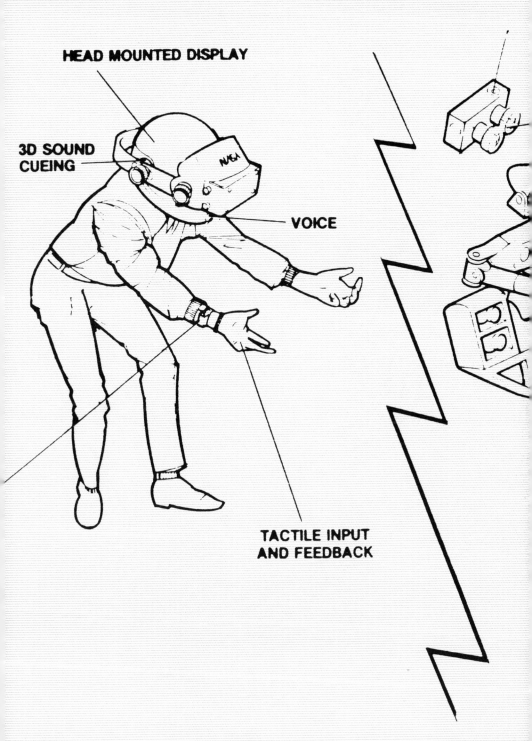

HEAD MOUNTED DISPLAY

3D SOUND CUEING

VOICE

TACTILE INPUT AND FEEDBACK

in ruins body in ruins body in ruin

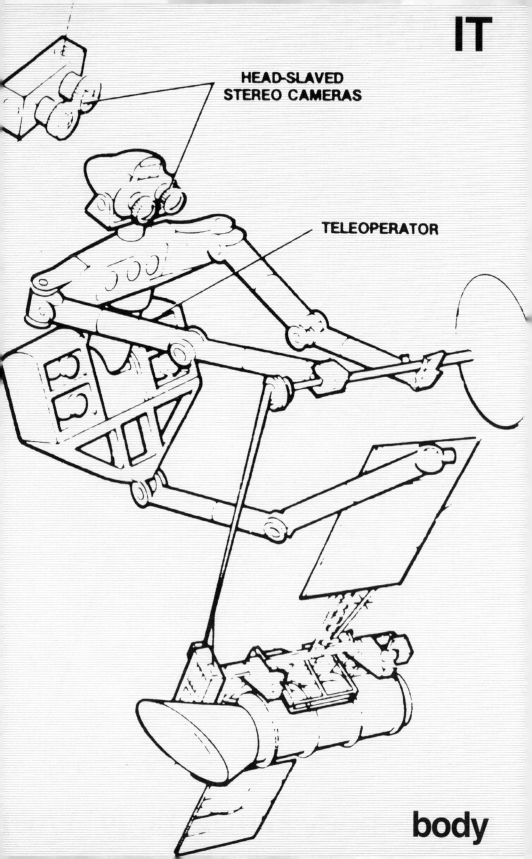

IT

HEAD-SLAVED
STEREO CAMERAS

TELEOPERATOR

body

OUT.

in ruins body in ruins body in ruin

Acknowledgements

Videotape: "Computer Access for Disabled Individuals",
Trace Research and Development Center, University of
Wisconsin – Madison, 1986.

Fisher S, "Virtual Interface Environment", Ames Research
Center, 1986.

Layout help from David Tomas, Anne Delson.
Gordon Morris: computer formating.

CATHERINE RICHARDS

18

━━━━◌◌◌◌◌◎◯◎◌◌◌◌◌◌━━━━

THE DANCE OF THE SCARECROW BRIDES

Rae Anderson

CROW.BRIDE.: a re-interpretation of a myth

The installation CROW.BRIDGE., mounted at the Centennial Gallery, Oakville, Canada, in May 1986, unites my interests in both masks and scarecrows. The installation comprises a circle of nine cruciform figures clothed in bridal gowns and veils; a series of nine masks of "Crow" are set to hang in a slightly wider circle between each bride.

The Dance of the Scarecrow Brides, Rae Anderson, Photo by Rae Anderson.

"The Dance of the Scarecrow Brides" is an outgrowth of a project begun in January of 1982 to experiment with the artform of the scarecrow. I am fascinated by the fact that we take our old clothes, stuff them, and place them out on the land as our representatives and watchdogs. When seen from a distance, they are startlingly human and alive.

I like to fashion objects from materials which may no longer be able to serve their original function. What new life can apparently useless things regain—useless things such as old wedding dresses? Where did all these dresses come from? Who wore these dresses, now yellowed with age? Do these brides not recall the day of your own wedding? Is it not a sacrilege that these gowns ended up in a musty bin in a secondhand shop? Where is your wedding dress? Have you kept it carefully wrapped, hidden away as a sacred vestment to be brought out perhaps for the marriage of your own daughter? Some of these dresses are very old—the brides who once wore them may now be dead. Is this a circle of ghosts—pale reflections of youth, health, and beauty? And yet they seem very alive.

Every bride is beautiful, so the saying goes—and every bride is beautiful because of this mask that she wears. Hours of love and care were lavished upon this lacy whiteness, this veil of seduction which holds out the promise of ripeness and fitness to bear children. Remember the dance of the seven veils. The veil also reminds us of christening clothes; this same veil then encompasses the final of life's ceremonial robes, the shroud.

Scarecrow Bride, Rae Anderson. Photo by Rae Anderson.

I can speak of how much the white circle of brides reminds me of the moon, one of the most female of symbols. There are the barely definable moments of approaching the circle, joining the dance, then daring to enter into the circle's centre. Each stage of participation has a different feeling about.

And what of the link between scarecrow and bride? To start from the very beginning, I bought my first secondhand wedding gown in January 1982, simply because it was a very beautiful piece of art. Then one grew to two, to three. Eventually I had a whole collection. I don't know when the idea came to put these clothes out to stand in the middle of the feild, but put them up we did... and it was breath-taking, an absolutely pure, strong image. They seemed to be waiting, watching as a silent chorus. It was only afterwards that the rationale, the historical basis for such a reinterpretation of scarecrows revealed itself. For the Greeks had a phallic scarecrow god named Priapus. He was a wooden fertility statue set up in the garden as a scarecrow, and offerings of wine and fruits were made to him to ensure protection of the garden. The original scarecrow as a fertility effigy overlaps the function of the bride as a fertile vessel.

Crow's Nest, Rae Anderson. Photo by Winston Romaine Fritz.

The black masks of Crow wait outside the white circle, never daring to enter. How doth the scarecrow scare the crow? The masks tell stories of that mythical creature, renowned in different cultures as the Trickster and the Creator. This is not the crow we know merely as a "pesky varmint". The masks offer a vision of Crow's birth, his youthful pranks, his maturation, and his own death in bringing forth new life. Dichotomies reverberate—the black and the white; the dark side of the moon, the full moon; the male and the female; the ambiguity of Crow's androgynous nature, the scarecrows as equally androgynous with their phallic cross structure and female overlay; Crow of many faces, the brides faceless; Crow's fertility as the mythical Creator of the world itself, the brides' circle as a pregnant image of fertility. Crow as harbinger of death and decay, an ill omen, echoes the brides' ghostly skeletal aspect. The concentric circles embody at once the womb that brings forth and the tomb that swallows all things.

Crow Howls at the Moon, Rae Anderson. Photo by Susan Ross.

Crow's Shadow, Rae Anderson. Photo by Susan Ross.

CONTRIBUTORS

Jean Baudrillard, who is himself *the* postmodern scene, has authored a large number of influential writings on postmodern theory and practice, including *America, Simulations, L'Echange symbolique et la mort, Le Système des objets, La Gauche divine, For a Critique of the Political Economy of the Sign, De La Séduction,* and *In the Shadow of the Silent Majorities.*

Julia Emberley is a contributing editor of *Impulse* magazine and has published in *Tessera* and *Feminist Studies.* She is now writing on the subject of negativity and transformation in contemporary women writers.

Kim Sawchuk has taught at the *International Institute for Studies in Semiotics* at the University of Toronto. She is a contributing editor of *Impulse* magazine and her present work focusses on the language of power.

Gail Faurschou is in the social and political thought programme at York University, Toronto, and writes in the area of the cultural production of postmodern fashion and advertising.

Charles Levin is the translator of Jean Baudrillard's *For a Critique of the Political Economy of the Sign* (St. Louis: Telos, 1981), and the author of many articles on social theory and psychoanalysis. He is currently a candidate at the *Canadian Institute of Psychoanalysis* in Montréal, and is writing a book on symbolization theory in psychoanalysis and social thought.

Andrew Haase, who works in the area of philosophy and social theory at Boston College, is engaged in the politics of avant-garde film-making.

Berkeley Kaite teaches sociology and mass communications and is completing her doctoral thesis on the subject, "A Semiotic Reading of Pornographic Imagery".

Greg Ostrander teaches critical social theory, and his current work is in the area of liberal political philosophy and its critics.

Eileen Manion teaches English and Women's Studies at Dawson College in Montréal. She is currently working on a follow-up essay, tentatively titled, "The Ms.-Directed Pregnancy," as well as a book on Mary Daly.

Elspeth Probyn currently teaches communication and cultural studies at Concordia University, Montréal, and is writing an epistemology of local bodies.

Stephan Anderson is a writer of both non-fiction and fiction in the area of body politics, and is a contributing editor of the *Montréal Mirror,* a cultural newspaper.

Stephen Pfohl and *Avery Gordon* teach sociology at Boston College and are the organizers of the *Parasite Café,* a theoretical and practical site of intervention within and against the postmodern culture of transnational capitalism. Pfohl, the author of *Predicting Dangerousness: The Social Contruction of Psychiatric Reality* and *Images of Deviance and Social Control,* is completing a collage text investigating the relationship between the electronic narration of desire and the conditions for a critical, postmodern practice of sociology. Gordon's current work concerns the intersection of feminist and poststructuralist interventions within the historical materiality of postmodern America.

Catherine Richards is a Montréal artist and engineer who works in the area of computer imaging systems.

Rae Anderson, a Toronto artist, is currently writing on the relationship between masks and women in different cultures.

Marilouise Kroker is editor of *Feminism Now: Theory and Practice,* (Montréal: New World Perspectives, 1984), and is managing editor of the *Canadian Journal of Political and Social Theory.* She is also co-editor of the *CultureTexts* series.

Arthur Kroker is co-author of *The Postmodern Scene: Excremental Culture and Hyper-Aesthetics* (New York: St. Martin's Press, 1987, and London: Macmillan, 1988). He is founding editor of the *Canadian Journal of Political and Social Theory,* and teaches political and cultural theory at Concordia University, Montréal. He is also co-editor of the *CultureTexts* series. Presently, he is writing a *Panic Encyclopedia.*